SOVIET POLICY FOR THE 1980s

SOVIET POLICY FOR THE 1980s

Edited by

Archie Brown
and
Michael Kaser

Indiana University Press
Bloomington

Manufactured in Great Britain

Library of Congress card catalog number: LC# 82-48593
ISBN 0-253-35412-9

Contents

List of the Contributors

ARCHIE BROWN, who was born in Annan, Scotland, in 1938, is a Fellow of St Antony's College, Oxford, and Lecturer in Soviet Institutions at the University of Oxford. He studied for five years as an undergraduate and graduate student at the London School of Economics and Political Science (University of London) and for an academic year at Moscow University, and has made a number of other study visits to Moscow and Leningrad Universities and to the Academy of Sciences of the USSR (most recently in 1980). He was Lecturer in Politics at Glasgow University from 1964 until 1971, when he moved to Oxford. He has been Visiting Professor of Political Science at the University of Connecticut and at Yale University and he gave the 1980 Henry L. Stimson Lectures at Yale. Mr Brown is the author of *Soviet Politics and Political Science* (1974) and *Political Change within Communist Systems* (forthcoming) and editor of and contributor to *The Soviet Union since the Fall of Khrushchev* (with Michael Kaser, 1975, 2nd edn, 1978), *Political Culture and Political Change in Communist States* (with Jack Gray, 1977, 2nd edn, 1979), *Authority, Power and Policy in the USSR* (with T. H. Rigby and Peter Reddaway, 1980) and *The Cambridge Encyclopedia of Russia and the Soviet Union* (with John Fennell, Michael Kaser and H. T. Willetts, 1982).

PHILIP HANSON, who was born in London in 1936, is Reader in Soviet Economics at the University of Birmingham. An economics graduate of Cambridge, he took his PhD at Birmingham and was Lecturer in Economics at Exeter University from 1961 to 1967. He worked for short spells in both the Treasury and the Foreign Office and has made several extended visits to the Soviet Union. He was Visiting Professor of Economics at the University of Michigan in 1977. Dr Hanson is the author of *The Consumer in the Soviet Economy* (1968), *Advertising and Socialism* (1974), *USSR: Foreign Trade Implications of the 1976–80 Plan* (1976) and *Trade and Technology in Soviet-Western Relations* (1981). He is co-editor (with Karen Dawisha) of *Soviet-East*

European Dilemmas: Coercion, Competition and Consent (1981), a contributor to US Congress Joint Economic Committee compendia on the Soviet Economy and the author of the Economist Intelligence Unit's *Quarterly Economic Review of the USSR*.

JOHN N. HAZARD was born in Syracuse in the state of New York in 1909. He studied at Yale, Harvard and at the University of Chicago, where he took his doctorate, and subsequently in the Soviet Union (from 1934–37) where he received the Certificate of the Moscow Juridical Institute. During the Second World War he worked for the United States government as Deputy Director of the USSR branch of the Foreign Economic Administration and was subsequently Adviser on Soviet Law to the US Prosecutor during the preparation of the indictment of Nazis at Nuremberg. Professor Hazard is Nash Professor of Law Emeritus of Columbia University, New York, and he spent the 1981–82 academic year as Goodhart Professor of Legal Science at Cambridge University. He is a Corresponding Fellow of the British Academy and Fellow of the American Academy of Arts and Sciences, and holds honorary doctorates from the Universities of Paris 1, Leyden, Freiburg and Louvain. Professor Hazard first set foot in the Soviet Union in 1930 and has been a frequent visitor over half a century. He is the author of *Soviet Housing Law* (1939), *Law and Social Change in the USSR* (1953), *Settling Disputes in Soviet Society* (1960), *Communists and their Law* (1969) and *The Soviet System of Government* (5th edn, 1980).

ANN HELGESON was born in Shenandoah, Iowa, in 1948. She took her first degree at Beloit College, Wisconsin, and her doctorate at the University of California at Berkeley. She has carried out research at both Leningrad and Moscow universities and spent the 1975–76 academic year in Moscow. Dr Helgeson was a Research Fellow at the University of Essex from 1979–81 and is currently Lecturer in the Centre for Russian and East European Studies at Birmingham University. She is the author of a number of contributions to books and academic journals, mainly concerned with Soviet population distribution and migration.

DAVID HOLLOWAY, who was born in Dublin in 1943, is Lecturer in Politics at the University of Edinburgh. He previously studied or taught at the universities of Cambridge, Oslo, Manchester and Lancaster and he has made several study visits to the Soviet Union. In

1978–79 he was Fellow of the Woodrow Wilson International Center, Washington DC, and he spent the 1981–82 academic year as Visiting Fellow, attached to the Peace Studies Programme, and Visiting Professor of Government at Cornell University. Mr Holloway is the author of *Technology, Management and the Soviet Military Establishment* (1971) and of numerous contributions to symposia and academic journals.

MICHAEL KASER, who was born in London in 1926, is a Fellow of St Antony's College and Reader in Economics at the University of Oxford. After taking the Economics Tripos as an Exhibitioner at King's College, Cambridge, he served in the British Foreign Service in London and Moscow from 1947 to 1951 and in the United Nations Secretariat (with the Economic Commission for Europe in Geneva) from 1951 to 1963, when he moved to Oxford to teach Soviet economics. He has made numerous visits to the Soviet Union and has participated in five out of the six Anglo-Soviet Round Table meetings including the first, held in London in 1975, and the latest, held in Moscow in November 1981. Mr Kaser is the author of *Comecon: Integration Problems of the Planned Economies* (1965; 2nd edn, 1967), *Soviet Economics* (1970), *Planning in East Europe* (with J. Zielinski, 1970) and *Health Care in the Soviet Union and Eastern Europe* (1976), and he is editor of and contributor to *Economic Development for Eastern Europe* (1968), *Planning and Market Relations* (ed. with R. Portes, 1971), *The New Economic Systems of East Europe* (ed. with H. Hohmann and K. Thalheim, 1975), *The Cambridge Encyclopedia of Russia and the Soviet Union* (with Archie Brown, John Fennell and H. T. Willetts, 1982) and *The Economic History of Eastern Europe since 1919* (with E. A. Radice), Vols. I and II, 1919–1949 (1982).

ALASTAIR McAULEY, who was born in Maidstone, Kent, in 1938, is Senior Lecturer in Economics at the University of Essex. After graduating from the London School of Economics and Political Science in 1962, he spent two years as a graduate student at Glasgow University and the 1964–65 academic year as an exchange scholar at Moscow University. He subsequently taught at Manchester University and at Princeton University before moving to Essex in 1968. In 1976–77 he was Visiting Assistant Professor at the University of Wisconsin, Madison, and in 1977 a Visiting Fellow of the Kennan Institute, Washington DC. Among his publications are *Economic Welfare in the Soviet Union: Poverty, Living Standards and Inequality*

(1979) and *Women's Work and Wages in the Soviet Union* (1981).

JOHN H. MILLER was born in Staveley, Derbyshire, in 1940. After studying as an undergraduate at St John's College, Cambridge, he made extended cultural exchange visits as a graduate student to Sofia (1963) and Moscow (1967–68) and also pursued graduate studies at the University of Glasgow. From 1968 until 1972, he was Lecturer in the Institute of Soviet and East European Studies at Glasgow. Since 1972 he has been Senior Lecturer in Politics at La Trobe University, Melbourne. In 1976 and in 1980–81 he was a visiting Senior Associate Member of St Antony's College, Oxford. Mr Miller is the author of several important articles in the field of Soviet politics and of a forthcoming monograph on the relationship between party and society within the Soviet Union.

ALEC NOVE was born in Petrograd in 1915 but educated in England, graduating from the London School of Economics and Political Science in 1936. Since 1963 he has been Professor of Economics at Glasgow University, a post which he combined until 1979 with the Directorship of the Institute of Soviet and East European Studies at Glasgow. Prior to that, he was in the Civil Service from 1947 to 1958 (mainly at the Board of Trade) and from 1958 to 1963 he was Reader in Russian Social and Economic Studies at the University of London. Professor Nove, who has made numerous visits to the Soviet Union, was awarded an honorary doctorate by the University of Giessen in 1977 and elected a Fellow of the British Academy in 1978. His publications include *The Soviet Economy* (1961; 3rd edn, 1969), *Was Stalin Really Necessary?* (1964), *The Soviet Middle East* (with J. A. Newth, 1965), *An Economic History of the USSR* (1969), *Socialist Economics* (co-editor with D. M. Nuti, 1972), *Efficiency Criteria for Nationalised Industries* (1973), *Stalinism and After* (1975), *The Soviet Economic System* (1977) and *Political Economy and Soviet Socialism* (1979).

Introduction

This book (a sequel to *The Soviet Union since the Fall of Khrushchev*,[1] which surveyed Soviet political, economic and social life from October 1964 to the mid-1970s) concentrates on the second half of the 1970s and the beginning of the 1980s, though authors of individual chapters have taken a longer historical perspective where this is helpful to an understanding of the issues or of major trends.

The authors of this collective work were, however, asked to do something more – and more in that respect than for the earlier work – namely, to discuss possible options in policy and the relative likelihood of change during the decade. It is clear that to examine trends and make projections is a more firmly-based enterprise in certain areas of Soviet studies than of others. Thus, to take one example from an area discussed in this book, population growth and its distribution can be fairly readily extrapolated from current trends to embrace the remaining years of the 1980s and beyond. In the realm of demographic *policy*, however, it becomes a matter for an author's judgement whether the present policies being pursued will be successful and whether they are likely to be supplemented by more radical measures. In the sphere of foreign policy, unforeseeable circumstances are inevitable; and when the topic is the succession to the top political leadership, there is immense scope for error, when much may hinge on the timely or untimely death of a contender or power broker within the elderly leadership.

The contributors have attempted to provide a context in which future developments may be understood and to make informed judgements about the limits of the probable. Each chapter except the final one is a revised version of a paper read in 1981 to a seminar which has been meeting weekly during Term in Oxford University for the past thirty years at St Antony's College. The time of this particular seminar series was chosen deliberately, since the unveiling of a new Five-year Plan and the holding of a Party Congress oblige the Soviet leadership to give an account of its stewardship, to assess 'the state of the union' and to look ahead.

While contributors have drawn upon materials made available by the 1981 Party Congress, the meeting itself is not the prime focus of the book, and authors took account of events during the remainder of the year. Thus the chapter on foreign and defence policy comments on the effect on East–West relations of the imposition of martial law in Poland in December 1981. The final two chapters, completed after the others in order to draw together some of their major points, bring the analysis into early 1982, and a Postscript has been added at a late stage of production to take account of the May 1982 plenary session of the Central Committee of the CPSU with its policy pronouncement on agriculture and the political promotion of Andropov and Dolgikh. The opportunity has also been taken to update the 'Calendar of Political Events', which is annexed, to July 1982.

Important as are the interconnections between political, economic and social relations in any society, they are nowhere more inextricable than in the Soviet Union. Central to the polity, the society and the economy is the role of the Communist Party. John Miller directs attention to some of the fundamental principles underlying Party 'management' of the country and goes on to provide a detailed analysis of trends in the social composition of the Party. After discussing the Party membership as a whole, he turns to Party officials, and examines the meaning and significance of the institution of *nomenklatura*, addresses the problem of rejuvenation of Party officialdom and analyses the composition of the new Central Committee elected at the XXVI Congress.

David Holloway surveys both East–West relations and Soviet relations with other Communist states and devotes attention to the setbacks to détente over the past five years. He notes a disturbing feature from a Soviet point of view – 'a potential or quasi-alliance' being formed among 'the Soviet Union's main adversaries'. Holloway pays special attention to two crises – Afghanistan and Poland – and also brings his expertise on the Soviet military to bear on the arms race, throwing light at the same time on the different perspectives on the superpowers' military strengths of Moscow and Washington.

Philip Hanson complements Holloway's discussion of foreign policy with an analysis of external economic relations. He examines the overall development of Soviet trade in the 1970s, finding integration with other CMEA (Comecon) countries taking precedence over trade with the West, but cautions against exaggerated expectations, 'just as it was unwise to project enormous consequences from the earlier commercial turn to the West'. He suggests that the basically unreformed Soviet economic system has 'performed relatively poorly in commercially acquiring, assimilating and diffusing western technology' and that though there have been benefits from the import of such technique, they are unlikely to have 'lived up to the expectations of the more enthusiastic advocates of import-led growth'.

John Hazard, the doyen of western specialists on Soviet law, discusses the connections between law and the economy and goes so far as to describe the encouragement for private farming in the most recent period as a 'neo-NEP'. More generally, he provides a broadly-based survey of Soviet legal trends, noting the incremental changes that have taken place in the law and its implementation in the post-Stalin period as a whole and in the years since the 1977 Constitution in particular. Hazard sees Soviet jurists in the 1980s as being likely to press with greater vigour the claims of the citizen when the latter is confronted by the 'arbitrary application of bureaucratic procedures'.

Alastair McAuley documents a change of programme with respect to socially-financed consumption; once promoted in preference to consumption paid out of personally-earned income, open social consumption is now 'being squeezed between a weakening in the growth of the economy on the one hand and increases in commitments to unacknowledged social programmes (notably food subsidies) on the other'. Social expenditure itself is, furthermore, committed to support of a higher dependency ratio – more pensioners among the Slavs, more children among the Central Asian nationalities than among the Russians.

Ann Helgeson documents the regional and ethnic shifts in demographic trends and concludes that government population policy (notably the 1981 family decree) can do little to reverse the downward trend in urban family size: 'the coming of the good life to the USSR has altered the "demand" for children, in comparison with the demand for other uses of time and money'. Nevertheless the present and worsening maldistribution of manpower with regard to existing industrial location and prospective sources of energy and raw materials has engendered measures on migration and on the abatement of excessive labour turnover.

Manpower could in past Soviet industrialisation be drawn from underproductive agriculture, but today, as Alec Nove shows, the inefficiency of collective farming means a serious drain on resources. Upwards of 15 million people are annually brought from outside to help with harvesting, 'a major burden to the rest of the economy, especially as 7.8 million are "workers from productive sectors"'.

Nove, like McAuley, notes the heavy cost of farm subsidies – some \$33,000 million (at the official exchange rate) in 1981.[2]

Another aspect of government finance is explored by Michael Kaser. His new interpretation of Soviet budget entries indicates that, with respect to expenditure on material goods, military uses have declined in proportion to civilian uses over the 1970s. This indicates that the 'defence burden' may not have been quite so heavy as some American estimates have suggested. Constraints there are on Soviet growth – labour and energy particularly on the input side – but the economic reform of 1979 tries for more efficiency at the production unit not by some devolution of authority (as in 1965) but by more sensitive central monitoring.

In the concluding chapter of the volume, Archie Brown discusses the style and structure of the top Soviet political leadership in recent years and assesses the potential significance in policy terms of the succession to Brezhnev as General Secretary, a succession which differs from every other leadership change in Soviet history. He devotes some attention to the contenders for the General Secretary-ship in terms of the precedents and the requirements of the office. He concludes with a survey of trends and dilemmas in a number of major areas of policy, in the course of which he draws together some of the major findings and prognoses of the other contributors to this book.

NOTE

1. *The Soviet Union since the Fall of Khrushchev* was first published in Britain (Macmillan, London) in 1975 and in the United States (The Free Press, New York) in 1976. A second, updated and enlarged edition was issued by the British publisher in 1978 and reprinted in 1982; five of its authors contribute also to the present work: Archie Brown, Philip Hanson, David Holloway, Michael Kaser and Alec Nove.
2. In addition to the Postscript to the entire volume mentioned on page xi (and which begins on page 267), a Postscript on the May 1982 'Food Programme' has been added by Alec Nove to his chapter on agriculture at page 185.

Glossary

CPSU	Communist Party of the Soviet Union
GKNT	State Committee for Science and Technology
GNP	Gross National product
ispolkom	executive committee
Itogi	*Itogi vsesoyuznoy perepisi naseleniya* (Results of the all-union population census)
JEC	Joint Economic Committee
kraykom	Territorial (*kray*) committee (of the CPSU)
Narkhoz	*Narodnoe khozyaystvo SSSR* (National economy of the USSR)
Naselenie SSSR	*Naselenie SSSR: statisticheskiy sbornik* (Population of the USSR: a statistical collection)
NASEES	National Association for Soviet and East European Studies
n.e.s.	not elsewhere specified
NFAC	National Foreign Assessment Center
NMP	Net material product
obkom	*oblast'* committee (of the CPSU)
oblast'	region
P. zh.	*Partiynaya zhizn* (Party Life)
raykom	*rayon* (district) committee (of the CPSU)
sovnarkhoz	regional economic council
Vest. stat.	*Vestnik statistiki* (Bulletin of statistics)

1 The Communist Party: Trends and Problems

John H. Miller

THE MANAGEMENT OF THE PARTY IN SOCIETY

It makes sense to picture Soviet leaders as convinced and thorough-going Hobbesians, so persuaded of the precariousness of social cohesion and so appalled at the prospect of social breakdown, as to rate the absolute position of the sovereign as a supreme value in politics.[1] They are Hobbesians, moreover, not Machiavellians, because they seek the bulwark against social breakdown in an institutional arrangement, the Communist Party of the Soviet Union, and not in the personal qualities of the sovereign.[2] If we imagine Soviet leaders proceeding from a serious conviction of the actual superiority of one-party (absolute) government over other forms, we find a great many of the familiar but characteristic features of Soviet politics, ideological, stylistic and institutional, taking their place in a coherent pattern.

First, it directs our attention away from the prevalent assumption that the essence of Marxist-Leninist ideology is to be sought in principles, priorities, ideals determining policy content or governmental output.[3] Following that line one becomes enmeshed in the attempt to disentangle 'sincere' beliefs from tactics and public relations. Yet, at the same time, commonsense and elementary testing[4] suggest that there *are* principles of government, which, in a simple and unambiguous sense, the Soviet leaders hold dear and act upon; and they suggest further that these principles lie in the field not of policy content, but of *social organisation and management*. They are beliefs, in fact, about how organised society holds, or is held, together, and they bear such familiar labels as 'party supremacy', the 'vanguard role of the party', 'democratic centralism', the ban on faction in the party. It is perfectly reasonable to treat these as the active, operative aspects of ideology for the Soviet leadership, and to suspend judgement on the

1

question of how these aspects relate to the rest of the ideological corpus.

Second, such stylistic features of Soviet politics as the intense (and utterly non-Marxist) concern with security, control and social order; the publicity given to political participation, but participation only in the implementation, not in the making of policy; the acknowledgement of interest-diversity[5] combined with the lack of institutional form for its public expression, and hence the tendency for political communication to develop along personalist and clientelist lines;[6] the half-heartedness of arrangements for the public arbitration of political disputes: all these are features that should be expected of politics conducted by, and within, a single and sovereign political organisation.

Institutionally the key elements of the party's position in society are also entailed in a thorough and radical application of the principle of one-party government. Crucial to the maintenance of the party's pre-eminent 'vanguard' role in society are: (i) the licensing of other, 'non-party' organisations and meetings;[7] (ii) the centralised control by party officials of all staffing, party and non-party, under the so-called *nomenklatura* system;[8] (iii) the penetration of other organisations and meetings by party members and the obligation of the latter to meet separately as a group;[9] (iv) the control of communications by means of standardised curricula and censorship of the media.[10]

Some of these procedures underpinning the party's vanguard position in society have to be worked by comparatively junior party officials, or by ordinary party members. So the maintenance of the party's position is linked closely with the maintenance of internal discipline and cohesiveness among party members. In fact the institutions for promoting the latter (listed below) often bear a strong resemblance to the institutions for maintaining the party's social position, allotting to party officials a role within the party analogous to the role of the party within society.

(1) The ban on groups with a distinct, organised platform within the party, the shorthand for which is 'factionalism'.[11] Although the original ban was on organised platforms (many of which are familiar by name from the 1918–21 period), its effect in practice would seem to have been to inhibit the ordinary party member from canvassing or lobbying for a position before meetings, and hence to hand over the dominant role in policy-planning and the steering of decisions to party officials, part of whose job it is to

draft policy (including policy alternatives and 'contingency' plans) and to organise its formal acceptance.

(2) The doctrine known as 'democratic centralism'.[12] This amounts in practice to the centralised, hierarchical management of party appointments and party communications, with permanent officials, not meetings, processing the important documents at all levels.[13] It is, however, a doctrine of 'informed centralism'; a positive effort is made to collect social information from all walks of life supplementary to that supplied by the state bureaucratic networks.[14]

(3) The careful regulation of admission to the party through a system of fourfold checks: references from party members of at least five-years' standing; approval by a party meeting usually at one's place of work; approval by party officials at the next highest administrative level; and a period of a year's probation.[15]

On the basis of all the above, a working definition of the CPSU might be: 'the One Political Organisation, into which the maximum of society's decision-makers, and the maximum of communications to and from them are drawn'.[16] Simply to state this as a claim made concerning a society of 270 million people is to invite the thought that there must be an immense investment in the promotion, maintenance and protection of such a role in society. Let us call the staff in charge of this sector of party tasks the party 'managers' as distinct from the party leaders.[17] It is reasonable to assume that the party managers have thought seriously, have accumulated and evaluated experience, and formulated rules and practices governing their work, and that we should see rules and practices being applied as the party responds to the challenges of the 1980s. Unfortunately, documentation of these guidelines for the post-Stalin period is sparse, and so the next stages of this argument have to be deductive[18]

First, it is entailed in the role that the party claims for itself in society that party membership will include certain types of people:

(1) All (or virtually all) persons who take, or interpret, decisions at any level in society, plus those who might be needed to replace them, and a substantial proportion of those who influence or communicate decisions. This will give the party a commanding presence, inter alia, among people who appoint or supervise the work of others; communicators in the media and education; the armed forces, police and security; and people in a position to

affect economic output.[19]

(2) A second, much larger group whose function is to permeate all walks of ordinary, non-party life, to gather and report information, to mobilise local opinion and lead local activity, and to verify performance.[20]

Party members in the first of these groups would number not less than two million, and those in the second group about twelve million.[21] The second group are important. Their information-gathering and local leadership are functions that have to be performed by someone in society; if not by party members, then by some other group or groups who could thereby encroach upon party supremacy.[22] And their qualifications and attributes as party members matter, if they are to do their job reliably, and serve as a field for recruitment into the first group.[23]

Thus far, functional imperatives seem to suggest a surprisingly large party presence in society, a good deal larger, for instance, than the proportion of people with tertiary degrees in Britain. The party managers are certainly aware that too exclusive or selective an admissions policy carries with it the risk of losing touch with social groupings or swings in the popular mood and, perhaps more importantly, the risk of driving talented and articulate persons into independent collective action, perhaps organised, perhaps oppositionist. The rise of dissidence since the mid-1960s must have reinforced this belief.

On the other hand, it is abundantly clear that the notion of the party as a vanguard is perceived as setting upper limits to the party's presence in society. If there were unrestricted entry into the party, it would sink from its position of the 'leading and guiding force of Soviet society'[24] to being the place where all social interests are pooled and aggregated, a sort of forum for collective bargaining. The warning that 'numerical growth is not an end in itself' and that neglect of this 'spreads dissension in the (party) ranks' (*zasoryayut eë ryady*) is sounded clearly in an important Central Committee decree of August 1965, one which signalled the end to a period of rapid expansion in party membership.[25] Similar diagnoses were apparently made three years later about the way in which Czechoslovak party membership had been managed.[26] It sounds very much therefore as if the party managers regard admission into the party as a matter of striking a delicate balance, between, on the one hand, the maximum engagement of society's influentials (with the concomitant risk of devaluation of its vanguard role) and, on the other hand, maintenance of admission standards (which could foster an isolated élitism). Thus it is likely that the party managers have a working notion of the optimum size of the party presence, in society as a whole, and perhaps also in particular social groups; in the latter case the optimum figure would vary with the group's political importance. The principal hypothesis of this chapter is that it will be policy to achieve and maintain an optimum party presence in society, and in individual social groups, particularly groups which can affect decisions, output or the public mood.

All the signs are that, with small exceptions, the party managers believe they have achieved this optimum, and that their current task is to maintain equilibrium.[27] This might seem a routine and unimportant task, but it is almost certainly not so; rapid social change, some planned and some not amenable to planning, and in particular social change affecting some groups more than others, has an immediate effect on people's understanding of their eligibility for party membership, or on the party managers' perceptions of the optimum party presence. So there arises what has been termed the 'dilemma of party growth'.[28]

Suppose that group X – an example of such a group would be the holders of tertiary degrees – had undergone above average growth in size or in eligibility for party membership, the latter being gauged from past practice. The party managers can then choose one of three alternative policies for party recruitment from group X:

(1) They can maintain what they see as optimum party 'saturation'[29] of society as a whole, but allow an increase in party admissions among group X. If this group is sizeable the consequence will sooner or later be a reduction in party admissions somewhere else in society.

(2) They can maintain current admission levels both in society and in group X. This carries with it the risk of disaffection in group X, particularly if those turned away from the party are articulate or have alternative foci of loyalty.

(3) They can concede increased recruitment in group X, and in other groups as well, so that overall party saturation increases. This was the course pursued under Khrushchev and repudiated by the Brezhnev leadership, seemingly because of the damage it could cause to the party's vanguard status.

As a problem for the 1980s the party managers may expect to encounter the dilemma of party growth among certain socio-economic groups as education and economic complexity increases; or among regional and ethnic groups in consequence of demographic trends.

If there is competition for admission to party membership – and all the signs are that this is the case in most parts of the USSR – then the word 'optimum' will have to be interpreted in a qualitative as well as a quantitative sense. People should be let into the party because an efficient purpose is thought to be served by this, rather than for such formal or routine reasons as that it goes with the job or runs in the family. To the precautions against the party losing touch through underrepresentation in certain areas of society, must be added precautions against those representatives becoming insensitive because they are too old, or have come to take their social and political position as a matter of right. These, too, are problems that a party in its seventh decade of sole power might be expected to encounter.

PARTY MEMBERSHIP IN THE 1970s AND 1980s: DATA AND TRENDS

Total Party Presence in Society

Table 1.1 reveals the rapid – one might almost say heedless – way in which the party expanded its ranks when N. S. Khrushchev was first secretary. If growth rates of that period had continued, there would

Table 1.1 CPSU Growth and Saturation of USSR Adult Population

	Party (members and candidates)	Growth over five-year period %	Adult population (aged 20 and above)	Percentage of adults in party (PSR[a])
1956	7,173,521	—	(125,885,000)	5.7
1961	9,275,826	+29.3	(135,246,000)	6.9
1966	12,357,308	33.2	(144,165,000)	8.6
1971	14,372,563	16.3	(152,281,000)	9.4
1976	15,638,891	8.8	(165,767,000)	9.4
1981	17,430,413	11.5	(178,874,000)	9.7

Figures in brackets are estimates.
[a]Party saturation rate.
Sources:[30] *P.zh.* 21/77, p. 21 and 14/18, p. 17; *Itogi . . . 1970*, vol. II, pp. 12–13; *Naselenie SSSR . . .*, pp. 69 and 141; *Narkhoz. SSSR 1975*, pp. 40 and 43.

now be 28 million persons (one in every six adults) in the party! Instead the growth rate was halved by the new leadership, and the public signal for this seems to have been the Central Committee decree of August 1965 mentioned above. The growth rate was halved again in the 1971–76 period. Examination of regional growth rates (of which more below) shows that they may vary quite considerably from the national figure; but whatever their absolute level, these growth rates were also generally halved around 1966 and again in 1971. This suggests the thought that party admissions targets were handed down for the five-year inter-congress periods (that they were five-year plans, in fact), and that they took the form of directives to halve current net growth rates.[31] In the latter part of the 1970s party growth rates have risen again somewhat, possible reasons for which will be touched on below.

The size of the party's presence among those eligible to join is most conveniently worked out as a percentage of those aged 20 or above in the population.[32] Table 1.1 shows how this 'party saturation rate' (PSR) increased dramatically during the Khrushchev administration, and then only very slowly during the 1970s. Table 1.4 shows that the party saturation of the employed population has also risen slowly during the Brezhnev period, from 10.5 per cent to about 11 per cent. At the most recent party congresses in the Union Republics mention was made by more than one party first secretary of the fact that the local party now included one in ten of the employed population (*kazhdyi desyatyi rabotayushchii*).[33] Is it possible that they were referring to the fulfilment of a target, and that 10 per cent of the employed population is the optimum party saturation figure aimed at by the party managers? As a target it would have the great advantage that it could be monitored where most party admissions occur – at the workplace; knowledge of demographic trends would not be required.

The Age of Party Members

Table 1.2 shows how the age distribution of party members and candidates has changed over the past 15 years. The mean age of Communists is still, probably, slightly lower than that of the adult population at large. Two age groups are increasing in absolute size, those under 30 and those over 40, whereas the 31–40 age group has been declining in numbers throughout the 1970s. In part this reflects the pattern of past recruitment rates: high in the Khrushchev years, low between 1966 and 1976 and rising since then. But it is difficult to interpret the absolute figures on which Table 1.2 is based without raising two other surmises.

Table 1.2 Age Distribution of Communists

% of party members and candidates aged:	1967	1973	1977	1981
25 or younger	5.0	5.7	5.8	6.5
26–30 }	46.5	7.4	10.8	11.1
31–40 }		31.0	25.9	21.2
41–50	25.6	29.2	26.4	26.1
51–60 }	22.9	16.3	18.1	20.8
Over 60 }		10.4	13.0	14.3
Absolute nos.	12,684,133	14,821,031	15,994,476	17,430,413

Sources: P.zh. 19/67, p. 16; 14/73, p. 19; 21/77, p.31; 14/81, p. 18.

First, the latest phase of party admissions would seem to have drawn substantially on employed people over 40.[34] Second, there seems to have been a large number of resignations or exclusions in the 31–40 age group and among the over 60s. In the latter case it is possible that many people's membership is allowed to lapse when they retire from employment; some confirmation of this may be found in the employment figures cited in Table 1.4.

Party Membership by Education and Occupation

For an understanding of the way in which the socio-economic composition of the CPSU is changing, Tables 1.3 and 1.4 need to be read in conjunction with each other. From Table 1.3 one of the most important of recent social developments is at once apparent: holders of tertiary qualifications have more than doubled in 14 years, and persons with the completed secondary qualification called 'secondary specialist' have increased nearly as fast. And the party managers' response to this is equally clear: they have adopted the first of the strategies foreshadowed on page 5, admitting tertiary graduates into the party at a rate almost commensurate with their output in society, and far outpacing overall party growth rates. So graduates have increased in 14 years from 16.5 per cent to 28 per cent of the party, and party saturation of the poorly educated – already low – is declining.[37] The change is massive and rapid; as Unger has pointed out,[38] annual increases in tertiary qualifications in the party – many acquired by people in the party, of course – were the equivalent of 80 per cent of overall party growth in the early 1970s. That figure seems to have slackened off in the late 1970s, because all-round party growth has increased; in terms of the above analysis, because an element of strategy (3), the Khrushchevian one, has been introduced. But the basic picture of the increasing dominance of the party, and especially of entrants to the party, by the highly qualified still stands.

Table 1.3 Party Membership and Levels of Education

	People with completed tertiary qualifications		PSR	% of whole party
	in the population	in the party		
1967	(6,674,000)	2,097,055	31.4	16.5
1970	8,261,541	(2,618,000)	31.7	18.7
1973	(10,040,000)	3,209,605	32.0	21.7
1977	(13,019,000)	4,008,986	30.8	25.1
1979	14,826,000	(4,424,000)	29.8	26.5
1981	(16,400,000?)	4,881,877	29.8?	28.0
	People with secondary specialist qualifications		PSR	% of whole party
	in the population	in the party		
1967	(11,603,000)	2,574,162	22.2	20.3
1970	13,420,241	(2,937,000)	21.9	21.0
1973	(16,162,000)	3,351,395	20.7	22.6
1977	(20,707,000)	3,915,346	18.9	24.5
1979	23,439,000	(4,129,000)	17.6	24.7
1981	(25,900,000?)	4,355,000	16.8	25.0
	People with primary, incomplete secondary or secondary general education		PSR	% of whole party
	in the population	in the party		
1967	(118,489,000)	7,686,931	6.5	60.6
1970	128,405,693	(8,017,000)	6.2	57.2
1973	(135,821,000)	7,931,538	5.8	53.5
1977	(146,378,000)	7,689,795	5.3	48.1
1979	151,960,000	(7,746,000)	5.1	46.3
1981	(156,900,000?)	7,802,000	5.0	44.8

Figures in brackets by interpolation or extrapolation[35]
Sources: Itogi . . . 1970, vol. III, pp. 6–7; *Vest. stat.* 6/80, p. 41; *P.zh.* 14/73, pp. 16–17; 21/77, pp. 29–30; 14/81, p. 17.

Table 1.4 Employment of Communists in Branches of the Economy

Party members and candidates employed in:	1967			1977			1981		
	No.	PSR	% of whole party	No.	PSR	% of whole party	No.	PSR	% of whole party
I *Material Production*									
Industry	3,195,718	11.0	25.2	3,968,712	11.2	24.8 ⎫			
Construction	666,380	8.7	5.3	1,069,939	9.8	6.7 ⎬	(6,697,000)	10.9	38.4
Transport	838,019	11.2	6.6	947,612	9.9	5.9			
Communications	(112,000)	10.0	0.9	(125,000)	7.9	0.8 ⎭			
Collective farms	1,330,316	7.3	10.5	1,371,435	9.5	8.6	(1,427,000)	11.0	8.2
State farms	1,006,096	10.7	7.9	1,273,194	11.6	8.0	(1,413,000)	12.0	8.1
Trade, catering and supply	(464,000)	7.1	3.7	(568,000)	6.2	3.6 ⎫			
Miscellaneous	(122,000)	6.9	1.0	(133,000)	7.4	0.8 ⎬	(820,000)	7.0	4.7
Subtotal	(7,735,000)	9.5	61.0	(9,457,000)	10.1	59.1	(10,357,000)	10.6	59.4
II *Non-material Branches of the Economy*									
Science, education, health and culture	(1,741,000)	12.0	13.7	(2,145,000)	10.7	13.4	(2,275,000)	10.3	13.1
Administration	(939,000)	47.4	7.4	(1,098,000)	38.3	6.9	(1,229,000)	38.0	7.1
Housing and services	139,386	5.2	1.1	222,014	5.5	1.4	(269,000)	5.7	1.5
Subtotal	(2,817,000)	14.7	22.2	(3,463,000)	12.9	21.7	(3,773,000)	12.6	21.6
Total Communists employed in the national economy:	(10,552,000)	10.5	83.2	(12,920,000)	10.7	80.8	(14,130,000)	11.0	81.1
Communists not employed in the national economy:	(2,132,000)	?	16.8	(3,074,000)	?	19.2	(3,300,000)	?	18.9
Total party personnel	12,684,133			15,994,476			17,430,413		

Figures in brackets by calculation.

Sources: P.zh., 21/77, pp. 33–5; 14/81, pp. 19–20; *Narkhoz 1967*, pp. 492, 648–9; *1977*, pp. 276, 378; *1979*, pp. 290, 387–8.[36]

Table 1.4 presents two puzzling features at first sight, one of which is resolved in part by the trends derived from Table 1.3. First, the party has presented it as a matter of urgency for many years that the working-class element in its membership be increased.[39] If this has been successful, why is it not reflected in an increased share in the party by workers in 'material production'? The answer to this is, in part, that such an increase has been masked by the other, less publicised, drive to maintain party saturation among the educated. When the latter slackened slightly, in the late 1970s, a tendency for material production to reassert its position can just be detected.

The second puzzle about Table 1.4 is as follows. Party saturation of different sectors of the economy has not changed dramatically, in the way that education statistics have, and such increases as have occurred – in construction and agriculture – and such decreases – in administration, science, education and health, transport and communications – are not such as to suggest particular recruitment among the skilled and qualified. But it must be remembered that these are data about sectors of the economy; *within* these sectors we have only the sketchiest idea about the distribution of skill or income.[40] The fact that Table 1.4 reflects virtually none of the immense changes revealed by Table 1.3 suggests that these have been changes *within* individual economic sectors.

Table 1.5, which concerns party members in white-collar employment (*sluzhashchie po rodu zanyatii*) throws light on the situation, even though we do not know the absolute numbers of white-collar employees involved.[41] It is clear that party membership has increased among two particular groups of white-collar employees: supervisory personnel (*rukovoditeli*) and the technically qualified. Whatever absolute number we attribute to the total of white-collar Communists

Table 1.5 Distribution of Communists in White-collar Employment

Of all Communists in white-collar employment:	1967 %	1977 %	1981 %
Heads of institutions, organisations and their structural subdivisions at county level or higher:	4.7	5.5 ⎫	
Heads and deputy heads of economic enterprises:	3.2	3.6 ⎭	9.4
Engineers and technical personnel, agricultural specialists:	34.9	40.4	42.0
Employees in science, education, health, literature and art:	23.6	24.2	23.4
Subtotal	66.4	73.7	74.8
Employees in trade, catering and supply:	5.5	4.3	4.1
Unspecified white-collar employees:	28.1	22.0	21.1
Subtotal	33.6	26.3	25.2
Grand total	100.0	100.0	100.0

Source: P.zh., 21/77, p. 28; 14/81, p. 17.

in Table 1.5, the number of them in routine clerical occupations, and also in the politically innocuous sectors of trade, catering and supply, has stayed static, or, quite possibly, fallen. That is, within all economic sectors, recruitment has been concentrated in the decision-making, supervisory and specialist grades and has ignored the less senior and the less qualified. This can be seen as an attempt to maximise the efficiency of the party presence (see above p. 6) and to serve notice to rank-and-file white-collar employees (who in Stalin's time would have had high expectations of entry into the party) that white-collar status (or parentage?) is no longer enough. To have increased the selectivity of party admissions along these lines without significant effects on party saturation by economic sector has arguably been an operation requiring care and skill.

Class and Social Mobility of Communists

It was noted above that we do not know how many Communists are in white-collar occupations. We do, of course, possess the standard Soviet threefold class breakdown – into workers, peasants, or employees (*sluzhashchie*) – of party members by what is termed their 'social position' (*sotsial'noe polozhenie*), that is their class affiliation at the time of joining the party, which must amount to a classification, typically, of their first job, or that of their parents, if they are not yet in employment. Extracts from such data are given in the top left quarter of Table 1.6. It has been taken for granted for a long time that these statistics of the social 'position' underestimate the proportion of Communists actually in white-collar employment; the discrepancies between the social position data and the education statistics in Table 1.3, for instance, seem insoluble, unless we make that assumption.[42] That is, it has been taken for granted that there is significant mobility of party members out of the worker and peasant classes into the white-collar, 'employee' class during – and connected with – their party membership.

It now seems possible to put an approximate figure to this mobility, using regional statistics, that have become available recently, which distribute party members both by social position and by class of current employment. Table 1.6 shows the sums of these data for 15 regional party organisations comprising about a quarter of the total member-ship.[43] A fairly regular picture emerges from the regional stastistics: that 10 or 11 per cent of employed Communists are persons of worker or peasant social position who have moved into white-collar employ-

Table 1.6 Communists by Class Background, Original and Current

All Communists		By social position		Employed Communists	
		Workers and peasants	Employees	Total	Employees
I *Party as a whole*					
1967	12,684,133	6,868,423 (54.1%)	5,815,710 (45.9%)	(10,552,000) (83%)	(6,000,000?) (57%)
1977	15,994,476	8,895,280 (55.6%)	7,099,196 (44.4%)	(12,920,000) (81%)	(7,250,000?) (56%)
1981	17,430,413	9,792,935 (56.2%)	7,637,478 (43.8%)	(14,130,000) (81%)	(7,750,000?) (55%)
II *15 Regional organisations*					
mid-1960s	3,122,430	1,669,075 (53.5%)	1,453,355 (46.6%)	2,738,077 (87.7%)	1,570,837 (57.4%)
mid-1970s	4,098,214	2,267,954 (55.3%)	1,830,260 (44.7%)	3,553,385 (86.7%)	2,001,349 (56.3%)

Sources: P.zh. 21/77, pp. 21, 28; 14/81, p. 16 plus note 43.

ment. Transposed into national terms, it is likely that about 56 per cent of employed Communists (or seven and a quarter million) were in white-collar occupations in the 1970s, and about 20 per cent of *these* were recruits from the other two classes. This last figure would seem to be rising very slowly.

Reducing the number of employees by social position and increasing the number of workers has, as noted above, figured large in party public relations during the 1970s. Clearly, one way to preserve both the social profile of the party and high party saturation of the ad-ministrative grades is to give preference in party recruitment to upwardly mobile workers and peasants, the sort who seem good prospects for qualifications and promotion. Like this, the party managers can evade, in a technical sense, the charge of blurring the party's 'proletarian social profile',[44] though increasingly the party's proletarians are the skilled and upwardly mobile working class. The policy has a further advantage. If one wanted to work against notions that party membership was the automatic perquisite of a desk job, or to reduce tendencies for son to follow father in party membership, one might introduce a substantial proportion of recruits from worker and peasant backgrounds into the market for senior positions and, at the same time, cut back the admission of routine clerical workers into the party. This would be to spell out that there is now more competition for

Soviet Policy for the 1980s

party membership in white-collar occupations. The party managers would seem to be observing one of the oldest rules of survival for a ruling group, the maintenance of channels of recruitment into it. Whether, of course, they are doing *enough* to counteract other tendencies towards the formation of a hereditary ruling group, is a different matter, one much less capable of investigation.

Ethnic Composition of the Party

Table 1.7 shows how CPSU membership has grown over the last ten years in the non-Russian Union Republics of the USSR. Two things are to be noted from this table. First, the parties in the non-Russian republics (with one exception) keep up a growth rate higher than that of the RSFSR or the USSR mean. This has been so since the death of Stalin, and can be accounted for either by the higher population growth rates of southern republics, or the later incorporation of western republics into the Union, so that the corresponding party organisations have had to catch up with 'normal' levels of party

Table 1.7 Party Membership in the Union Republics, 1971–81

Party (members plus candidates) in:	1971	PSR	Growth	1976	Growth	1981
Ukraine	2,386,789	7.5	+10.0%	2,625,808	+11.7%	2,933,564
Belorussia	434,527	7.7	16.5	506,229	17.6	595,311
Uzbekistan	428,507	7.6	13.8	487,507	16.6	568,243
Kazakhstan	575,439	8.3	14.2	657,141	11.0	729,498
Georgia	296,375	10.3	7.4	318,371	10.1	350,435
Azerbaydzhan	258,549	10.6	11.3	287,823	14.8	330,319
Lithuania	122,469	5.9	18.9	145,557	17.4	170,935
Moldavia	115,164	5.5	17.5	135,303	21.1	163,902
Latvia	127,753	7.5	12.2	143,305	12.5	161,264
Kirghizia	104,632	7.1	4.9	109,746	15.2	126,402
Tadzhikistan	86,491	6.5	11.8	96,716	12.7	108,974
Armenia	130,353	10.1	9.7	142,959	15.2	164,738
Turkmenistan	69,862	6.9	11.5	77,910	20.1	93,556
Estonia	73,168	7.6	15.2	84,250	16.2	97,923
Remainder	9,162,485	?	7.2	9,819,266	10.3	10,835,349
USSR	14,372,563	9.4	8.8	15,638,891	11.5	17,430,413

Sources: Entries concerning the Union Republics in *Ezhegodnik Bol'shoy sovetskoy entsiklopedii,* 1971 and 1976; *P.zh.* 14/81, p. 14.[45]

saturation. In the case of the southern republics, where 'native' adolescents have been reaching adulthood, and formal eligibility for party membership, twice as fast as in Russia proper, the party managers must have faced another form of the 'dilemma of party growth'. They could have tried to keep pace with the surge in potential recruits, risking a lowering of entry standards and, possibly, pressure against local European minorities, who are disproportionately urbanised and disproportionately represented in white-collar jobs. Alternatively, admission standards could have been maintained, leading to a fall in the already low party saturation levels of the non-European population, with the risk that communism might come to be identified increasingly with Europeans, and the native élites pushed towards the Islamic revival.

Uzbekistan provides the best documentation on this issue. Party growth rates have been about 3 per cent per annum (as compared with an all-Union mean of 2 per cent), and it would seem that this growth has been concentrated on the non-European population, such that, though party saturation in Uzbekistan is almost certainly down, it has fallen only marginally among Uzbeks, and faster among Europeans. In other words, greater efforts (or responsiveness) are being devoted to the party recruitment of non-Europeans. And a side-effect of this would seem to be that education levels in the Uzbekistan party are falling – in contrast to the all-Union trend.[46]

The second conclusion to be drawn from Table 1.7 is that party growth rates in the Union Republics show considerable variation among themselves, only some of which is readily explicable. That Uzbekistan and Turkmenistan (with their higher population growth rates) and Belorussia (with its record industrial growth rate[47]) should also show rapid party increase is plausible; that Kazakhstan should move from above average to below average party growth during the 1970s, that Kirghizia should move strikingly in the opposite direction, and that Georgia should show the slowest growth rates of all republics since 1956 is less obvious. Mary McAuley has recently marshalled evidence suggesting that republican central committees may have a considerable measure of responsibility for the planning of their local party membership (whether those plans succeed or fail!)[48] and her approach is probably the most sensible one to the figures in Table 1.7. One is left, though, with the lingering suspicion that Georgia was instructed centrally after 1953 to lower its 'profile' in the all-Union party; it is difficult to see how its low party growth rates can have been the outcome of any perceived interest within Georgia itself.[49]

The Union Republics are not, of course, ethnically homogeneous, so that trends discerned in Table 1.7 may be quite different from trends affecting ethnic groups *stricto sensu*. Table 1.8, which simplifies the available data on the latter, reveals some curious developments. Russians still have a disproportionate share in party membership compared with their share in the population (a little over 52 per cent); this share is declining, but not so rapidly in the 1970s as it did in the late Khrushchev period. For reasons noted immediately above, the share in party membership of the non-Russian 'titular' nationalities – that is, those nationalities which give their name to a Union Republic – continues to increase. But it should be noted that it is their share of

Table 1.8 Share in Party Membership of Major Soviet Nationalities

% share of party taken by	1961	1967	1977	1981
Russians	65.9	61.9	60.5	60.0
Other titular nationalities				
Ukrainians, Belorussians, Moldavians	18.6	19.3	20.1	20.3
Transcaucasians	4.7	4.5	4.7	4.8
Central Asians	4.1	4.3	5.0	5.3
Balts	1.1	1.3	1.4	1.5
Subtotal	28.5	29.4	31.2	31.8
Non-titular nationalities	5.6	8.8	8.3	8.2
Total	100.0	100.0	100.0	100.0

Sources: calculated from *P.zh.* 1/62, p. 49; 19/67, pp. 14–15; 21/77, p. 31; 14/81, p. 18.

total party membership that is increasing, not their party saturation, which may well be falling among the titular nationalities of the southern republics.

This expansion in party membership among the non-Russian titular nationalities, combined with a tendency among Russians (however caused) to cling to their dominant position in the party, has occurred at the same time as a general cutting back in party growth. Table 1.8 suggests how this feat was achieved. The share in party membership of nationalities not associated with Union Republics – the largest of these being the Tatars, Jews, Germans and Chuvash – is falling, and their party saturation is probably virtually static. Whether this sluggishness in the recruitment to the party of 'non-titular' nationalities is to be attributed to someone's plan, or to their own reluctance to join, strength is added to McAuley's argument that some aspects of party recruitment are being controlled at republican level. Titular nationalities appear to be at an advantage in party admissions; and, by the same token, minorities at a disadvantage.

The largest local minority in republics outside the RSFSR is often the Russian one, and it has, of course, been normal in the post-Stalin period for these Russians to have a larger share in the local party than would be warranted on population grounds, and for this share to be declining. But there are odd divergences from this pattern. In Belorussia and the Ukraine, for instance, the Russian share in net increase during the 1970s is well above their share in the population.[50] In Georgia, Azerbaydzhan, Kazakhstan and Uzbekistan, it is below that share, and declining.[51] And in the first two of these republics the decline in party recruitment of Russians has been accompanied by a substantial emigration of Russians.[52] It is difficult not to invoke anti-Russian tension in part explanation of this and, if this is correct, it is highly interesting that party membership should provide us with an early signal of such developments.

What is striking about trends in the ethnic composition of the CPSU is how varied they are. There would seem to be no underlying pattern to them, and in some cases – such as the sharp decline in Russian admissions in four southern republics – things may be taking place that are unwelcome in Moscow. There seems to be something of a contrast between the party's handling of socio-economic features of its membership, and of ethnic ones; the former certainly present problems but the response to them seems to be a deliberate and coherent one; the response to ethnic pressure does not.

Internal Migration and Party Membership

Table 1.9 reveals an important trend in party membership which has received little attention. Four northern provinces of the RSFSR in which agriculture – and poor agriculture at that – is an important source of employment are contrasted against four urbanised and industrialised provinces. Massive emigration, since confirmed by the results of the 1979 census,[53] stands out as a feature of the former type of province.

It is reasonable to assume that this migration has been disproportionately one of young, adult, rural males, and that urbanised provinces like Gor'ky or Kuibyshev have been beneficiaries of this

migration. Party growth, on the other hand, is about the same in each
group of provinces, and not very different from the overall RSFSR
level; that is, admissions into the party have proceeded at a standard
rate irrespective of demographic trends, and it looks suspiciously as if
the plans for these admissions have been based on data about the party
organisation, not about the population, something that was hinted at
above, p. 7. Although our ignorance of age distribution makes

Table 1.9 Impact of Rural Depopulation on Party Membership

Province	1966		1976	
	Party (full members)	*Population*	*Party (full members)*	*Population*
Kirov	80,000	1,775,000	96,000	1,662,000
Kostroma	55,000	870,000	66,000	802,000
Novgorod	42,500	724,000	60,000	719,000
Vologda	70,000	1,308,000	87,000	1,286,000
Subtotal	247,500	4,677,000	309,000	4,469,000
% increase			+24.9%	−4.4%
Gor'ky	197,500	3,668,000	234,000	3,658,000
Kuibyshev	155,000	2,559,000	207,000	3,043,000
Saratov	155,000	2,386,000	192,000	2,522,000
Volgograd	150,000	2,163,000	180,000	2,434,000
Subtotal	657,500	10,758,000	813,000	11,657,000
% increase			+23.7%	+8.4%
Approx. % increase for RSFSR	—	—	+21.6%	+6.4%

Sources: XXIII S˝ezd KPSS: stenograficheskii otchet, vol. II, pp. 389–607;
XXV S˝ezd KPSS: sten. otch., vol. II, pp. 329–596.[54] *Narkhoz* 1965 and 1975.

accurate measurement difficult, it is virtually certain that the party
saturation of adults in rural provinces undergoing depopulation has
risen very fast, whereas that of urbanised areas, the recipients of
immigrants, has been sluggish.[55] On p. 12 above, it was argued that
the party managers have made serious efforts to hold steady party
saturation in some white-collar occupations. No such efforts are in
evidence among the agricultural workers of North Russia – perhaps
because they *are* agricultural workers, or perhaps because they are also
disproportionately female.

Women in the Party

The proportion of party members and candidates who are women has increased from 19.7 per cent in 1957 to 26.5 per cent in 1981, but the latter figure still entails an adult party saturation rate of only about 4.7 per cent among females, and 16.1 per cent among males. Not unnaturally, therefore, increasing or high levels of female party membership are presented as matters of importance and success. The 1977 source lists twenty provinces where women are 30–40 per cent of party membership, and one, Ivanovo, where the figure is 43 per cent.[56] At the same time, in many southern parts of the USSR, the proportion of women in the party is below or just above 20 per cent and has remained virtually unchanged since the mid-1950s.[57] This tends to suggest that, if there has been a plan to boost female membership, it may not have been an entirely successful one. The provinces which show the highest female participation in the party are (with one exception) all provinces where there is a high component of light industry (Ivanovo, the Baltic republics) or agricultural provinces to the north and west of Moscow, from which there has been high emigration. Although it is difficult to prove, it seems likely that in both cases we have to deal with a workforce which is disproportionately female. If this is correct, high rates of female party membership can be accounted for satisfactorily by postulating that party recruitment plans are plans for the *employed* population (as was suggested above, p. 7); there is no need to postulate specific targets for female admissions.

Female membership of *obkomy* and *raykomy* is only slightly lower than that for the party as a whole.[58] It is well known, of course, that women hold only an insignificant number of the most senior party positions, amounting to 3.8 per cent of the members and candidates of the 1981 all-Union Central Committee, and being unrepresented among *obkom* first secretaries; in this, however, the party leadership corresponds to senior positions in Soviet life generally.

Problems of Party Membership in the 1980s

The detailed examination of the composition of the 'outer', non-official, circle of party members has pointed up two trends which are likely to become more pronounced in the 1980s, and suggested one provisional conclusion about the party's arrangements for handling problems. First, the educated and the qualified are increasingly becoming the typical CPSU members, and the party presence among the poorly educated is falling. Risks are entailed in the withdrawal of the party presence from any area of society, and it would seem to be in recognition of such risks that the party is now making admission more difficult for many white-collar employees.

Second, an increasing proportion of the party are non-Russians and non-Slavs; and legitimately so, given the demographic trends of the last 30 years (quite apart from the much older Russian preponderance in the party). Yet side-by-side with this trend, party saturation among many non-Slav groups is falling, and in some overwhelmingly Russian regions, that of the local population is rising fast. It might easily be that party saturation of groups is a better indicator of popular perceptions within and towards such groups than the absolute share of party membership they provide. In addition, the share in party membership of the 'non-titular' ethnic groups, and of some Russian minority groups outside Russia, is falling, with just a hint that community tensions may be linked with this.

Finally, the most plausible hypothesis concerning the mechanism for controlling the party's presence in society is that primary party organisations are set admission targets based on the size of their existing organisation and the nature of their workforce.[59] Such targets would be easy to plan, to implement and to monitor. Admission targets planned on the basis of the workforce and implemented mainly at the workplace could explain why the socio-economic aspects of the party presence in society appear to be managed in a smoother and more regular manner than do its ethnic aspects.

TRENDS AMONG OFFICIALDOM

The Nature and Significance of *Nomenklatura*

The suggestion was raised above (p. 6) that the party managers need to maintain not only an optimum presence in society, but also an efficient and responsive presence. With the latter phrase we are shifting attention to that inner circle of party members who hold society's most responsible and influential positions, and who may be labelled, very loosely, 'officialdom'. Only a fraction of the posts they hold are party posts, of course, but they have in common the fact that party membership is a prerequisite for holding these posts, and that they are all on the *nomenklatura* of a party committee at some level.

The word *nomenklatura* requires some clarification. Strictly and in origin it denotes a list or register of posts, occupancy of which must be ratified by a particular person or group. In this sense most people employed in organisations in any society would be said, in Soviet parlance, to be on someone's *nomenklatura*.[60] There are two things which are distinctive about Soviet staffing practices. First, a very high proportion of posts, and the most senior at that, are ratified not by administrative superiors in the organisation (a Ministry, for example) where the posts are located, but by a *party* committee at a superior administrative level. It is this party control of *nomenklatura*, not the supervision of staffing establishments as such, that is so important for the position of the party in society. Second, the party *nomenklatura* extends to posts in the everyday workplace – factory, farm and office – and in this way, the party has achieved a deeper and more comprehensive penetration of society than any previous rulers of Russia.

The present author disagrees fundamentally, therefore, with a recent development in academic shorthand, that of deeming 'the' *nomenklatura* to be equivalent to 'the' ruling class.[61] It is true that this usage reflects colloquial developments in more than one Slavonic language. To adopt the colloquial usage as a technical term, however, obscures two important points about Soviet politics: that the party *nomenklatura* is more important than all others combined; and that it includes positions at *rayon* level which, by no stretch of imagination can be called 'ruling class' positions. There may well be an identifiable group in Soviet society whose internal cohesion and disproportionate access to power would earn them the label 'ruling class'; if so, they would be a subset of, not identical with, those on party *nomenklatury*, let alone those on every *nomenklatura*.[62]

The number of persons on party *nomenklatury* (*nomenklaturnye*) would seem to be in the region of two million or more.[63] It is an immense number. The attempt to centralise and co-ordinate the principles whereby two million posts are filled is a powerful illustration of the 'Hobbesian' urgency with which the party has approached the problem of government effectiveness. But the *nomenklatura* system has now been in operation since the 1930s, and it would be reasonable to ask whether it has not evolved. *A priori* such evolution could have proceeded in either – or indeed both – of two directions.

First, the centralised nature of the system may have weakened. It is an inherent problem of centralised government that it cannot get enough detailed, undistorted information about local situations, and there is thus systemic pressure to delegate to the man on the spot who is in a position to know. The staffing equivalent of this is pressure to hire, other things being equal, local men to handle local problems and to let them represent their localities in dealings with the centre. If this is acceded to, centralised and co-ordinated staffing practices are eroded, to be replaced by a network of diverse patronage systems.[64]

Second, central insistence on the necessity for centrally organised staffing may have won through, but with the side-effect of reinforcing bonds of common group interest and identity among *nomenklaturnye*. We have already seen that it is colloquial usage to perceive *nomenklaturnye* as a class, that is, to suggest that the children of *nomenklaturnye* are likely to succeed them in that sort of job. Another common allegation is that *nomenklatura* status, once acquired, is not easily lost, that it is a tenured status in fact.[65]

The fact that the last two paragraphs have touched on some of the most basic and well-known critiques of the Soviet system, should prepare one for the fact that research progress on the issues involved is difficult and inconclusive. All the publicly available evidence is that the social characteristics of officialdom under Brezhnev have been extraordinarily stable. Such trends as we can detect can be said to illuminate the broad lines of critique but they certainly do not falsify or confirm them. Three relevant issues will be examined, the appointment of local personnel to local posts, the rejuvenation of officialdom, and the balance of interests within the new Central Committee.

Nomenklatura and Local Appointments

Centralised staffing principles will be of particular usefulness – and face their hardest testing – in provincial areas of the multiethnic USSR. Of the four institutional controls for the maintenance of party supremacy listed on p. 2 above, three could easily become less effective in areas of homogeneous subculture where local officials and ordinary citizens shared differences from central policy.[66] The fourth control is the centralised party *nomenklatura*; from the perspective of the centre it might seem imperative that at least some officials be brought into a provincial locality from the outside, and the party *nomenklatura* would be a mechanism for ensuring this.

This expectation is borne out when staffing in the provinces is examined, but the presence of non-locals is less obtrusive and more discriminating than might be imagined, and in one important respect it is declining.

The situation is clearest in the non-Russian Union Republics.[67] A majority of senior positions and, in particular, publicly visible ones are held by 'natives' of the Union Republic in question, but virtually reserved for outsiders are either a small number of key, and usually inconspicuous posts, or a presence among the top half-dozen officials in a given policy sector.[68] These outsiders are almost always Russians (or Russianised Slavs) and a significant proportion of them are secondments direct from Moscow, often from the all-Union Central Committee *apparat*. Movement from one provincial post to another across republican boundaries is very rare, for natives and Russians alike.[69] The most important change over time that can be detected is that the above rules have become more standard under Brezhnev than they were under Khrushchev.

In the RSFSR a preliminary investigation[70] suggests that the proportion of outsiders – as measured by promotions across province lines – is *lower* than it is in the other Union Republics, and that it is decreasing under Brezhnev; more careers are made locally and a longer proportion of careers are spent locally. This seems to have been in fulfilment of an undertaking given by Brezhnev.[71]

The broad interpretation would seem to be that the party managers do not seek to use *nomenklatura* procedures to prevent the identification of officials with local interests and the development of experienced regional lobbies, and perhaps more may be heard of these during the 1980s. Central controls are instead, first, on the accumulation of comparative experience of different kinds of regional problem (with the exception of a specialised group of officials based on Moscow); and second, the monitoring of regional interest group activity by these seconded specialists and, in the case of the RSFSR, this second control has been considerably scaled down. The workings of the *nomenklatura* system would seem to be considerably less interventionist than they were under Stalin or Khrushchev, in part because of local pressure against such interventions. However, there are no signs hitherto of diverse staffing practices growing up in the regions; the centre would seem to be accepting local recommendations more than formerly in making its appointments, but not to have waived its right of veto.

Rejuvenation among Officials

The high and rapidly rising average age of the Politburo and Central Committee Secretariat, and the way in which these bodies have during the 1970s released some of the most junior among their number from their membership, have focused attention on problems of ageing among Soviet officialdom. As was outlined above, the development of party *nomenklatura* institutions could have involved the development of an expectation of tenure among *nomenklaturnye*, and this could adversely affect the efficiency and responsiveness of officialdom and generate frustrations among junior officials who can no longer foresee the career advancement they might have expected a generation earlier. The average age of officials in almost any sector and at almost any level has risen markedly since the death of Stalin; this process has gone beyond the restoration of an age distribution 'normal' by the standards of bureaucracies elsewhere, and has created the suspicion in some minds that the party managers are reluctant to see power handed on to a younger generation.

As Jerry Hough has demonstrated,[72] the problem as perceived by the party managers may be more difficult than this last sentence suggests. In 1981 we might reasonably expect recruits anywhere into top political positions to be aged, say, between 55 and 60, that is, to have been born between 1921 and 1926. This is precisely the generation in the Soviet Union which suffered the most casualties in the Second World War and, in so far as it survived, the most disruption to its education and the most competition from juniors. The problem, as the party managers see it, may well be the difficulty in 'skipping a generation' and handing power to a group on average *ten* or more years younger, substantially different from the present one in experience, assumptions and conventions, and by implication, in potential policy.[73]

There tends to be an increase in turnover of offices immediately prior to a Party Congress. Table 1.10 summarises available data on the age of senior officials before and after the XXVI Congress and of persons recruited to senior positions in the last five years.[74]

Voting members of the Central Committee are on average nearly two years and four months older in 1981 than they were in 1976; new recruits or replacements amounting to a quarter of the membership have had the effect of slowing down that ageing, but not of reversing it, nor is there any prospect that this will happen in the early 1980s, given current rates of turnover. The same interpretation emerges from the data on the 500 or so most senior officials – members and candidates of the Central Committee and members of the Central Auditing Commission – and on what are basically two subsets of this group, *obkom* first secretaries and members of the Council of Ministers. However it can also be noticed that it is the two oldest groups (Central Committee voting members, the Council of Ministers) which have co-opted new

Table 1.10 Ageing of Senior Officials

	Mean age		New appointments 1976–81	
	After 1976 Congress	After 1981 Congress	Age in March 1981	Of whom aged 55 or less
Central Committee: members	60.0 years	62.3 years	57.2 years	42.5%
N =	(287)	(310)	(80)	(34)
Central Committee: candidates	56.4	58.4	55.7	53.4%
N =	(139)	(133)	(73)	(39)
Central Auditing Commission	53.1	56.9	53.2	60.0%
N =	(85)	(55)	(25)	(15)
Central Committee and Central Auditing Commission	57.9	60.7	54.4	57.5%
N =	(511)	(498)	(106)	(61)
Obkom first secretaries	53.6	56.5	53.0	70.6%
N =	(156)	(151)	(51)	(36)
Council of Ministers	62.9	63.6	58.8	42.2%
N =	(103)	(110)	(45)	(19)

members younger than the present incumbents by the greatest margin, and that there does not seem to be an inhibition against the co-optation of persons aged 55 or younger, that is, born since 1925. All this can be labelled a policy of caution and conservatism, certainly, but hardly one of intransigence or petrification; and in this sense, the pattern of developments within the Politburo would seem to be *sui generis* and not characteristic of the whole system.

Obkom first secretaries show a considerable contrast in Table 1.10 with Ministers; the former are much younger on average and receive younger new appointees;[75] and such rejuvenation as has occurred in the Council of Ministers is largely the outcome of a substantial re-shuffle of government posts in the period October to December 1980. When one looks at the 46 persons born before 1920 whose change of status led to their being counted among 'New appointments, 1976–81', only three of them are *obkom* first secretaries; 28 are Ministers or from Ministries, and a further 10 are senior *apparatchiki* of the Central Committee. An attempt to maintain administrative vigour through the induction of younger officials might be expected to concentrate on the important provincial 'line' officials, before it affected the Central Committee or Council of Ministers 'staff' positions. Once again, a policy of extreme caution, but not immobility, would seem to be indicated.

Voting Members of the New Central Committee

It has been laid down in the Party Rules since 1966 that the full members of the Central Committee elect the General Secretary; on two occasions (July 1957 and October 1964) this vote would seem to have been more than a formality. So in proposing the membership of the new, March 1981 Central Committee, the party managers were drawing up a list of people who may vote on the succession to L. I. Brezhnev, and who *might* play a decisive role in this. It is relevant, therefore, to see whether any trends in the background or interests of this electorate can be discerned. Of the two most obvious indicators of such interests, occupation and clientele, the latter is exceedingly difficult to process and will not be attempted here.[76] Table 1.11 shows changes in the current occupation of Central Committee members, and in the locality or administrative level where they work.

Table 1.11 shows interesting, but slight increases in percentage terms in the representation of security and of workers and peasants in the Central Committee, and slight decreases in the representation of Councils of Ministers, Supreme Soviets and diplomacy. But the significant change is the increase in the representation of the all-Union Central Committee *apparat* from 18 to 30 persons (or from 6.3 per cent to 9.4 per cent). Thus, the Central Committee members who can be formally associated with the all-Union rather than lower levels of administration have risen from just under to more than half of the total membership.

Another way of looking at the same trend is as follows. The majority of Central Committee members appear to get their membership *ex officio*; the party managers influence, through the party *nomenklatura*, who is appointed to senior positions, but have rather less short-term control over the balance of these senior positions on the Central Committee. They can, however, modify this balance of power by increasing the size of the Committee. There are 89 persons among the 319 Central Committee members in 1981 who were not members in March 1976; of these 89, 44 are new incumbents of posts whose former occupants were members in 1976; and 45 have jobs which did not carry this status in 1976. Of these 45, 9 hold positions in the Central

Table 1.11 Occupational Representation among 1976 and 1981 Central Committee Members

	1976			1981		
	All-Union	RSFSR	Other Republics	All-Union	RSFSR	Other Republics
Party apparatus	18	65	37	30	67	41
Government apparatus	65	11	7	71	9	5
Supreme Soviets	3	1	5	3	1	5
Military	17	1	2	17	4	1
Security and law	4	—	—	7	—	—
Foreign affairs	17	—	—	16	—	—
Academy, media and writers	10	2	2	11	2	2
Trade unions	3	—	—	5	—	—
Economic management	—	4	—	—	3	—
Workers and peasants	—	7	3	—	12	4
Others	3	—	—	3	—	—
	140	91	56	163	98	58
Total		287			319	

Notes: Government apparatus means, above all, Ministers, but includes a few chairmen of *ispolkomy*; Security and law covers the KGB, the MVD, the Procuracy and Supreme Court; Others are voluntary organisations and the Komsomol. Commanders of military districts are classified under RSFSR or Other Republics; military commanders abroad and ambassadors are included in the all-Union figures.

Committee *apparat*, 9 in the all-Union Council of Ministers, 3 are from the military, 3 from the KGB and two are institute directors associated with foreign policy;[77] on the other hand only 8 are regional party secretaries and 11 are workers (9 from outside Moscow). Thus the majority of the net additions to the Central Committee, and the most effective of them, are likely to be defenders of all-Union as opposed to regional interests, and the most important effect of the expansion of Central Committee membership would seem to be a proportional cut-back in regional representation. Indeed, an attempt to curb the influence at the centre of regional lobbies might well have been the purpose behind this expansion.

The foregoing survey of trends in party membership and among party officials in the late 1970s has revealed little that is dramatic, still less evidence of failure to come to grips with problems. Perhaps ethnicity and regionalism come closest to falling into that latter category. The most sensible interpretation to be put on developments is that, in so far as matters can be managed, the party managers have handled them with caution, deliberation and strategy; and that they have also shown considerable acceptance of evolutionary change in both party and society. This may sound an unremarkable conclusion, but it is one remarkably close to the platform on which the Brezhnev administration came to power in October 1964.

NOTES

1. Interestingly, Maria Hirszowicz entitles a book *The Bureaucratic Leviathan* (Oxford, 1980); she does not, however, refer to Hobbes by name in the book. Archie Brown has gathered material on the fear of social breakdown as a salient theme in Russian political thought; see his *Soviet Politics and Political Science* (London, 1974), p. 93, and in Archie Brown and Michael Kaser (eds), *The Soviet Union since the Fall of Khrushchev* (London, 1975), p. 268.

2. The reverse was true, of course, of Stalin and Stalinists! The subject of this chapter is the CPSU in its position as staked out by N. S. Khrushchev and consolidated under L. I. Brezhnev. One of this author's criticisms of the use of the word 'totalitarian' is its identification of absolutism with personal autocracy.

3. The standard treatment in almost any textbook on the USSR is to the effect that Lenin refined *tactics* for realising a version of Marx's *ideals*. Is this approach not, first, overgenerous to the practicality of Karl Marx, and second, a slight on the distinguished political philosophers whose central concern has been the *organisational form* of the state, and not its policy? For a stimulating but, for this reader, ultimately unsatisfactory discussion of the role of ideology in Soviet politics, see *Soviet Studies*, XVII, no. 3 (January 1966), 273–85 and subsequent issues.

4. We might be confident that we had identified 'sincerely held' beliefs if we found people treating beliefs as interconnected parts of a coherent whole, taking measures against incoherence or inconsistency and taking *risks* for the sake of this coherence. In 1968 a logical connection was perceived between the relaxation of censorship, the rise in power of non-party organisations and the election of congress delegates in Czecholovakia, and risky intervention embarked upon. It would be difficult to argue an analogous attitude to, say, the rights, freedoms and duties in Chapter 7 of the Soviet Constitution.

5. For an interesting example, see L. I. Brezhnev in *Pravda*, 4 November 1967, p. 6, col. 2.

6. Papers on clientelism and staffing practices in Soviet politics presented at the Second World Congress for Soviet and East European Studies in 1980 will be published in T. H. Rigby and Bohdan Harasymiw (eds), *Leadership Selection and Patron-Client Relations in the USSR and Yugoslavia* (forthcoming).

7. Such licensing was widely reported in the case of the Polish organisations Solidarity and Rural Solidarity. The rules governing registration of organisations in the USSR seem to have been laid down in *Polozhenie o dobrovol'nykh obshchestvakh i soyuzakh* (utverzhdeno postanovleniem VTsIK i SNK RSFSR ot 10.7.1932 g.) paragraphs 11–16, and quoted in A. G. Khazikov (ed.): *Sbornik normativnykh aktov po sovetskomu administrativnomu pravu* (Moscow, Vysshaya shkola, 1964), pp. 111–12.

8. The best specific treatment of this is still Bohdan Harasymiw, '*Nomenklatura*: The Soviet Communist Party's Leadership Recruitment System', *Canadian Journal of Political Science*, II, no. 4 (December 1969), 493–512. Subsequent textbooks cite but do not amplify Harasymiw's work. For a relatively explicit Soviet document on the origins of the practice, dated April 1920, see Mervyn Matthews: *Soviet Government: A Selection of Official Documents on Internal Policies* (London, 1974), pp. 145–6.

9. *Ustav KPSS* (Rules of the CPSU), paragraphs 68 and 34. These cannot be interpreted otherwise than as an instruction to form 'steering committees' in non-party gatherings. The right of non-party members of non-party bodies to copy this practice would seem to be precluded by Article 6 of the 1977 Constitution.

10. For the last published Soviet directive on this, see Matthews, op. cit., pp. 71–3. Paragraphs 34, 42b, 45, 49 of *Ustav KPSS* refer in veiled terms to the practice.

11. See Matthews, op. cit., pp. 149–51 for the original March 1921 ban. References in the contemporary party rules are in the Preamble and in paragraph 26.

12. *Ustav KPSS*, paragraph 19.

13. In theory, rule 19 could be worked differently; but it has been conventional since the 1920s for candidates for party office to be 'recommended' by the permanent officials of a party committee at the next highest administrative level; elections are then, so far as we know, uncontested. That it is party 'organs' or committees which prepare and receive reports would be a matter of commonsense, but is confirmed by the rules, for example paragraphs 19 (b), 42 (f), 47, 50.

14. *Ustav KPSS*, paragraphs 2 (g), 42 (f), 60.

15. *Ustav KPSS*, paragraphs 4, 5, 14–16.

16. Two elements in this definition need pointing out: the word 'maximum' is important because claims such as that made by the CPSU can rarely be realised totally; 'decision-makers' is used rather than administrators because the party makes a serious (if not wholly successful) effort not to take over the implementation of decisions but to consign them to the 'state' bureaucracy; see *Ustav KPSS*, paragraph 42 (c).

17. The word 'managers' is adopted from Grey Hodnett, *Leadership in the Soviet National Republics* (Oakville, Ontario, 1978). One assumes that the persons concerned are mainly employed in the Department of Organisa-

tional Party Work of the Central Committee.
18. Party documents of the late 1940s and early 1950s provide abundant examples of pressure to achieve the goal of a party cell in every collective farm. We know much less about equivalent campaigns nowadays (if there are any).
19. For a much fuller, empirical account of the party presence in different occupational groups, see T. H. Rigby: *Communist Party Membership in the USSR, 1917–67* (Princeton, NJ, 1968), ch. 14.
20. *Ustav KPSS*, paragraphs 2, 68.
21. These figures are meant to indicate an order of magnitude only; they are however not inconsistent with numerical estimates given below.
22. One could view the MVD under Beria as having supplanted the party in some of its 'grass-roots' functions; from this perspective Khrushchev's expansion of party membership at the same time as he downgraded the MVD network was logical.
23. The CPSU thus does not fit easily into the distinction between a 'mass' and a 'cadre' party, as Duverger himself pointed out, in *Political Parties* (London, 1964), p. 70. What is significant about the 'outer' group of party members is that, through them, the administration achieves deeper and more systematic penetration of society than had previously been experienced in Russia. Rigby, op. cit., p. 7, gives the historical reasons for the emergence of this group. What is here being argued is that its emergence was functionally entailed in a serious application of the 'vanguard' notion; something which the theorists of totalitarianism were correct in perceiving as a characteristic of modern authoritarianism.
24. *Ustav KPSS*, Preamble, and *Constitution of the USSR*, Article 6.
25. 'On Serious Inadequacies in the Work of the Khar'kov Oblast Party Organisation on Party Admission and the Training of Young Communists', *Partiinaya zhizn'* 1965, no. 15, pp. 23–5.
26. G. Wightman and A. H. Brown, 'Changes in the Levels of Membership and Social Composition of the Communist Party of Czechoslovakia' in *Soviet Studies*, XXVII, no. 3 (July 1975), 413; also D. P. Hammer in note 28 below, p. 21.
27. Thus the present situation differs in principle from that in the early 1950s, for which see above note 18. The possible exceptions are newly important economic sectors such as retail distribution and urban services where there is some slight evidence of an increase in traditionally low levels of party membership; see below, Table 1.2.
28. Darrell P. Hammer appears to have coined the phrase in *Problems of Communism*, July–August 1971, pp. 16–21. It is applied in this chapter in a somewhat more detailed sense than Hammer's.
29. The word is Rigby's; for example, op. cit., p. 416.
30. To avoid repetition the following note on principal sources is in order. Most data on the party are taken, or calculated, from articles entitled *KPSS v tsifrakh* (CPSU in figures) in *Partiinaya zhizn'* (Party Life; hereafter *P. zh.*), 1973, no. 14, pp. 9–26; 1976, no. 10, pp. 13–23; 1977, no. 21, pp. 20–43; and 1981, no. 14, pp. 13–26. Demographic data are taken, interpolated or extrapolated from various volumes of *Itogi vsesoyuznoy perepisi naseleniya* (Results of the all-Union Population Census; hereafter

Itogi . . .) of 1959 and 1970; from *Naselenie SSSR: statisticheskiy sbornik* (Moscow, 1975); from Chapter 1 of various editions of *Narodnoe khozyaistvo SSSR;* and from various editions of *Vestnik statistiki* for 1980 and 1981 summarising results of the 1979 census.

A good deal of the ensuing discussion of party membership is similar to the treatment by T. H. Rigby in 'Soviet Communist Party Membership under Brezhnev', *Soviet Studies*, XXVIII, no. 3 (July 1976), 317–37, and by Jerry F. Hough and Merle Fainsod in *How the Soviet Union is Governed* (Cambridge, Mass., 1979), pp. 320–61. Specifically on party membership in the armed forces and in the regions, however, conclusions have been summarised from a larger work in preparation by the present author on *The Party Presence in Soviet Society*.

31. If correct, this picture will have been complicated by the recall and reissue of party membership cards in 1973–74, in which, allegedly, 347,000 members were expelled. For details and interpretation of this, see Rigby, loc. cit., pp. 321–2 and A. Unger 'Soviet Communist Party Membership under Brezhnev: A Comment' in *Soviet Studies.*, XXIX, no. 2 (April 1977), 308.

32. Immense variations in the birth rate, and hence in the shape of the population pyramid, between different regions of the USSR, make party saturation figures of the *total* population highly misleading.

33. See, for example, V. V. Scherbitsky in *Pravda Ukrainy* 11 February 1981 and Sh. R. Rashidov in *Pravda Vostoka* 4 February 1981.

34. 2,300,000 candidates were admitted from the Komsomol between 1976 and 1981 (*P.zh.* 14/81, p. 16) which agrees well with the present number of Communists aged up to 30. But total admissions for the same period were 3,160,000; not many of the 860,000 admitted otherwise than through the Komsomol can have been from the declining 31-40 age group.

35. In Tables 1.3 and 1.4 education and employment figures for the total population in 1981 are extrapolated from the trends of the late 1970s and should thus be used with more caution than other parts of these tables.

36. Administration in Table 1.4 covers the party, state and economic bureaucracies, and also those of the social organisations such as the Komsomol and Trade Unions. Communists not employed in the national economy include not only pensioners, housewives and students, but, almost certainly, Communists in the armed forces (about 900,000); see above, note 30, The calculation of Communists by branches of the economy for 1981 is more difficult than for previous years, because *P.zh.* 14/81 provides less information; again, these 1981 figures should be used with caution.

37. This trend is probably due more than anything to the fact that poorly educated Communists are concentrated in the older age groups and are decreasing by natural causes quite quickly.

38. A. Unger, loc. cit., 313. Attention should be drawn to an error in this otherwise provocative article corrected by T. H. Rigby, op. cit., no. 3 (July 1977), 453.

39. See, for instance, Rigby, op. cit., XXVIII, no. 3, (July 1976), 329–32; Unger, loc. cit., 310–13; *P.zh.* 19/67, p. 11; 14/73, p. 13; 14/81, p. 15.

40. See, for example, *Itogi . . . 1970*, vol. V, p. 194, or *Narkhoz. 1975*, pp. 533

and 538 for what is offered on the class breakdown of sectors of the economy.

41. We know that about 44 per cent of the party are 'white-collar by social position' (*sluzhashchie po sotsial'nomu polozheniyu*). We do *not* know how many are 'white-collar by occupation' (*sluzhashchie po rodu zanyatii*). It is unlikely to be lower than 44 per cent or higher than 70 per cent of employed Communists; that is in 1977 there could have been between 5,700,000 and 9,000,000 Communists who were white-collar by occupation. A plausible figure for 1981 would be 7,750,000 (55 per cent), for which see p. 13.

42. Party people with tertiary or secondary specialist qualifications in 1977 amounted to 7,924,332 or nearly 50 per cent. It is difficult not to believe that the overwhelming majority of these were in occupations classified as *sluzhashchie*.

43. These are Azerbaydzhan, Georgia, Krasnodar, Kuibyshev, Leningrad, Lithuania, Moldavia, Moscow City, Rostov, Saratov, Tataria, Tomsk, Turkmenistan, Uzbekistan, Volgograd. For bibliographical data on all but the last of these, see Mary McAuley, 'Party Recruitment and the Nationalities in the USSR: A Study in Centre-Republican Relationships' in *British Journal of Political Science*, 10, part 4 (October 1980), 486–7. In addition see *Volgogradskaya obl. org. KPSS v tsifrakh, 1917–1978* (Volgograd, 1979). As will be seen, the data on social position for these regions correspond well with that for the Union as a whole; this gives one confidence that the data on occupational distribution are also representative. The data cannot always be gathered for an identical date; those for the mid-1960s are from 1964–66; for the mid-1970s, from 1970–78 but principally from 1975–78. The reason why a higher proportion of Communists appear to be in employment in the regions than in the Union as a whole is as follows: regional party statistics do not include members of the armed forces at any point; employment figures for the party as a whole also exclude them, but they are, of course, still present in the grand total and social position figures for the party.

44. See Unger, loc. cit., 314–15.

45. It is often assumed that the residue left after deducting Union Republican party membership figures from the all-Union total is a figure for the RSFSR. This is not so. Because Union Republican figures are for civilian organisations only, the residue includes all Communists in the armed forces, outside and inside the RSFSR (and, indeed, the Soviet Union!). However, the growth rates calculated from these residues are unlikely to be very far from the growth rates of party organisations in the RSFSR. For figures for the 1960s comparable to those in Table 1.7, see Rigby, *Communist Party Membership* . . . ., p. 507.

46. Calculated from data in *K. P. Uzbekistana v tsifrakh* (Tashkent, 1979), pp. 279–80, 327-8, using demographic data from *Itogi . . . 1970*, vol. II, p. 29; vol. III, p. 12; vol. IV, pp. 202, 378 and *Vest. stat.* 6/80, p. 41; 9/80, p. 61.

47. See *Narkhoz 1979*, pp. 143–4.

48. Mary McAuley, 'Party Recruitment and the Nationalities in the USSR', in *British Journal of Political Science*, 10, part 4 (October 1980), 461–87.

49. Unless, that is, one postulates demoralisation within the Georgian party,

after loss of its special relationship with the all-Union administration.

50. See *K. P. Belorussii v tsifrakh, 1918–1978* (Minsk, 1978), pp. 102–4; *K. P. Ukrainy – boevoy otryad KPSS* (Kiev, 1976), p. 25; *K. P. Ukrainy: naochnii posibnyk* (Kiev, 1972), p. 13; *Itogi . . . 1970*, vol. IV, pp. 152, 192.

51. See *K. P. Azerbaydzhana v tsifrakh* (Baku, 1970), pp. 44–5; *K. P. Gruzii v tsifrakh* (Tbilisi, 1971), pp. 199, 268; *Kompartiya Kazakhstana za 50 let* (Alma Ata, 1972), pp. 280–324; *K. P. Uzbekistana v tsifrakh*, pp. 279, 327; *Itogi . . . 1970*, vol. IV, pp. 202, 223, 253, 263.

52. Compare the figures in *Itogi . . . 1970*, vol. IV, with those in *Vest. stat.*, 10/80, pp. 67–70.

53. *Vest. stat.* 2/80, pp. 12–16.

54. Party membership by province is calculated from the size of the delegation sent by a province to a Party Congress.

55. See my forthcoming work cited in note 30. Some of the highest party saturation rates in the Union are now to be found in the outer Moscow hinterland, for example Kalinin or Kostroma provinces.

56. *P. zh.* 21/77, pp. 26, 32–3.

57. This is true of Kazakhstan, Kirghizia, Tadzhikistan, Turkmenistan and Azerbaydzhan. For bibliography, see McAuley, loc. cit.

58. *P. zh.*, loc. cit. This is occasionally confirmed by the regional sources, for example *Lietuvos Komunistu Partija Skaiciais 1918–1973* (Vil'nyus, 1976), pp. 203–4.

59. Since most primary party organisations are based on a place of work, it would not be difficult for superior authorities to hand down a target of, say, 10 per cent saturation of the workforce to an organisation in an industrial enterprise, but one of 30 per cent to an institution employing mainly graduates.

60. Thus I would explain staffing at my place of work to a Soviet visitor by saying that a tutor is on the *nomenklatura* of a head of department, a lecturer on that of a dean, and a professor on that of the Vice-Chancellor, the latter being the persons who convene and chair the respective selection committees.

61. The major attempt at such a redefinition has been M. Voslensky: *La Nomenklatura: Les privilégiés en URSS* (Paris, 1980). For his exclusion of *the raykom* level of the party *nomenklatura* from his discussion, see ibid., pp. 121–5.

62. Alec Nove, for instance, has suggested that such an identifiable subset is the *nomenklaturnye* of the all-Union Central Committee. See his 'Is There a Ruling Class in the USSR?', *Soviet Studies*, XXVII, no. 4 (October 1975), 615–38.

63. The basic available data on the party *nomenklatura* are collected by Harasymiw, op. cit., in note 8 above, and *Osteuropa*, 27, no. 7 (July 1977), 583–98. The figure of approximately two million was obtained by taking the posts named by Harasymiw as being on a party *nomenklatura* at some level and ascertaining, from *Itogi . . . 1970*, vol. VI, pp. 20–3, how many persons belonged to these occupations in 1970. Rigby, in his introduction to Rigby and Harasymiw, op. cit., in note 6 above, arrives at a similar figure for the whole of the USSR by extrapolating from the known size of the *nomenklatura* in two regions.

64. The USSR has, of course, never lacked for charges of patronage and clientelism, and the latter are not in principle incompatible with *nomenklatura* staffing procedures. What *would* constitute an erosion of the present *nomenklatura* system would be loss of *standardised* staffing procedures.

65. See, for example, Nove, op. cit., 618; Rigby in Rigby and Harasymiw, op. cit.; Harasymiw, op. cit (1969), 510.

66. The public use of Stalin's name and image in Georgia is a case in point.

67. For several reasons, among them the size of their Supreme Soviets relative to population and the possession of their 'own' Central Committees and *apparaty*, we simply have much more biographical data for areas other than the RSFSR.

68. For this and subsequent points, see John H. Miller, 'Cadres Policy in Nationality Areas' in *Soviet Studies*, XXIX, no. 1 (January 1977), 3–36, and – a study of much greater scope and detail – Grey Hodnett, *Leadership in the Soviet National Republics* (Oakville, Ontario, 1978), especially Chapters 2 and 8.

69. For more on this, and its interpretation, see John H. Miller, 'Nomenklatura: Check on Localism?' in Rigby and Harasymiw (eds), op cit.

70. Ibid.

71. Explicitly recalled at the 1971 Party Congress. See XXIV *S˝ezd KPSS, sten. otchet.*, I, p. 124.

72. Jerry F. Hough, 'The Generation Gap and the Brezhnev Succession' in *Problems of Communism*, July-August 1979, 1–18, especially 3–5.

73. For a much more searching investigation of this issue, and a provisional interpretation, see Seweryn Bialer: *Stalin's Successors: Leadership, stability and change in the Soviet Union* (Cambridge, 1980), Ch. 6, especially pp. 102 and 114–24.

74. The absolute numbers given do not always correspond to the total size of the group concerned because of missing data on age, particularly concerning recent appointments. In summing 'new appointments' to the Central Committee (members and candidates) and the Central Auditing Commission internal promotions *between* these bodies have been ignored.

75. RSFSR *obkom* first secretaries (data available for 77 in 1981) are on average 1.6 years older than the all-Union mean, and first secretaries outside the RSFSR (N = 74) 1.7 years younger. This difference has hardly changed over the last decade. However, among the new appointments to this position in Table 1.10, RSFSR first secretaries (N = 19) are slightly *younger* than those from elsewhere (N = 32).

76. For an interesting attempt, see J. P. Willerton, Jr., 'Clientelism in the Soviet Union: an Initial Examination' in *Studies in Comparative Communism*, XII, nos. 2–3, Summer/Autumn 1979, 159–83. The principal difficulties (which Willerton does not blink) are that two-thirds of his sample could not be associated with any patron, even in a formal sense, and that the fall from grace of patrons did not have a marked adverse effect on the careers of their apparent clients.

77. G. A. Arbatov and N. N. Inozemtsev.

2 Foreign and Defence Policy

David Holloway

Soviet Party Congresses do not provide a forum for real public debate about policy, but they are the stage from which authoritative statements of policy are made. At the XXIV Congress in 1971 Leonid Brezhnev outlined the Peace Programme that has been a central feature of Soviet detente policy over the last ten years. This Programme was further elaborated at the XXV Congress in 1976. But since then, and in particular since the Soviet intervention in Afghanistan in December 1979, East–West relations have taken a sharp turn for the worse. The XXVI Party Congress in February 1981 provided an opportunity for the Soviet leadership to make clear its attitude to the worsening climate of international relations. It was unlikely that Brezhnev would renounce the policy of detente with which he personally has been so closely associated (the XXIV Congress marked his emergence as the dominant figure in Soviet foreign policy). In the event, his report to the Congress attempted to breathe new life into the policy first advanced ten years before, and to portray the Soviet Union as the champion of peace in a troubled world.

The origins of Soviet detente policy in the 1970s can be traced back to 1969–71, when major changes in international relations and in the Soviet Union itself created the impetus for a new foreign policy line. The state of world politics was changed by the Sino-Soviet border clashes of 1969, which helped to push China out of the self-imposed isolation of the Cultural Revolution; by the foreign policy of the Nixon Administration, which was intent on exploiting the Sino-Soviet rift to put pressure on the Soviet Union; and by the election of the SPD-FPD government in West Germany, which wished to settle outstanding disputes with the Soviet Union and other Eastern European countries. The domestic sources of Soviet policy also changed in those years. At the end of the 1960s the Soviet Union attained strategic parity with the

United States, and this raised an important question for Soviet policy: should the Soviet Union pursue significant strategic superiority, or should it try to stabilise the strategic relationship at parity? The second major issue was economic. The Czechoslovak crisis of 1968 set back the cause of economic reform in the Soviet Union because it seemed to show that such reform would create pressure for political change. The Soviet leadership now put greater stress on the acquisition of foreign technology as a way of improving economic performance.

Detente was seen by the Soviet leaders as following from an increase in Soviet power and a shift in the international 'correlation of forces' in favour of the socialist camp. Strategic parity would prevent the West from trying to deal with the Soviet Union from a position of strength, and encourage it to adopt more 'realistic' policies. This in turn would lead to a relaxation of tension and to a reduction in the risk of war. It would also lead to greater access to western credits and technology, and to greater opportunities for advancing Soviet influence in the world. Moreover, by pursuing a policy of detente towards the West, the Soviet Union hoped to forestall too close a rapprochement between China and the United States. In Soviet eyes, therefore, detente not only resulted from growing Soviet power, but would provide a favourable context in which to pursue Soviet objectives, some of which entailed co-operation with the West, and some conflict.[1]

This broad framework allowed for differences of emphasis and priority. At the Soviet-American Summit in Moscow in 1972 the three top Soviet leaders, Brezhnev, Kosygin and Podgorny, disagreed about the relative priority to be given to arms limitation and economic relations. Differences have been evident within the Soviet leadership about the need to acquire foreign technology. And in the early 1970s debate took place about the use of military power as an instrument of policy in the Third World. Moreover, the framework of detente policy has been able to accommodate ambiguous or divergent motives: arms limitation talks, for example, can be seen as a way of curbing the arms race, or as a tactic to restrain western defence policies and allow the Soviet Union to pursue military superiority. This ambiguity is important because, as many commentators have noted, different foreign policy tendencies exist in the Soviet Union, and these may have supported detente for different reasons. Besides, in the formation of policy different interests have been balanced: arms limitation has been pursued alongside high levels of arms procurement; a heavy military burden has coexisted with the effort to improve economic performance by importing technology; closer ties with the West have been accompanied by repression at home to minimise the political effects of such contact. As a result, Soviet policy has often seemed to foreign governments to be inconsistent and internally contradictory.[2]

In the early 1970s detente was marked by significant results in arms limitation (for example the SALT I Agreements of 1972), in East–West economic relations (for example the Soviet-American Trade Agreement of 1972) and in the settlement of political disputes (for example the Four-Power Agreement on Berlin of 1971). It also gave rise, in the Soviet Union as well as in the West, to hopes of further agreement and co-operation. But if the five years following the XXIV Party Congress saw definite if unsteady improvement in East–West relations, the five years preceding the XXVI Congress were, as Brezhnev said in his report, a 'complex and stormy' period in international affairs.[3]

A NEW ENCIRCLEMENT?

In the interwar period Soviet leaders viewed the international position of the Soviet Union primarily in terms of 'capitalist encirclement'. That concept was dropped from Soviet analyses after Stalin's death. But in the late 1970s the Soviet Union faced the prospect of a new encirclement as its chief adversaries – the United States, Western Europe, China and Japan – formed a quasi-alliance.

The main impetus to this realignment came from the steady deterioration of Soviet-American relations in the latter half of the decade. Brezhnev pointed to the central role of these relations when he declared at the XXVI Congress that 'it is universally recognised that in many ways the international situation depends on the policy of the USSR and the USA'. The crisis over Afghanistan caused the deepest rift, but it had already become clear that Soviet and American conceptions of detente were at odds. The aim of the Nixon–Kissinger detente policy had been to link different aspects of the Soviet-American relationship so that the United States could use leverage in one area (for example, trade) to influence Soviet policy in another (for example, in the Third World). But the Soviet leaders, while anxious for co-operation in some fields, and willing to make some concessions, were determined to retain their freedom to pursue goals which conflicted with western interests.

Two events in 1975 marked a serious setback for the process of Soviet-American detente. In January the US Senate adopted the

Jackson–Vanik Amendment to the Soviet-American Trade Bill,
requiring explicit Soviet undertakings about emigration. As a result,
the Soviet Union abrogated the Trade Agreement that had been
signed in Moscow in 1972. Later in the year the Soviet Union delivered
large supplies of arms to the MPLA in Angola and provided support
for the Cuban forces operating there. Soviet and Cuban help was
decisive in securing the victory of the MPLA over the forces backed by
South Africa, China and the United States.[4]

To domestic critics of American policy these events indicated that
the Soviet Union would not change its repressive policies at home in
return for better trade relations, and that detente would merely
encourage an expansionist Soviet policy in the Third World; in other
words, that the Nixon–Kissinger policy of detente would not work. To
the Soviet leaders the Senate Amendment showed that the United
States was trying to interfere in Soviet domestic affairs, and the outcry
over Angola that the United States was trying to restrict Soviet
activities abroad. In February 1976 Brezhnev told the XXV Party
Congress that

> detente does not in the slightest abolish and cannot abolish or alter
> the laws of the class struggle. Some bourgeois leaders affect surprise
> over the solidarity of Soviet Communists, of the Soviet people, with
> the struggle of other people for freedom and progress. This is either
> outright naivete or more likely a deliberate befuddling of minds.[5]

It was clear that there was a marked divergence between Soviet and
American conceptions of the process of detente.

President Carter took office in January 1977 with a firm commitment
to make the Soviet Union contribute more to detente, and in particular
to win concessions on human rights and on arms control. The Soviet
leaders regarded the policy of the new Administration as no more than
a further attempt to put pressure on them. More at home with
Realpolitik than with moral politics, they were profoundly annoyed by
Carter's stress on human rights. In March 1977 they rejected an
American proposal for major cuts in the Soviet and American strategic
arsenals, on the grounds that it was one-sided and that it moved away
from the provisions of the Vladivostok Accord, which Party General
Secretary Brezhnev and President Ford had concluded in November
1974. This false start set back the negotiations, and it was not until June
1979 that the SALT II Treaty was signed, at the Vienna Summit. By
that time, however, opposition to SALT had grown in the United

States, based on specific objections to the Treaty and on a general anxiety about the course of Soviet policy.[6]

In 1977 the Soviet Union airlifted arms to Ethiopia and sent military advisers to help the revolutionary government to put down rebellion in Eritrea and to defeat Somalia, which was trying (with its Soviet-armed and -trained forces) to seize the province of Ogaden. Cuban forces also came to the aid of the Ethiopian revolution.[7] Once again the Soviet-Cuban intervention angered American opinion and stimulated pressure for a tougher foreign policy. The Soviet Union was increasingly seen as a global power, willing and able to use military force around the world to further its political ambitions. Since the chief aim of American detente policy was to restrain Soviet expansion by linking co-operation in arms control and trade to Soviet behaviour abroad, Soviet activities in Africa inevitably undermined American faith in co-operation.

As relations with the Soviet Union deteriorated, the United States' ties with China grew stronger. After Mao's death in 1976 the Soviet Union put out feelers to see whether the new leadership was ready for an improvement in relations. But it was soon clear that, in spite of major changes in domestic affairs, hostility towards the Soviet Union would remain a feature of Chinese policy. The new Chinese leadership was determined to make China a modern industrial state by the year 2000 and sought closer contact with the United States, Western Europe and Japan.

In August 1978, disregarding the dire Soviet warnings, China and Japan signed a Treaty of Peace and Friendship. This included an 'anti-hegemony' clause that, in spite of disavowals, was clearly directed against the Soviet Union. The Soviet government denounced the Treaty as 'a threat to stability in Asia'.[8] In November (within weeks of signing a Treaty of Friendship and Co-operation with the Soviet Union) Vietnam invaded Kampuchea, which was aligned with China. In December the United States and China announced that they had reached agreement on the position of Taiwan and would now proceed to establish normal diplomatic relations. In February 1979 China invaded Vietnam in order to punish it for its invasion of Kampuchea, but withdrew its forces within a month. The Soviet Union both gained and lost from this flurry of Friendship Treaties and invasions. Vietnam and the Vietnamese-backed government in Kampuchea were now firmly allied with the Soviet Union against China. But in June Brezhnev had warned the United States not to play the 'China card' against the USSR, declaring that this was a 'short-sighted and dangerous policy' which its architects might bitterly regret.[9] Six months later Japan, China and the United States had drawn much closer together.

The Soviet intervention in Afghanistan gave further impetus to these realignments. President Carter abandoned the now hopeless effort to have the SALT II Treaty ratified by the Senate. He also imposed an embargo on grain shipments to the Soviet Union and adopted various other economic sanctions.[10] In January 1980 the United States tilted further towards China: Congress approved the granting of Most Favoured Nation trading status to China (the Soviet Union had lost the chance of such status by abrogating the Trade Agreement in 1975); the US Secretary of Defense stated, after a visit to Beijing, that the two countries shared similar strategic assessments and would broaden their military contacts; the United States agreed to sell 'non-lethal' military equipment to China (and had announced in 1978 that it would not oppose the sale of arms to China by its Western European allies). In January 1981 President Reagan took office with a commitment to reassess East–West relations, redress an alleged Soviet military superiority, and to assert American power more vigorously throughout the world. In spite of some differences over the status of Taiwan it seems likely that Sino-American relations will continue to grow closer.

Soviet relations with Western Europe have not deteriorated in the same way. This is partly because the achievements of detente have been more tangible in Europe. Trade with the Soviet Union has become important for the Western European economies; the benefits in terms of individual and family contacts have been more clearly felt, especially in West Germany; and no major political crisis had erupted in Europe itself before the military crackdown in Poland in December 1981. But there have been disappointments. The Helsinki Final Act of 1975, which ratified existing territorial boundaries in Europe and called for expanded cultural and scientific ties, has not created a new pattern of East–West relations in Europe. The two follow-up meetings, in Belgrade (1977–78) and Madrid (1980–81) proved acrimonious, especially on the subject of human rights, and provided no new impetus for detente. Similarly, the negotiations on Mutual and Balanced Force Reductions (MBFR) in Europe, which have been taking place in Vienna since 1973, have so far borne no fruit.

More recently, Soviet relations with Western Europe have been strained by the crisis over Afghanistan and by the issue of theatre nuclear forces (TNF) in Europe. The Western European governments joined the United States in condemning the Soviet action in Afghanistan. They also agreed to the deployment of US Ground-Launched Cruise Missiles (GLCMs) and Pershing II missiles in Europe, as a response to the Soviet deployment of the SS-20 Intermediate Range Ballistic Missile (IRBM) and the *Backfire* bomber. Yet these issues have also caused difficulties in the Western Alliance. Because trade with the Soviet Union has been more important for Western European governments, they have been less willing than the United States to impose economic sanctions on the Soviet Union; and because disillusionment with arms control is not so deep, they have been more anxious than the United States to enter into negotiations with the Soviet Union on the limitation of TNF. These differences were evident in the western response to General Jaruzelski's imposition of martial law in Poland in December 1981. NATO had issued stern warnings to the Soviet Union about the consequences of military intervention, but the Polish government's repressive action appears to have caught western governments off guard. The United States imposed sanctions on both Poland and the Soviet Union, but the Western European governments did not follow the American lead.

By 1978 it was clear that a potential or quasi-alliance, based on anxiety about the growth of Soviet power and the assertiveness of Soviet policy, was being formed between the Soviet Union's main adversaries. This has been a serious setback for the Soviet Union, and Soviet efforts to forestall it have been clumsy and ineffective. In February 1978, for example, the Soviet Union tried to head off the Sino-Japanese Treaty by publishing a draft treaty on 'Good Neighbourly Relations and Co-operation' with Japan. But the draft angered the Japanese government because it made no reference to the four Kurile islands whose jurisdiction is in dispute between the two countries. Japan claims these as its own, but the Soviet Union has held them since the end of the Second World War. The Soviet leaders were unwilling to make any concession on this issue to prevent a Sino-Japanese rapprochement; perhaps they felt that a concession would be taken as a sign of weakness and provoke claims from other governments, in particular from China.

It would be wrong, however, to overemphasise the threat that this potential alliance poses to the Soviet Union. There are differences of interest among the Soviet Union's adversaries. The western response to the Soviet action in Afghanistan, for example, was badly co-ordinated, and ineffective in its immediate aim of securing the withdrawal of Soviet forces; the repression in Poland in December 1981 left

the Western Alliance in similar disarray. Western European governments have run into difficulties in meeting the commitment they made
in May 1978 to raise their defence expenditure by 3 per cent a year.
China faces formidable problems in achieving its modernisation
programme and, for all its warnings about the Soviet threat, is concentrating on industrial development rather than on a military build-
up. Japan, in spite of anxiety about Soviet actions and prodding from
the United States, has not yet raised its military expenditure above 1
per cent of GNP. And although the commitment of the Reagan
Administration to increasing American military power is clear, the
final shape of its policy towards the Soviet Union is not. Yet for all
these qualifications it remains true that Soviet policy in the decade of
detente has drawn the Soviet Union's adversaries closer together; and
this must be considered a major failure of that policy.

The Soviet leaders have disclaimed all responsibility for the failure
of detente. At the XXVI Party Congress Mr Brezhnev blamed the
deepening crisis of capitalism and the rising influence of reactionary
circles in the West for the poor state of East–West relations. He
presented the Soviet Union as the injured party. Western governments
have not shared this assessment, and have seen the growth of Soviet
military power, and the use of that power to expand Soviet influence,
as the chief cause of the worsening international situation.

Whatever the truth of these arguments, it is important to note that
the United States and the Soviet Union have had different conceptions
of detente. The United States has seen detente as a form of behaviour
modification, the key aim of which is to restrain Soviet expansion by
offering the Soviet Union co-operation in areas of mutual interest.[11]
The Soviet leaders, on the other hand, have seen detente as a relationship of both co-operation and conflict. They have rejected the
American conception of linkage, arguing that co-operation in such
areas as arms control and trade is mutually beneficial, and that therefore the Soviet Union should not be expected to pay an extra price by
changing its political system or modifying its foreign policy to conform
to American ideas about the norms of international behaviour. When
President Reagan lifted the grain embargo in June 1981, the Soviet
leaders did not see this as a favour, but as an action taken in pursuit of
American self-interest.

Of course, linkage is not merely a theoretical construct; co-operation between the United States and the Soviet Union is likely to be
made more difficult by conflict between them, no matter what conceptions they hold. But the difference in conceptions of detente has

had important political effects, because Soviet actions in Africa and Asia have undermined American belief in the value of co-operation, and because agreement is harder to achieve when the two sides do not share the same frame of reference. The Carter Administration in particular found it difficult to devise a policy combining co-operation and conflict. Indeed, by the end of the decade it appeared to some observers that the Soviet Union had little to gain from restraint, and little to fear from conflict, in its relationship with the United States.[12] The Soviet leaders do not appear to have been altogether happy in dealing with a President they regarded as inept and impulsive, for co-operation had become difficult and conflict unpredictable.[13] The Reagan Administration has declared its intention to build up American power, the better to pursue conflict with the Soviet Union; it is not yet so clear what it will offer in the way of co-operation.

MILITARY POLICY

There have been no signs in the last five years of a slackening of the Soviet military effort. The Soviet Union does not reveal how much it spends on defence, but western estimates (which are subject to considerable error) point to a continuing growth in defence expenditure. At the XXVI Congress Brezhnev asserted that the Warsaw Pact had fewer men under arms than NATO, and western estimates bear this out.[14] But the Soviet Union plays a larger role in the Pact than the United States does in NATO, and according to American estimates the Soviet Union spends considerably more on defence than the United States, although its GNP is only about 60 per cent as large.[15] This commitment to military power has worried western governments, which see the Soviet Union striving to achieve military superiority.

Soviet leaders have been at pains to stress that military superiority is not their aim. In a speech in Tula in January 1977 Brezhnev declared that

the Soviet Union's defence potential must be sufficient to deter anyone from taking the risk of interfering with our peaceful life. Not a policy aimed at superiority in armaments, but a policy aimed at reducing them, at lessening military confrontation – that is our policy.[16]

At the XXVI Congress Brezhnev stated even more categorically that the military and strategic equilibrium prevailing between the USSR and the USA, between the Warsaw Pact and NATO, is objectively a safeguard of world peace. We have not sought, and do not now seek, military superiority over the other side. That is not our policy.

These statements mark a shift in Soviet thinking about military policy.

In the early 1960s, when the Soviet Union lagged behind the United States in strategic forces, Soviet military thought stressed the importance of preparing to fight and win a nuclear war, and superiority was seen to be of great importance.[17] At the end of the decade, when the Soviet Union achieved strategic parity, some military theorists came to accept that this relationship, while far from ideal, was the best that could be attained in the circumstances. The pursuit of superiority would be costly and would probably not succeed, because the United States would respond.[18] Since Brezhnev's Tula speech in January 1977 Soviet leaders have emphasised that their doctrine is defensive and that the aim of their policy is to deter attacks on the Soviet Union, not to seek superiority over the United States in order to fight and win a nuclear war. Brezhnev told the XXVI Congress that

to try to outstrip each other in the arms race or to expect to win a nuclear war is dangerous madness.

It may seem paradoxical (and suspicious) that Soviet leaders have denied that superiority is their goal just at the time when the growth of Soviet strategic power has given most concern in the West. Two factors help to explain this apparent paradox. The first is that the Soviet leadership apparently accepts that with no effective defences available against ballistic missiles, and with large numbers of warheads on either side, nuclear war would have devastating consequences, which civil defence might lessen, but could not prevent.[19] The second is that the Soviet leaders appear to have become more confident of the ability of Soviet military power to deter a nuclear attack: growing Soviet power has, in their eyes, made a general nuclear war less likely. Clearly the General Staff does plan for the conduct of such a war, and would try to win it if it took place. But there is little evidence to suggest that the Soviet leaders think that victory would be anything other than catastrophic, for the victors as well as the vanquished.[20]

This new emphasis in Soviet military doctrine has been accompanied by a clear assertion of the Party's primacy in military affairs. On the death of Marshal Grechko in April 1976, D. F. Ustinov, who had spent most of his career in the defence industry and had been a Central Committee Secretary since 1966, was appointed Minister of Defence. Although Ustinov is hardly the archetypal 'civilian', his appointment meant that for the first time in twenty-one years the Minister was not a professional soldier. Since then the Soviet Union has let it be known that Brezhnev is Supreme Commander-in-Chief and Chairman of the Defence Council, the highest defence policy-making body; he has been made a Marshal of the Soviet Union and showered with military honours. In January 1977 Marshal Ogarkov, apparently a protégé of Ustinov's, was made Chief of the General Staff.[21] Ogarkov, who has been described by one of his colleagues as 'by no means a run-of-the-mill army officer',[22] was a leading figure in the early stages of SALT and may therefore have a special knowledge of strategic matters.

The consequences of these developments are difficult to assess, and may not be clear for some time. Although Soviet doctrine may be defensive in intention, Soviet military strategy stresses the importance of taking the offensive in the event of war, and Soviet forces are deployed with this in mind; hence the policy implications of the shift in doctrine are not clear. Moreover, it is not always evident what the new statements of doctrine mean in practical terms. Parity, to which the Soviet leaders now declare themselves committed, is hard to define precisely, because no agreed way of measuring strategic power exists. Brezhnev told the XXVI Congress that 'approximate parity' existed in the Soviet-American strategic relationship and in medium-range nuclear weapons in Europe. But western governments have argued that the Soviet Union enjoys superiority in both areas and justify their arms programmes in terms of the need to redress the imbalance.

American military planners are worried by the increasing vulnerability of the US land-based missiles to attack by the latest generation of Soviet ICBMs.[23] They argue that the greater accuracy of the new Soviet missiles would allow the Soviet Union to destroy a large proportion (up to 95 per cent) of the American Minuteman land-based missiles in a first strike. The President would then be forced either to capitulate or to retaliate against Soviet cities, in the knowledge that the Soviet Union would still be able to destroy American cities after the American strike. While the Soviet leaders might not exploit this vulnerability by launching a nuclear strike, it is said, the knowledge that it exists will give them a political advantage in any crisis and thus encourage them to pursue an adventuristic foreign policy. This is especially so because, in one current view, the Soviet leaders believe that they can fight and win a nuclear war. The failure of negotiations to restrict the deployment of the new Soviet ICBMs was one of the main reasons for opposition to SALT II in the United States, and the need for an invulnerable ICBM has been the main rationale for the mobile MX missile, which is due to be deployed in the late 1980s.

There are, however, a number of reasons for doubting that the Soviet leaders think that what has been called the 'window of vulnerability' exists. To achieve a successful first strike against Minuteman silos the Soviet leaders would have to assume, first, that the United States has not adopted a 'launch-on-warning' policy and that the missiles would still be in their silos when the Soviet warheads arrived; second, that the Soviet missiles would function as well as they have on their best test flights, even though they would be flying over a different part of the earth, where different geodetic effects would be felt (and the assumption of Minuteman vulnerability is highly sensitive to assumptions about the accuracy of Soviet warheads); third, that the American President would not retaliate with SLBMs and strategic bombers, since these could wreak devastation on the Soviet Union (Marshal Ogarkov has written that American expressions of concern about Soviet ICBMs frequently leave American SLBMs and bombers out of account[24] – though the Soviet General Staff could hardly do so). There is little evidence in Soviet thinking of the kind of technological hubris that would be required to launch such a strike. Moreover, it is by no means clear that the Soviet leaders contemplate nuclear war as readily as this argument seems to assume. It is hard to see, therefore, that the 'window of vulnerability' thesis has much validity in terms of Soviet foreign policy.

The Soviet Union does, however, see the attainment of parity as imposing restraints on the ability of the United States to use its strategic forces in a crisis. One Soviet commentator has noted that the United States has been much less ready to put its strategic forces on alert during crises since the Soviet Union attained parity.[25] In Soviet eyes, the build-up of Soviet strategic power has deprived the American strategic forces of much of their political and military utility. Soviet writers have interpreted changes in American strategic doctrine in the 1970s as an effort to escape from the consequences of parity, and they portray the new American strategic weapons programmes as a drive for superiority.[26] Brezhnev told the XXVI Congress that attempts to attain superiority over the Soviet Union were 'absolutely futile'.

The second major issue to have caused concern in the West is the balance of nuclear forces in Europe. In the mid-1970s the Soviet Union began to deploy the SS-20 mobile IRBM and the *Backfire* bomber. The

Soviet Union argues that these systems represent no more than a modernisation of Soviet forces. Western governments view them as part of a Soviet drive for superiority. Western European governments, in particular, fear that the American nuclear guarantee is no longer credible now that the Soviet Union has attained parity, and that the Soviet leaders might come to believe that they could attack Western Europe without any nuclear response from the United States.

In December 1979 NATO decided to deploy 464 GLCMs and 108 Pershing II missiles in Western Europe (deployment is to begin in 1983). In October 1979 Brezhnev tried to head off the NATO decision by saying that if NATO did not go ahead with it, unilateral but unspecified reductions would be made in the medium-range nuclear weapons based in the European part of the Soviet Union; but his offer was not taken up. Again at the XXVI Congress he proposed a moratorium on the deployment of such weapons, but NATO has rejected this on the grounds that it would merely ratify Soviet superiority in this area and that it would not cover those SS-20s deployed east of the Urals which could strike targets in Europe.[27]

The Soviet Union has pursued a vigorous campaign against the NATO decision, trying to capitalise on the opposition that the new missiles have aroused in Western Europe. This campaign has at least two aims: to worsen relations between the United States and Western Europe, and to prevent deployment of the missiles. The Soviet Union evidently regards the issue as an opportunity for sowing disarray in the West. But it also has real anxieties about the new weapons. From the Soviet point of view, the new American missiles represent not so much a change in the theatre balance as an addition to American strategic power. The Pershing II missile is of special importance here because it is highly accurate and could reach Moscow and other targets within range in four to six minutes. By themselves, 108 of these missiles would not constitute an effective first-strike force, but in the context of other American weapons programmes they look more dangerous.[28] The NATO decision has been portrayed in the Soviet press as part of the general American drive for superiority.

In November 1981 the Soviet Union and the United States began negotiations to limit medium-range nuclear forces in Europe, but major obstacles have to be surmounted before an agreement is reached. NATO claims that the Soviet Union has superiority in theatre nuclear forces, while the Soviet Union insists that parity exists. There is no agreement on what systems to weigh in the balance. Besides, the problem of verifying an agreement which limits mobile missiles (as both the Soviet and American systems are) will be considerable, if not insuperable. The whole issue shows how difficult it is to agree what parity means in practice, and how definitions of the military balance can be manipulated for political purposes.

The issues of Minuteman vulnerability and theatre nuclear forces in Europe show that what is taking place is not merely a competition in arms, but also a competition in strategies, with each side trying to make the strategy of the other unworkable. NATO decided to deploy American missiles in Europe because it is feared that its strategy of flexible response was no longer credible in view of the build-up of Soviet forces. Soviet leaders have declared that their doctrine is defensive, but their military strategy remains committed to the offensive. It is an object of Soviet policy to make NATO strategy more difficult to implement, and this has contributed to the anxiety that western governments feel about Soviet policy. At the same time, however, the Soviet Union has worries of its own. Current western policy is seen as an attempt to escape from parity and to regain superiority. Moreover, Soviet commentators point out that of the five nuclear weapons states four are hostile to the Soviet Union, and that over the last ten years relations between the Soviet Union's adversaries have grown closer.

With the attainment of strategic parity, Soviet theorists turned their attention to the utility of military force as an instrument of policy outside the central military relationships with NATO and China. The Soviet leaders have not accepted that detente obliges them to restrain their efforts to increase Soviet influence in the world. They have assumed that they have (in the words of one Soviet official) an 'equal right to meddle in Third Areas'.[29] As Marshal Grechko put it (less pithily) in 1974:

at the present stage the historic function of the Soviet Armed Forces is not restricted to their function in defending our Motherland and the other socialist countries. In its foreign policy activity the Soviet state purposefully opposes the export of counter-revolution and the policy of oppression, supports the struggle for national liberation, and resolutely resists imperialist aggression in whatever distant region of our planet it may appear.[30]

Active Soviet interest in the Third World is not new, for the Soviet Union has supported anti-colonial struggles from its earliest days. But in the 1970s a growing naval presence and airlift capability have provided the Soviet Union with new instruments of policy.

During the 1970s the Soviet leaders evidently felt that they had attained a new international status, and a new ability to influence events around the world. They have used arms transfers, military advisers and their Cuban allies to help governments and movements that turned to them for support. But Soviet actions should not be seen merely as the result of a policy decision taken in the early 1970s, for contingent factors have played a great role. The collapse of three empires – the Portuguese (1974), Ethiopian (1974) and Iranian (1979) – created opportunities which the Soviet Union felt able to exploit. Moreover, Soviet policy has been guided not only by the desire to assert Soviet status as a global power, but also by more specific objectives: the security of its own frontiers, the containment of China, the restriction of western power and influence. Soviet policy has to be interpreted not merely in terms of Soviet ambitions, but also in the context of the regions where it intervenes. The Soviet Union is indeed an important actor in international politics, but it does not devise the plot, write the script, set the scene or direct the play as well.

TWO CRISES: AFGHANISTAN AND POLAND

At the turn of the decade the Soviet leaders faced two major crises. In Afghanistan they used military force to instal a new, subservient government in a neighbouring country. In Poland they threatened to use force to stop political change and reimpose an order of which they approved. The Soviet action in Afghanistan has been widely interpreted as symptomatic of growing Soviet power and assertiveness. The situation in Poland was seen as a sign of Soviet weakness, and even of the decay of the Soviet model of political and economic organisation.

Close observers of Afghanistan foresaw in 1979 that the Soviet Union might feel impelled to send combat troops to save the government which had seized power in April 1978. That *coup*, which was apparently neither planned nor instigated by the Soviet Union, brought to power a pro-Soviet Marxist-Leninist government that was bitterly divided by factional politics. The new government provoked widespread rebellion by launching far-reaching reforms in a brutal and disorganised way. Before December 1979 there were 7000 Soviet military and civilian advisers in Afghanistan, but the government had called for further Soviet military aid to repress the insurgents. In an effort to restore stability the Soviet Union urged President Taraki to remove his Prime Minister, Hafizullah Amin, moderate his policies and form a more broadly-based government. This plan was thwarted by Amin, who appears to have been forwarned of Taraki's intention. He eliminated Taraki and took over power himself in September 1979. The Soviet leaders apparently regarded Amin as untrustworthy (as he no doubt regarded them) and feared that he might take the country out of the Soviet sphere of influence. On 24 December the Soviet Union began to airlift troops into Kabul, claiming it was responding to an appeal from the government to suppress a counter-revolution which was being fomented from outside the country. On 28 December Kabul Radio broadcast a speech by Babrak Karmal announcing that Amin had been deposed and that he had taken power. Babrak Karmal had been in the original post-*coup* government, but had fallen victim to factional in-fighting and had been 'exiled' to the Ambassadorship in Prague. He was in the Soviet Union at the time of the invasion, but was soon brought to Kabul and installed as president; Amin was killed in the early stages of the invasion.[31]

In the event, the Soviet occupation appears to have stiffened resistance to the government in Kabul. The Soviet forces, now said by western governments to number nearly 100,000, are in no danger of being defeated, but they have not extended their control much beyond the main towns and roads. Soviet casualties by mid-1981 were estimated to be between 8000 and 12,000 killed and injured.[32] The Soviet Union seems to be set for a long period of 'normalisation', and is neither so embarrassed nor so troubled by the resistance as to seek a face-saving way of withdrawing its forces. The Soviet government has insisted that any settlement of the international crisis over Afghanistan must be based on recognition of the existing government in Kabul, and it is on this point that the European Communities' initiative for a peace conference foundered in July 1981.[33]

Some western observers have seen the Soviet action as primarily defensive, and accept the point made by Brezhnev at the XXVI Congress, that the situation in Afghanistan posed 'a direct threat to the security of our southern frontier'. Others have interpreted the Soviet action in a more offensive light, seeing it as a step towards Soviet domination of the Persian Gulf region.[34] It is impossible to say with certainty what considerations were uppermost in Soviet minds; nor indeed are defensive and offensive aims mutually exclusive. The Soviet leaders evidently feared that an anti-Soviet government would emerge in Afghanistan, either under Amin or following his defeat by the rebels. Soviet intervention would not only prevent that, but would also provide the Soviet Union with a stronger position in an unstable area. Poor American relations with Iran and with Pakistan (over Pakistan's nuclear programme) precluded the possibility of military reaction from outside, while the American opposition to ratification of SALT II and the NATO decision to deploy American missiles in Europe seemed to indicate that the Soviet Union had little to gain from restraint. Occupation of Afghanistan would also contribute to the Soviet aim of surrounding China with Soviet allies.

There is some evidence that the whole operation misfired, and that the killing of Amin was not planned; perhaps the Soviet leaders expected to carry it off with fewer political repercussions.[35] In the event they found themselves isolated to an unprecedented degree at the United Nations and subjected to severe criticism, not only from the western powers, but also from Islamic and Third World countries. But Soviet leaders have traditionally given more weight to physical guarantees of security than to the less tangible factor of international opinion, and the former may well prove more durable in this case than the latter. Soviet policy at the moment is to sit tight, to show a willingness to talk about the international position of Afghanistan but not to make any substantial concessions, and to hope that world opinion will forget about the invasion as other crises come to occupy its attention.

If the Soviet leaders saw the occupation as contributing to their own security, the western powers saw it as a threat to the supply of oil from the Gulf. In 1979 25 per cent of US, 66 per cent of Western European, and 75 per cent of Japanese oil imports passed through the Straits of Hormuz.[36] The collapse of the Shah's regime had already weakened the western position in the region. The invasion of Afghanistan worsened the regional balance of power, brought Soviet forces closer to the Strait, and perhaps most important, demonstrated Soviet willingness to use combat troops outside Eastern Europe. On 23 January 1980 President Carter warned that

> an attempt by any outside force to gain control of the Persian Gulf region will be regarded as an assault on the vital interests of the U.S.A., and such an assault will be repelled by any means necessary, including military force.[37]

The Soviet invasion gave new impetus to the creation by the United States of a Rapid Deployment Force, ready to intervene in distant areas of the globe, and in particular in the Persian Gulf.

In this region Soviet concern about security cuts across the vulnerability of western interests, and the danger of confrontation is heightened by the rivalries and instabilities of the regional powers.[38] In December 1980 Brezhnev proposed an international treaty on the Persian Gulf, but it was rejected by the United States on the grounds that it would legitimate Soviet interference in the region.[39] This is likely to be one of the most dangerous areas of superpower confrontation in the 1980s.

The crisis in Afghanistan presented the Soviet Union with opportunities as well as dangers. But the crisis in Poland was profoundly worrying for the Soviet leaders, and offered no gain, no matter what course of action they pursued. Twice they appear to have come close to using Soviet forces, in December 1980 and March 1981. Past experience shows that they are willing to use force in Eastern Europe to suppress political movements they consider hostile to Soviet interests. But, as in other crises in the region, the threat of force (as opposed to its use) did little to arrest the process of political change.[40]

The Soviet leaders viewed the emergence of Solidarity with anxiety, for the very idea of an independent trade union is fundamentally anti-Leninist. The Polish Party lost control of events and thereby became incapable of performing the basic role of a Leninist Party, of acting as the 'leading and directing' force in society. By the summer of 1981 the Party itself had been affected by the process of change. In June the Soviet leadership warned its Polish counterpart that the situation in the Polish Party had 'recently become a subject of special alarm'.[41]

The political and economic aspects of the crisis have been inseparable. The movement for political change was sparked off by strikes protesting against food price increases. The political institutions lacked the authority to take measures to revive the economy. It seemed for a time in 1980 and 1981 that the state would acquire authority through the process of political renewal. But the political leaders found themselves in a difficult position, and needed the support of two constituencies: the Soviet Union and the Polish people. In the event they proved unable (or unwilling) to satisfy both at the same time.

Long before the military crackdown of December 1981 events in Poland had reached the point at which, on past experience, the Soviet Union might have been expected to use force. By speaking of the 'onslaught of the internal counter-revolution, which relies on the support of imperialist subversive centres abroad'[42] the Soviet authorities had provided themselves with as much justification as they usually have for intervening. It seemed, however, in the summer of 1981 that they were willing to accept some change in Poland. Polish socialism has always had special features: the Party State has not been able to dominate society as completely as in other Eastern European countries; the Church has provided a powerful focus of loyalty and identity; Polish agriculture remains largely in private hands; and popular unrest has been a significant factor in Polish politics, precipitating changes in the Party leadership in 1956, 1970 and 1980. The Soviet leaders may have been reluctant to use their own forces to reimpose order, for fear that they would meet with resistance.[43]

The repression imposed by the Polish government in December 1981 was perhaps the best outcome the Soviet leaders could hope for. The precise role of the Soviet Union in the decision to impose martial law is not clear, but it is evident that the government's action was a response, whether direct or indirect, to Soviet pressure. The Soviet Union has been able to play down its own involvement, and to present General Jaruzelski's action as an internal Polish affair. The Polish action has destroyed the movement for political renewal, at least in the short term.

The long-term consequences of General Jaruzelski's action are not apparent. The economy is in a critical state, with food shortages, falling production and a huge foreign debt, and it is not evident that repression will make things better. The state still faces powerful social forces, and it is not clear whether it can achieve some accommodation with them, or rule without such accommodation. Moreover, it is not, in the immediate aftermath of the repression, clear who rules – the Army, the Party, or a small clique of military and political leaders; nor can one say how far they will base their rule on the appeal to Polish nationalism, thus raising the possibility of conflict with the USSR.

Nevertheless, the Soviet leaders may feel that the crisis has been resolved, in the short term, with the least possible damage to their own interests. Although General Jaruzelski's action has become an issue in East–West relations, the international repercussions are less severe than would have followed direct Soviet intervention. Western European governments are apparently willing to continue business much as usual, and even the United States has not gone as far as imposing a grain embargo or suspending the TNF talks. In a more profound way, however, the crisis in Poland (which falls into the cyclical pattern of East European crises: Hungary in 1956, Czechoslovakia in 1968 and Poland in 1980–81) shows once again how difficult it is for East European governments to serve the two masters of Soviet power and their own people.

FOREIGN POLICY AND DOMESTIC POLITICS

Discussion of Soviet foreign policy leads quickly to questions of domestic politics. The whole issue of future Soviet development has become a central one in western debates about the appropriate policy to pursue towards the Soviet Union. The relationship between Soviet foreign and domestic policies is broad and complex, and only one aspect of it can be touched on here: economic constraints on the Soviet military effort.

In 1976 the CIA changed its estimate of the proportion of GNP that the Soviet Union spends on defence from 6–7 per cent to 11–13 per cent. Although there are considerable difficulties in estimating Soviet defence outlays, most observers agree that the revised figure is more plausible than the earlier one. The new estimate does not imply that Soviet forces are larger or more capable than had previously been thought, just that they cost more to produce and maintain. According to the CIA, Soviet military expenditure in the 1970s has grown at about 4–5 per cent a year, slightly faster than the GNP.[44]

Over the last fifteen years the Soviet Union has been successful in building up its armed forces, while at the same time raising living standards and ensuring economic growth. But in the 1980s resource allocation is becoming more difficult because the rate of economic growth has been declining and is likely to continue to fall. The problem is recognised in the Soviet Union. Academician N. Inozemtsev, a leading economist, who is also a member of the Central Committee, has written that

> in the '80s we will have to solve simultaneously such large-scale tasks as further raising the standard of living of the people, continuously increasing the economic and scientific-technical might of the country, reliably ensuring its security. And these tasks will have to be solved, as was emphasised at the Congress, in conditions that are far from easy, since several factors which complicate economic development will be operative. Among them are the reduction in the growth of labour resources, the increasing cost of exploiting the East and the North, expenditure on preserving the environment and on the infrastructure, above all transport and communications, and the necessity for more rapid renewal of productive funds.[45]

In this context the CIA's estimate of the economic burden of the defence effort can be read two ways: as indicating that the Soviet leaders are seriously committed to increasing their military power and hence likely to ignore the economic costs; or as showing that the costs of the defence effort are high and might therefore have to be cut if other needs are to be met. The first of these views has some validity in as much as the Soviet leaders have given, and still give, high priority to defence. But it would be wrong to suppose that priorities cannot be changed, for the present leadership has in fact made major changes in the pattern of resource allocation – by increasing investment in agriculture, for example. The possibility of a change in the priority of defence spending cannot be dismissed out of hand.

The choices that the Soviet leaders will face in the 1980s cannot be discussed in detail here. It is difficult to be precise because we cannot be certain how the Soviet economy will perform (witness the conflicting western estimates of Soviet energy production in the 1980s) and because our knowledge of the actual level of Soviet military expenditure is so poor. Nevertheless, it is reasonable to suppose that a shift of resources away from defence could result in a rise in investment or in consumption. How great the benefit would be depends on how efficiently the resources would be used compared to the way in which they are being used now. But the loosening of supply constraints that would follow a cutback in defence spending would benefit the economy in the short term. For longer term benefit, some reform of the economic system might be necessary as well as the change in priorities. But Brezhnev made it clear at the XXVI Congress that the Soviet Union intends to maintain the present military relationship with the West, and this will entail increases in defence expenditure to match the increased western effort. In this context the prospect of a reduction in defence outlays looks rather remote.

Some observers portray the choices facing the Soviet leaders in very stark terms, arguing that while the Soviet Union now enjoys a military advantage over the West, it will be unable, for economic reasons, to match the increase in American military power that will result from the Reagan Administration's policies. This combination of present strength and future weakness is seen to pose a particular danger to the West.[46] The Soviet Union, it is argued, might try to exploit its temporary advantage to make some lasting foreign policy gain – for example, by destroying China's nuclear forces, or by seizing control of the Persian Gulf.

There are several difficulties with this argument. In portraying the Soviet Union as a military giant with feet of clay it overestimates the strength of the Soviet Union's external position (strong though that is) and exaggerates the rigidities and weaknesses of the Soviet economic and political system (great though those are). A Soviet commentator has argued that American policy has been guided by a contradictory view of the Soviet Union: advances in military technology are asserted to be necessary to meet the Soviet threat, but at the same time it is assumed that the Soviet Union will not be able to catch up.[47] In Soviet eyes, neither the assertion nor the assumption are justified.

There is no evidence that the Soviet leaders see the choices facing them in drastic terms. Certainly they see problems, but manageable ones; Brezhnev's speech to the XXVI Congress conveyed neither an impression of overweening arrogance nor a sense of panic about the problems to come. It may be, of course, that the present leaders are too sanguine about the prospects for economic development, and that the problems will turn out to be less tractable than they say. But they would have to see their choices in a stark way if they were to act as this thesis suggests. Besides, if the Soviet Union's problem is indeed present strength and future weakness a daring strike now might only exacerbate the problem by provoking a strong reaction and even greater cohesion among the Soviet Union's adversaries.

There is a related thesis which argues that the Soviet Union must keep expanding its power abroad because otherwise the system will lose its legitimacy.[48] There is considerable force in this argument. The creation of military power is the area in which the Soviet Union has most clearly attained the goal of 'catching up and overtaking' the advanced capitalist powers. The Soviet Union's international influence demonstrates the power and prestige of the state, and a serious foreign policy setback would diminish the legitimacy of the state by showing it to be weak or incompetent; the traditional pattern of Russian development has been for domestic reform to follow military failure abroad. But legitimacy might also be lost if the rate of economic growth continues to decline, for rapid growth has been a major goal of Soviet policy, and has been claimed as a mark of the system's success. A serious drop in living standards might also affect support for the Soviet state. Raising living standards has been a central element in the present leadership's policy, and the situation in Poland serves as a pointed reminder of the dangers of neglecting this aspect of policy. Thus the thesis about legitimation through expansion is not a sound basis on which to predict the policies of the Soviet Union.

It is conceivable that the Soviet Union might pursue adventures abroad to divert attention from problems at home. But there is little evidence that this has been done. The Soviet invasion of Afghanistan does not appear to have been undertaken for this reason; nor has it been used to stir up nationalist sentiment inside the Soviet Union. On the other hand, the Soviet leaders can point towards the worsening state of international politics to justify the continuing high level of military effort, and can explain economic difficulties in terms of the need to ensure the defence of the Soviet Union and its allies. The appeal to Soviet patriotism is likely to be effective, because Soviet people appear to accept that strong armed forces are needed to maintain peace and security.[49]

This discussion does not of course give a full picture of western thinking about the interrelationship of domestic and foreign policies in the Soviet Union. But the thesis about present Soviet strength and future weakness does appear to colour the policy of the Reagan Administration towards the Soviet Union and is thus an important factor in East–West relations. Both President Reagan and Secretary of State Haig have said that they foresee the collapse of Communism in the Soviet Union. This view is held by many people not only on the right, but also on the left, of the politicial spectrum in the United States and Western Europe (though it is usually phrased differently on the left). The possibility of sudden change in the Soviet Union should not be ruled out, but there are two difficulties with the prognosis that the system will soon collapse. The first is that collapse has been predicted many times since 1917 and has not yet happened; the evidence for it does not appear to be stronger now than before. The second and more serious difficulty is that this prognosis does not solve the problem of how to establish a satisfactory policy towards the Soviet Union; it merely defines it out of existence.

Although some western analyses of the choices facing the Soviet leaders present these choices in a way that seems too stark and dramatic, it remains true that the Soviet Union will face difficult decisions about resource allocation in the 1980s. These decisions are likely to become the focus of a wider debate embracing domestic and foreign policies. It is most likely that such a debate will take place during a period of leadership change, when contenders for power may advance different programmes for Soviet policy.

CONCLUSION

Since the mid-1970s the Soviet Union has achieved some notable successes in its foreign and defence policy. It has continued to build up its military power, and has used that power to gain influence in Africa and Asia. It lost Somalia as an ally, but gained other friends. It helped the MPLA to win the Civil War in Angola. It has sustained the revolutionary government in Ethiopia. It has cemented its ties with Vietnam, and with the Vietnamese-backed government in Kampuchea. The Soviet leaders evidently feel that they have acquired a new international stature, and the capacity to carry out a global policy. A sense of power, rather than of desperation, lay behind the decision to intervene in Afghanistan.

In the last five years the Soviet leaders have tried to spell out the rationale for their military power. They have argued that their forces are defensive, and are designed to serve four main purposes: to deter a nuclear attack; to defend the Soviet Union if attacked; to hold the socialist camp together (the Brezhnev doctrine); and to support struggles for national liberation and independence (when that suits Soviet purposes). At the XXVI Congress Brezhnev stated that the danger of war

> originates not from the Soviet Union, not from any mythical Soviet superiority, but from the arms race and from the tension that still obtains in the world.

Western governments do not see Soviet military power in quite the same light. They regard the continuing growth of the Soviet military effort as a threat to western security. The military balance has become a very contentious issue in Soviet-American and Soviet-West European relations. The assertion of Soviet power in Africa and Asia helped to undermine the prospects of detente with the United States. The build-up of forces in the Far East led to a worsening of relations with Japan. The Soviet search for security has aroused insecurity in other states.

Soviet policy has also suffered serious setbacks in the last five years. The most important has been the formation of a quasi-alliance between the Soviet Union's main adversaries. Soviet policy shows no signs of being able to reverse this setback. There are, it is true, many conflicts of interest between the Soviet Union's potential enemies, and the continued existence of their close relations cannot be taken for granted; but if the Soviet Union continues its present policy it is only likely to drive them closer together. Soviet detente policy has failed to attain some of its most important aims: relations with the United States are worse than they have been since the 1960s; Sino-Soviet rapprochement has not been prevented; foreign technology has not reinvigorated the Soviet economy; a major new round of the arms race appears now to be under way. Moreover, some of the areas where the Soviet Union or its allies have intervened remain at the centre of international crises – Angola, Ethiopia, Kampuchea, Afghanistan, Poland. Although we know in principle that East-West relations are not a zero-sum game, that one side's loss is not necessarily the other's gain, we tend in practice to forget it, and to assume that because the world now appears more dangerous for the West, it must be safer for the Soviet Union. But that is not necessarily so, and the failure of detente in the 1970s is a setback for the Soviet Union as well as for the West.

Soviet policy in the 1970s can be seen as a move away from isolation towards greater involvement in the international system: foreign trade has been given greater weight in economic policy; there has been some recognition that security depends not only on one's own efforts, but also on co-operation with potential enemies; Soviet power has been asserted more actively throughout the world. None of these aspects of Soviet policy is wholly new, but taken together they have raised the question of the Soviet Union's place in the world in a new way.

Four different tendencies can be identified in Soviet foreign policy.[50] The first is an autarkist tendency, which urges reliance on the Soviet Union's resources to ensure economic development and provide security. This is based on a deep suspicion of involvement with the rest of the world: anxiety about the dangers of dependency on foreign grain and technology, fear of co-operative arrangements for security, and worry about the costs and risks of using military force in the Third World. A second tendency stresses the importance of detente with the West as a way of slowing down the arms race, reducing the risk of war and furthering Soviet economic development. The third – 'activist' or 'internationalist' – tendency points to the opportunities for expanding Soviet power and influence and increasing Soviet security by restricting the power of the major Soviet adversaries. The fourth and most ambitious tendency – the 'globalist' – looks beyond the expansion of Soviet power to the creation of a new world order.

Soviet policy should not be seen simply as a struggle between groups representing the different schools of thought; the influence of these ideas is more diffuse than that. It is helpful, nevertheless, to view Soviet policy in these terms. In the mid-1970s a shift of emphasis can be discerned from detente to activism. This prompts the question: might Soviet policy have developed differently if the West, and in particular the United States, had pursued detente more vigorously, giving the Soviet Union more to hope for from co-operation and perhaps also more to fear from conflict? The question cannot be answered on the available evidence, but the existence of different currents in Soviet thinking makes the question worth asking.

Soviet policy has shown a great fear of dependency, and events in the last two years have increased that fear. Academician Inozemtsev has stated that the Soviet Union has drawn two conclusions from the sanctions imposed by the United States after the invasion of Afghanistan: that no important sector of the Soviet economy should become dependent on imports of machinery from the capitalist countries, but that, at the same time, the Soviet Union should not forego the benefits of international economic and scientific-technical collaboration.[51] The Soviet Union has not shown the same disillusionment with arms control as the United States, perhaps because it never shared the same illusions; but recent Soviet statements show an awareness that effective arms control is going to become more difficult to achieve.

Alongside the fear of dependency there exists a great ambition to create a new world order. Soviet globalists argue that the post-war order created by the United States had now collapsed, and that a new order – economic, political and military – must be created. They maintain that there are global problems which require international co-operation for their solution, but that at present these problems are a source of conflict between East and West. A solution can be found only through a restructuring of international relations. Because of growing Soviet power, a new order cannot be created without the participation of the Soviet Union; and the creation of a new world order provides a purpose for Soviet power to pursue. Soviet writings do not give a clear picture of such an order, but they do indicate a more subtle vision than is provided by the pattern of Soviet domination in Eastern Europe.[52] This tendency may become more important in Soviet policy in the 1980s, with the nature of world order itself the main issue in East–West relations.

The Soviet position in the world presents a contradictory picture: expanding power, linked to ambitions to play a global role and even to create a new world order; foreign policy setbacks, domestic economic difficulties and the fear of a new encirclement. The XXVI Congress did not, however, initiate a major change of course: it reaffirmed the policy of detente and presented the Soviet Union as the champion of peace. The worsening state of international relations was noted more in sorrow than in anger (though anger has been more evident in Soviet commentary since the Congress). Brezhnev declared the Soviet Union ready for dialogue with the United States, and spelt out more clearly the defensive rationale for the build-up of Soviet military power. He also advanced a wide range of proposals for arms limitation and regional security negotiations. It is not clear how much flexibility there is in Soviet policy; there were, in any event, no signs of major concessions. The Congress did not mark a major turning-point in Soviet foreign and defence policy, not did it give a clear indication of how policy might develop under a new leadership. The present leaders apparently believe that their foreign policy problems are manageable, and that they can rely on Soviet power to ward off threats and dangers. They seem willing to leave to the next generation of leaders any major choices about the direction of policy, and to pass on to them a powerful and secure state.

NOTES

1. See P. M. E. Volten, *Brezhnev's 'Peace Program': Success or Failure? Soviet Domestic Political Process and Power*, Doctoral Dissertation, Free University of Amsterdam, 1981, Ch. 2.
2. Henry Kissinger, *White House Years* (Boston and Toronto, 1979), p. 1213; Bruce Parrott, 'Technological Progress and Soviet Politics', in John R. Thomas and Ursula Kruse-Vaucienne (eds), *Soviet Science and Technology*, published for the National Science Foundation by the George Washington University, 1977, pp. 305–28; Michael MccGwire, 'The Overseas Role of a "Soviet Military Presence", in Michael MccGwire and John McDonnell (eds), *Soviet Naval Influence. Domestic and Foreign Dimensions* (New York and London, 1977); Walter C. Clemens Jr., *The USSR and Global Interdependence: alternative futures*, American Enterprise Institute for Public Policy Research, Washington DC, 1978.
3. *Pravda*, 24 February 1981; all references in this chapter to Brezhnev's Report are to pp. 2–4.
4. Colin Legum, 'Angola and the Horn of Africa', in Stephen S. Kaplan (ed.), *Diplomacy of Power: Soviet Armed Forces as a Political Instrument*, The Brookings Institution, Washington DC, 1981, pp. 573–605.
5. *Pravda*, 25 February 1976.
6. For a good account of this phase of the talks see Strobe Talbott, *Endgame. The Inside Story of SALT II* (New York, 1979).
7. Colin Legum, op. cit., pp. 605–37.
8. *Pravda*, 13 August 1978.
9. *Pravda*, 26 June 1978.
10. For a discussion of the measures and their impact see Committee on Foreign Affairs, US House of Representatives, *An Assessment of the Afghanistan Sanctions: Implications for Trade and Diplomacy in the 1980s*, Report prepared for the Subcommittee on Europe and the Middle East,

April 1981, Washington DC, US Government Printing Office.

11. See the discussion in Stanley Hoffmann, *Primacy or World Order* (New York, 1978), p. 60ff.

12. Seweryn Bialer, *Stalin's Successors* (Cambridge, 1980), p. 2.

13. In January 1980 Brezhnev described the United States 'as an absolutely unreliable partner in interstate ties, as a state whose leadership, prompted by some whim, caprice, or emotional outbursts, or by considerations of narrowly understood immediate advantages, is capable at any moment of violating its international obligations, and cancelling treaties and agreements signed by it'. *New York Times*, 13 January 1980, quoted by Vernon Aspaturian in *The Soviet Invasion of Afghanistan*, ACIS Working Paper No. 27, Center for International and Strategic Affairs, UCLA, September 1980, p. 33.

14. See *The Military Balance 1980–81*, The International Institute for Strategic Studies (London, 1980), p. 96.

15. The CIA has estimated that during the period 1967–77 defence spending consumed an almost constant share of Soviet GNP – 11–12 per cent, or 12–13 per cent, depending on how defence spending is defined. *Estimated Soviet Defense Spending: Trends and Prospects*, CIA: SR 78-10121, June 1978, p. i.

16. *Pravda*, 19 January 1977.

17. The most important statement of this view is given in V. D. Sokolovsky (ed), *Voennaya Strategiya* (Voenizdat, Moscow), 1962, 1963 and 1968.

18. See Raymond L. Garthoff, 'Mutual Deterrence and Strategic Arms Limitation in Soviet Policy', *International Security*, Summer 1978.

19. See Robert L. Arnett, 'Soviet Attitudes Towards Nuclear War: Do They Really Believe They Can Win?', *Journal of Strategic Studies*, September 1979.

20. For further discussion see David Holloway, 'Military Power and Political Purpose in Soviet Policy', *Daedalus*, Fall 1980.

21. *Der Spiegel*, 7 July 1980, p. 22.

22. Gerard Smith, *Doubletalk. The Story of SALT I* (New York, 1980), p. 46.

23. See, for example, *Challenges for U.S. National Security. Defense Spending and the Economy. The Strategic Balance and Strategic Arms Limitation*. A preliminary report, prepared by the Staff of the Carnegie Panel on US Security and the Future of Arms Control. Carnegie Endowment for International Peace, 1981, Washington DC, especially pp. 77–81.

24. *Pravda*, 2 August 1979.

25. V. Zhurkin, in *Literaturnaya gazeta*, 17 September 1980.

26. See, for example, M. A. Mil'shteyn, 'Nekotorye kharakternye cherty sovremennoy voennoy doktriny SShA', in *SShA*, 1980, no. 5; and R. G. Bogdanov, 'Ogranichenie i sokrashchenie vooruzhenii – serdtsevina mezhdunarodnoy bezopasnosti, problema chrezvychaynaya, *SShA*, 1981, no. 5.

27. *The Times*, 6 May 1981.

28. Raymond L. Garthoff, 'The TNF Tangle', *Foreign Policy*, no. 41, Winter 1980, Winter 1980–81, 92–3.

29. Quoted by Alexander Dallin, in 'The Road to Kabul: Soviet Perceptions of World Affairs and the Afghan Crisis', in *The Soviet Invasion of*

Afghanistan, ACIS Working Paper No. 27, op. cit., p. 57.

30. *Voprosy istorii KPSS*, May 1974, quoted in Harriet Fast Scott and William F. Scott, *The Armed Forces of the USSR* (Boulder, Colorado, 1979), p. 57.
31. For speculation about possible Soviet military intervention see Louis Dupree, 'Afghanistan Under the Khalq', *Problems of Communism*, July–August 1979, 49–50; David Chaffetz, 'Afghanistan in Turmoil', *International Affairs*, January 1980. On the invasion see Fred Halliday, 'War and Revolution in Afghanistan', *New Left Review*, 119, January–February 1980; Zalmay Khalilzad, 'Soviet-Occupied Afghanistan', *Problems of Communism*, November–December 1980; Dev Murarka, 'The Russian Intervention: A Moscow Analysis', *The Round Table*, April 1981; and *The Soviet Invasion of Afghanistan*, ACIS Working Paper No. 27, op. cit.
32. *New York Times*, 7 August 1981, p. A4.
33. *Pravda*, 5 August 1981.
34. See the discussion of the various interpretations in Committee on Foreign Relations, US House of Representatives, op. cit., pp. 11–19. President Carter stressed the threat posed to the Persian Gulf in his State of the Union Address on 23 January 1980.
35. Murarka, op. cit., p. 131.
36. *BP Statistical Review of World Oil Industry, 1979*.
37. State of the Union Address, 23 January 1980.
38. In November 1978, when the Shah was in deep political trouble, Brezhnev warned against military intervention in Iran, declaring that it would be regarded by the Soviet Union as a matter affecting its security interests. *Pravda*, 19 November 1978.
39. The text of the speech is given in *Soviet News*, 16 December 1980.
40. Michel Tatu, 'Intervention in Eastern Europe', in Kaplan (ed.), op. cit., pp. 262–3.
41. Letter sent by the Central Committee of the CPSU to the Central Committee of the Polish United Workers Party on 5 June 1981. Text in *Soviet News*, 1981.
42. Ibid.
43. This seems to have been a consideration in the Soviet decision not to use force in Poland in 1956. See Tatu, op. cit., pp. 214, 259.
44. The CIA has estimated that in 1979 the military share of GNP was 12–14 per cent. See Joint Economic Committee, US Congress, *Allocation of Resources in the Soviet Union and China – 1980*, Hearings before the Subcommittee on Priorities and Economy in Government, Part 6, Washington DC, US Government Printing Office, 1981, p. 8.
45. Academician N. Inozemtsev, 'XXVI s''yezd KPSS i nashi zadachi', *Mirovaya ekonomika i mezhdunarodnye otnosheniya*, 1981, no. 3, 7.
46. Speech of Secretary of State Haig, *New York Times*, 12 August 1981, p. A4.
47. Zhurkin, loc. cit.
48. See Adam Ulam, 'Russian Nationalism', in Seweryn Bialer (ed.), *The Domestic Context of Soviet Foreign Policy* (Boulder, Colorado, 1981), pp. 3–17.
49. I have tried to explore the domestic sources of Soviet military power in 'War, Militarism and the Soviet State', in E. P. Thompson and Dan Smith

(eds), *Protest and Survive* (Harmondsworth, London, 1980).
50. Clemens, op. cit.; Franklyn Griffiths, 'Ideological Development and Foreign Policy', in Seweryn Bialer, op. cit., pp. 41–5.
51. Inozemtsev, op. cit., pp. 12–13.
52. See Elizabeth Kridl Valkenier, 'The USSR, the Third World, and the Global Economy', *Problems of Communism*, July–August 1979; and also M. Maksimova, 'Global'nye problemy mirovogo razvitiya', in *Mirovaya ekonomika i mezhdunarodnye otnosheniya*, 1981, no. 1; and I. Ivanov, 'Perestroika mezhdunarodnykh otnoshenii i global'nye problemy', ibid., 1981, no. 2.

3 Foreign Economic Relations

Philip Hanson

INTRODUCTION

Between the mid-1950s and the mid-1970s Soviet policy-makers conducted an economic 'turn to the West': at first gradual, then strongly accelerating in the late 1960s and early 1970s.[1] During the last five years or so they have in certain respects turned away again. Why? And is this turn away from the West essentially a short-term tactical manoeuvre or something more enduring? These are the questions to which this chapter is directed.

Table 3.1 Shares of USSR Trade Turnover with Socialist, Western and Developing Countries
(percentages)

	1970	1971	1972	1973	1974	1975	1976	1977	1978	1979	1980
Socialist	65.2	65.4	65.5	58.5	54.1	56.3	55.6	57.3	59.8	56.1	53.7
of which:											
CMEA members	55.6	56.2	59.6	54.0	48.9	51.8	50.8	52.5	55.7	51.9	48.6
Industrial West	21.3	21.5	22.6	26.6	31.3	31.3	32.9	29.6	28.1	32.1	33.6
Developing	13.5	13.1	12.9	14.9	14.6	11.5	11.5	13.1	12.1	11.8	12.7

Source: Vneshnyaya torgovlya SSSR za 1971–1980 g. (Moscow, annual).

To focus on trade with the West may seem an unduly subjective way of proceeding. Table 3.1 shows, after all, that the West accounts for only a quarter to a third of Soviet merchandise trade. But the West has a general importance for Soviet society that gives particular significance to Soviet-western trade. For the USSR, the western world is both the main political adversary and the main economic competitor. It is also more than just an adversary and a rival: it is the true outside world in Soviet thinking: the 'Over There' that looms so large in the

65

conversations in Alexander Zinoviev's *Yawning Heights*. In particular, it is, in my view, the source of most Soviet economic aspirations,
both official and popular. One could make little sense of Soviet
commercial relations with the West, however, if one did not take
Soviet trade with Eastern Europe into account. A useful way of
looking at Soviet foreign trade policies is to visualise a triangular
relationship: USSR, Eastern Europe,[2] West. Moscow conducts about
four-fifths of its trade with the members of the Council for Mutual
Economic Assistance (CMEA) and the West (Table 3.1). Developments in economic relations between any two of these trade partners
generally have quite strong implications for the third party. The
implications can be complicated and sometimes unexpected, and I
have tried to allow for them in the discussion that follows.

The first section reviews the overall development of Soviet trade in
the 1970s. The second considers Soviet economic relations with the
rest of CMEA, but does so mainly as background to the third section,
which is on economic relations with the West. In the conclusions
something is said about trade with the developing countries which is
otherwise (perhaps unjustly) neglected here.

SOVIET TRADE AND PAYMENTS IN THE 1970s

Soviet external transactions in the 1970s combined rapid growth with
minimal organisational change. Several recently published western
studies describe these developments, and this section draws heavily on
them.[3]

The rapid growth of total Soviet trade in the 1970s is shown in Table
3.2. This rapid growth must be seen in perspective. First of all, about
half of it reflects volume increases (rather less than half for exports,
rather more than half for imports). Thus total exports in current
foreign trade roubles rose about three-and-a-half times in 1970–80 but
Soviet official volume estimates show an increase of only 62 per cent.[4]
Second, the increase in Soviet trade was at about the same pace as that
of western trade (in current prices), and the former remained tiny in
comparison with the latter. Soviet exports (from Soviet foreign trade
returns, converted into dollars) were equivalent to 5.8 per cent of total
OECD exports in 1970 and to 6.1 per cent in 1980. Third, while Soviet
trade grew faster than the Soviet domestic economy (whose real GNP
rose at about 3.4 per cent p.a. on average in the 1970s), trade remained
relatively small in relation to total Soviet economic activity. An export

Table 3.2 Total Soviet Merchandise Trade in
Current Prices 1970–80

| | *Thousand millions of valuta roubles* | |
	Exports	*Imports*
1970	11.5	10.6
1971	12.4	11.2
1972	12.7	13.3
1973	15.8	15.5
1974	20.8	18.8
1975	24.0	26.7
1976	28.0	28.8
1977	33.2	30.1
1978	35.7	34.7
1979	42.4	37.9
1980	49.6	44.5

Source: Vneshnyaya torgovlya SSSR v 1980 g. (Moscow, 1981), p. 6.

share in GNP of about 4 per cent can be derived for 1978 by relating Soviet exports in dollars to CIA estimates of Soviet GNP in current (1978) US dollars. It is true that figures of this sort are not very informative; it is the valuation of exports and total output in prices reflecting Soviet relative scarcities that is needed to show the 'real' importance of exporting in the Soviet economy. Still, the elementary observation holds true, that this huge and resource-rich country is, for good reasons of economic geography, much less concerned than are most nation-states with foreign trade. Finally, it must also be remembered that merchandise trade flows in much of the world are intimately linked with labour and capital movements. This is not the case for the USSR. The Soviet Union remains a country the economic relations of which with the rest of the world are concentrated to an unusual degree on merchandise trade. Few of its citizens travel abroad and very few emigrate.[5] The number of foreigners resident in the USSR almost certainly increased in the 1970s but it remains small; and hardly anybody migrates to the Soviet Union to reside there permanently. Foreign equity capital continues to be totally excluded from any undertakings on Soviet territory, and western credits to the USSR are small in relation to total Soviet investment. Soviet direct investment abroad, it is true, is not negligible: McMillan identified 117 Soviet wholly or jointly owned companies in non-socialist countries at March 1979, mostly in banking, marketing and transport.[6] But this is still small beer by western standards. To complete this almost-blank picture of non-merchandise-trade activities, Soviet official data on foreign transactions other than merchandise ('visible') trade remain unpublished. Everything that is said below about the rest of the Soviet balance of payments is based on western estimates.

Table 3.1 shows the division of Soviet trade turnover among major groups of trade partners during the 1970s. Other CMEA countries remained Moscow's main trading partners, but their share fell somewhat, to just under a half in 1980. The share of the west rose from about a fifth at the beginning of the decade to almost a third in 1976 and then fluctuated close to that level. The share of the Third World fluctuated around one-eighth, tending slightly to decline.

These developments were the outcome of rather different price and volume changes in the separate geopolitical segments of Soviet trade. The degree to which these segments are separated from one another is considerable. The Soviet domestic economy is heavily insulated from foreign transactions by the planning system, the separate domestic and foreign trade price structures and the inconvertibility of the rouble.[7] By the same token Soviet trade is itself divided into somewhat separate compartments, between which unit values for a specific product can vary widely and can move quite differently over time. From a narrowly economic point of view, the two major compartments are 'hard-currency' (multilateral-settlement) and 'soft-currency' (bilateral-settlement) trade. Soviet trade partners in the first compartment of Soviet trade are nearly all western and Third World market economies.[8] The trade partners in the second compartment are predominantly (in terms of mutual trade turnover) administrative economies more or less *à la Russe*. But several market economies, including Finland and India, also have bilateral settlement arrangements with the USSR. The major trade-partner groupings employed in the Soviet foreign trade returns are those shown in Table 3.1. They cut across the hard-currency/soft-currency division. The picture is further complicated by the emergence in the 1970s of an element of hard-currency settlement, covering about 10–15 per cent of intra-CMEA trade towards the end of the decade.[9]

The Soviet Union was throughout the decade a substantial net energy exporter to both its socialist and its capitalist trade partners. It therefore stood to benefit greatly from the 1973–74 energy price rises engineered by OPEC. In its trade with the West and with many Third World countries, the benefit was direct. The Soviet Union sold in these markets at prevailing world prices. Raw materials, metals and gems

Table 3.3 USSR Terms of Trade with Non-socialist Countries
(index numbers 1970 = 100)

	1971	*1972*	*1973*	*1974*	*1975*	*1976*	*1977*	*1978*	*1979*	*1980*
Soviet exports:										
Value	108	110	165	243	235	288	353	361	471	597
Volume	101	97	138	170	155	180	200	208	201	198
Price Index	107	113	120	143	152	160	177	174	234	302
Soviet imports:										
Value	108	133	175	236	352	378	358	375	446	529
Volume	106	129	168	189	216	238	223	257	268	295
Price Index	102	103	104	125	163	159	161	146	166	179
Net barter terms of trade	105	110	115	114	93	101	110	119	141	169

Note: The 'price index' is the unit-value implied by the official series for volume and for value. The volume index for 1980 is shifted from a 1970 to a 1975 base and has been chainlinked to approximate a continued 1970-base series.
Source: Vneshnyaya torgovlya SSSR, annual issues, *1971* to *1980.*

also figure prominently in Soviet exports to non-socialist partners. Since terms-of-trade changes in much of the decade favoured raw-materials as well as fuel exporters, the Soviet Union had substantial windfall terms-of-trade gains in total in the 1970s vis-à-vis the West (Table 3.3).[10]

Excluded from the tables of terms-of-trade changes, moreover, is gold, of which the USSR is the world's second largest producer.[11] With average annual gold prices rising from $35 a fine ounce in 1970 to $613 in 1980, Moscow made a killing on the gold market, too, but from a peak in September 1980, the price fell and by January 1982 was half that peak. In general, Soviet terms-of-trade gains vis-à-vis the non-socialist countries enabled the Soviet Union to increase the volume of its imports nearly twice as much (in relation to 1970) as its volume of exports (Table 3.3), while running only briefly – in 1972, 1975 and 1976 – into hard-currency current account deficits (Table 3.4).

On balance, Soviet terms of trade vis-à-vis Moscow's CMEA trade partners changed in a similar direction over the decade (Table 3.5). For reasons to be considered in the next section, however, the dimensions and time-profiles of these changes differed from those experienced in trade with the West.

Certain features of the rapid growth of Soviet foreign trade in the 1970s are worth stressing. First, the growth of exports to the West,

Table 3.4 Soviet Hard-currency Trade and Payments 1970–79
(millions of US dollars)

	1970	1971	1972	1973	1974	1975	1976	1977	1978	1979
Reported merchandise imports	−2,701	−2,943	−4,157	−6,547	−8,448	−14,247	−15,316	−14,645	−16,951	−21,593
Reported merchandise exports	2,201	2,630	2,801	4,790	7,470	7,835	9,721	11,345	13,157	19,524
Gold sales[a]	0	79	380	900	1,178	725	1,369	1,597	2,673	2,200
Arms sales for hard currency[a]	100	87	122	1,345	1,000	793	1,108	1,500	1,644 }	3,980
Net invisibles[a]	422	307	267	663	814	190	187	954	743 }	
Current account balance[a]	22	160	−587	1,151	2,016	−4,714	−2,931	751	1,266	4,111
Net new borrowing (new drawings less principal repayments)[a]	291	288	602	1,340	1,426	5,402	4,694	1,777	1,785	−27
Net outstanding debt, end-year[a]	—	582	555	1,166	1,654	7,451	10,115	11,230	11,217	10,200
Debt service ÷ total exports (percentages)[a]	—	—	12	8	9	15	15	16	(17)	19
End-year gold reserves[a]	1,835	2,400	3,500	5,600	9,600	9,800	7,200	8,000	9,500	15,600

[a]Estimated.

Source: All except gold reserves from Ericson and Miller, op. cit. (endnote 3) and CIA, *The Soviet Economy* (same note). Gold reserves are those by weight in CIA, *Handbook of Economic Statistics 1980*, ER 80-10452, October 1980, Table 46, multiplied by the average London gold price for each year; their proper meaning is, however, uncertain, for they are based on output series below those estimated by Kaser (see endnote 11) and the price at which any large portion could be sold would be well below that at which smaller transactions have been conducted.

Table 3.5 USSR–CMEA Terms of Trade
(index numbers 1970 = 100)

	1971	1972	1973	1974	1975	1976	1977	1978	1979	1980
Soviet exports:										
Value	107	121	132	158	213	239	279	316	347	389
Volume	105	115	114	137	143	134	145	152	156	161
Price Index	102	105	116	115	149	178	192	208	222	242
Soviet imports:										
Value	110	113	143	157	214	231	262	320	331	356
Volume	110	126	128	140	156	148	162	186	184	185
Price Index	100	106	112	112	137	156	162	172	180	192
Net barter terms of trade	102	99	104	103	109	114	119	121	123	126

Note: On the 'price index', see note to Table 3.3.
Source: Vneshnyaya torgovlya SSSR, annual issues, *1971* to *1980*.

though rapid, did not stem from a dynamic exporting performance such as several Third World countries achieved. As Table 3.3 shows, a large part of this growth consisted of windfall price gains. Yet despite these gains the Soviet share of total OECD imports (in current prices) rose only from 1.3 to 1.6 per cent between 1970 and 1978. Over that period the really dynamic exporting countries of the 1970s achieved a significant growth in market share without the benefit of large windfall price increases. Thus the combined share of Brazil, Singapore, Hong Kong and South Korea in total OECD imports rose from 1.5 to 3.3 per cent.[12] Second, the growth of Soviet total hard-currency earnings was nonetheless sufficient to allow a rapid growth of hard-currency imports (Table 3.4). There was a strong concentration, among these imports, on two categories of goods: agricultural products and capital goods. Both these inflows represent an exploitation of systemic comparative advantage: compared to the capitalist economies of the West, the Soviet centrally-administered economy has proved to be relatively weak in agriculture and in technological innovation. By the same token, Eastern Europe could not be a very effective alternative source of these items. Capital goods, accounting for 41–45 per cent of Soviet imports from the West in 1971–76,[13] were the main channel for commercial acquisition of advanced western technology – both embodied in the capital goods themselves and accompanying them in the form of licences, know-how and training supplied as part of large package deals, especially for turnkey projects. Third, trade with the

West had certain trade-creating effects on Soviet trade with Eastern Europe. In particular, technology imports were often key inputs into CMEA integration programmes. The Orenburg gas pipeline, jointly constructed by European CMEA states, is a striking example. East European labour was employed (exceptionally) on Soviet territory to exploit Soviet natural resources with the help of western imported technology in the form of large-diameter pipe and the compressor equipment to pump the gas along the pipeline. There are numerous other examples including the whole development of the motor industry in CMEA[14] and the CMEA late-1970s target programme under which the most energy-intensive chemicals production was to be concentrated in the USSR: specifically, ammonia, ethylene and methanol, all of which have been receiving very large injections of western plant and process technology.[15] Experience in the late 1970s showed that East-West and East-East trade, though substitutes in the short run, are in many respects complementary to one another in the longer run.

Finally, the influences on the triangular relationship between the USSR, Eastern Europe and the West changed in certain important respects in the mid-1970s. Worsening East–West payments difficulties and changing terms of trade in different 'compartments' of Soviet trade conspired to induce a certain reversion towards a more inward-looking CMEA. This cluster of events is considered in more detail below.

SOVIET TRADE WITH EASTERN EUROPE

Developments in Soviet trade with other socialist (very largely, other CMEA) countries have differed in important respects from developments in Soviet trade with the non-socialist world. In this compartment of Soviet trade prices for the great bulk of transactions are set by bargaining within a set of price-fixing rules. Broadly, the rules required, up to 1975, that intra-CMEA prices be based, for each five-year-plan period, on the average of 'world-market' prices, with some adjustments, in the preceding five-year period. From the start of 1975 the rules were changed to require intra-CMEA prices to alter each year to reflect a moving average of the preceding five-years' 'world-market' prices (for 1975 only, the preceding three years). Thus in principle intra-CMEA prices lagged behind western world prices throughout the decade, but the lag was considerably shorter after the end of 1974.

The changes in world market prices from 1973 and in CMEA pricing rules from 1975 affected the relative attractiveness of CMEA and western trade to the USSR. Intra-CMEA trade had, at least in a short-term and narrowly economic sense, been unattractive to Moscow. The 'costs of empire' may have extended to absolute losses from trade with Eastern Europe, in the sense that a million roubles' worth (in foreign trade prices) of items imported from Eastern Europe may have been capable of being produced in the USSR at a resource cost below that required to produce the exports to pay for them.[16] At all events – and with greater confidence – it can be said that intra-CMEA trade was at prices which represented a considerable opportunity cost to Moscow in comparison with trading with the West. For example, the USSR obtained considerably less for a barrel of oil delivered to Poland than for a barrel of oil delivered to the Netherlands. The leap in world energy prices in 1973–74 made this opportunity cost still higher, under the existing CMEA pricing rules. By negotiating successfully to amend the rules from the end of 1974, the USSR managed to set about reducing this opportunity cost. The sequence of events with respect to oil prices is shown in Table 3.6.

But at this time (1975–76) Eastern Europe and the USSR were encountering balance of payments problems with the West, attributable in part to the combination of recession and inflation in the western world economy at that time. The East European countries had less international liquidity than the Soviet Union and were less able to generate hard-currency-earning exports. They could not simply be forced to deal with the USSR at the same prices as they would face on world markets. So the adjustment to world price levels was a matter of reducing, rather than eliminating, the lag of intra-CMEA behind world prices. And the USSR in effect extended credit to Eastern Europe (and to the non-European CMEA countries) by running surpluses with them where in the past it had generally aimed at something close to bilateral balance (see Table 3.7).[17] Thus the Soviet gross barter terms of trade with the rest of CMEA improved less than the net barter terms of trade: 115 in 1980 compared with 126 (1970 = 100). In other words, the increased purchasing power of a unit of Soviet exports in terms of Soviet imports from the rest of CMEA was less than fully reflected in the numbers of units of imports obtained in relation to the total volume of exports.

Nonetheless, in the period 1975–78 the share of Soviet trade that was with the rest of CMEA increased at the expense of Soviet trade with

Table 3.6 Intra-CMEA and World Prices of Crude Oil, 1975–80
(transferable roubles per tonne)

	1975	*1976*	*1977*	*1978*	*1979*	*1980*
Effective price of Soviet exports to other members of CMEA	31–38	34–41	44–50	54–60	65–72	about 76
(percentage increase over previous year)	(131)	(8)	(22)	(20)	(17)	(9)
Simulated price of Soviet exports to other member of CMEA	32.3	34.5	45.3	55.7	64.1	67–72
(percentage increase over previous year)	—	(7)	(31)	(22)	(15)	(8)
World price	61.3	68.4	66.8	64.8	81.6	143.0

Source: M. Lavigne, op. cit, Table 1 (see endnote 9): her simulated price is that calculated according to the CMEA agreement of January 1975; and *Annual Register 1980* (London, 1981), p. 491 for the price of Ras Tanura light petroleum, dollars per barrel being converted to valuta roubles per tonne according to the exchange rates published in *Ekonomicheskaya gazeta* (monthly, later fortnightly) and in *Moscow Narodny Bank Press Bulletin* (monthly): valuta roubles (at par with the transferable rouble) per US dollar, yearly averages:

1970	0.9000	1973	0.7380	1976	0.7540	1979	0.6558
1971	0.9000	1974	0.7567	1977	0.7370	1980	0.6496
1972	0.8241	1975	0.7219	1978	0.6841	1981	0.7185

the West (Table 3.1). And the volume of Soviet imports from the rest of CMEA increased marginally faster than the volume of Soviet imports from the West (Tables 3.3 and 3.5). (The sharp rises in energy prices in 1979–80 again compressed the CMEA current-price share somewhat in those years.)

The resumption by CMEA of a more-inward-looking trade pattern was accompanied by the elaboration in the late 1970s of new programmes of CMEA production specialisation. These included the joint nuclear power programme and the programme, already referred to, for concentrating production of the most energy-intensive chemicals in the USSR. These seem *prima facie* to be sensible measures for coping with East European shortages of energy and of the hard currency to purchase large amounts of non-Soviet primary fuel.

It is tempting for the western observer to assume that these developments are in all respects in Moscow's interests. They may have their political attractions, but they are at the same time economically problematic. The USSR is having the greatest difficulty, for instance, in providing Eastern Europe with a necessary minimum of energy supplies. A careful analysis by McMillan and Hannigan suggests that Kosygin's 1979 public undertaking of a 20 per cent increase in Soviet

Table 3.7 Soviet Trade with other CMEA Members,
1970–80
(millions of valuta roubles)

	Exports	*Imports*
1970	6,261	6,023
1971	6,681	6,603
1972	7,553	7,970
1973	8,311	8,611
1974	9,917	9,436
1975	13,363	12,885
1976	14,933	13,887
1977	17,452	15,795
1978	19,794	21,703
1979	21,703	19,934
1980	24,339	21,438

Source: As Table 3.1.

energy supplies to the rest of CMEA between 1976–80 and 1981–85 probably consists of maintaining crude oil and natural gas deliveries to Eastern Europe at about 1980 levels (which would account for 16.5 of the 20 per cent); a small increase in electricity supplies to Eastern Europe, and some increase in energy supplies to Cuba, Vietnam and Mongolia.[18] And they show that there is indeed very little scope for volume increases in Soviet supplies to Eastern Europe of natural gas, as well as of oil. (Some increase might accrue in the mid-1980s as a spin off from the giant Yamal'/Urengoy pipeline project for which contracts were signed with West-German-led consortia in autumn 1981.)

Thus Soviet policy-makers' attitudes to a more inward-looking development of CMEA may well be equivocal. Eastern Europe may represent a net drain on Soviet resources; at least it still represents a very large deviation from the most cost-effective pattern of total Soviet trade. In particular, it urgently needs specific inputs of fuel which the USSR can ill afford to spare and for which Eastern Europe can offer only inadequate recompense. And in the absence of a strong growth of East-West trade, with its trade-creating effects on intra-CMEA transactions, CMEA integration programmes may have rather little to offer. The difficulties involved even in maintaining oil deliveries to Eastern Europe were indicated by reports from Budapest in late 1981 that the USSR was seeking a 10 per cent cut in its oil supplies to the region in 1982.

Are there offsetting political benefits for Moscow from a more inward-looking CMEA? Presumably worries about excessively close links between, say, Hungary and West Germany would be reduced. But on the other hand the economic dependence of the East European countries on the USSR – measured by the percentage reduction in an East European country's GNP that the Soviet Union could engineer within a year by (say) cuts in its supplies to that country – was generally high even around 1975. Soviet policy-makers may already have all the 'dependence' on the part of Eastern Europe they desire, and may be positively reluctant to acquire more, on present terms.

SOVIET TRADE WITH THE WEST

Soviet-western trade is dominated by two influences: East–West political relations and eastern hard-currency finance. To the first of these, bilateral relations between Moscow and Washington are crucial. In discussing Soviet-western commercial relations, it is useful therefore to focus initially on the US. The Soviet-US trade agreements of 1972 came at a time when the volume of Soviet-western trade was rising rapidly. They appeared at the time to bring the United States in from the cold; for Western Europe and Japan the era of commercial detente had started long before. In extending MFN tariff treatment to Soviet exports, making US government credit support available for US exports to the USSR, and allowing substantial sales to the USSR of US grain, the US was rightly described at the time as 'normalising' its trade relations with the other superpowers; basically, Washington was coming into line with its western allies.[19]

Political normality, however, soon reasserted itself over commercial normalisation. The US Senate refusal to ratify the trade agreements except on condition of a Soviet public commitment to allow increased Jewish emigration was followed by Soviet abrogation of the agreements at the start of 1975. Subsequently President Carter's stance on human rights emphasised the political obstacles to trade.

The Soviet-Cuban involvement in Angola in 1978 further exacerbated relations and the Soviet invasion of Afghanistan at Christmas 1979 was the last straw. Nonetheless, by 1977 the US and the USSR had in certain respects achieved closer commercial and technological relations: some 30 US firms had permanent representative offices in Moscow (the number was marginally reduced to 29 by December 1980); contacts between US and Soviet officials and academics, as well as between industrial and commercial executives, had become more frequent and systematic; US official promotion of East-West trade was much more active than in the 1960s; Soviet imports of US grain (covered by the 1975–81 grain agreement subsequently extended to September 1982) and other agricultural products had greatly increased. On the other hand, relations had in other respects not been normalised. MFN arrangements and US official credit support for US capital-goods exports had failed to materialise; the monster US-Soviet energy projects that had been mooted for Siberian development had come to nothing; and if agricultural products were excluded, the US was still only a minor participant in Soviet-western trade.

The subsequent further deterioration in Soviet-US political relations hardened, rather than altered, this situation. In 1980, after Afghanistan, the US took the lead in devising western commercial 'retaliation'. The main elements were the partial embargo on US grain exports (abrogated by President Reagan in April 1981) and the Western allies' agreement to seek no exceptions that would allow the export of strategically sensitive items to USSR. The channel for such agreement is the Co-ordinating Committee for Multilateral Export Controls (CoCom), with headquarters in Paris, which comprises NATO states other than Iceland plus Japan, and the western 'economic summit meeting' in Ottawa in July 1981 accepted that the list of items should be reassessed. A proposal by the US Department of Defense, the 'Initial List of Militarily Critical Technologies,' was criticised on its appearance in October 1980 as likely to be too cumbersome (because too extensive) to operate efficiently, but opinion among NATO governments changed following the coup in Poland that December. The US Administration declared unilateral sanctions on the USSR, which included the complete suspension of licences for 'high-technology' items (presumably those on the US Commodity Control List) and the stoppage of all technology for oil and gas. CoCom followed by tightening its multilateral list at a session in January 1982.[20] The United States had contributed around a tenth of Soviet capital-goods imports from the West in 1971–76: well up from the 1–5 per cent US contribution of the 1960s, but still only about a half of the US share in the 14 OECD countries' capital goods sales world-wide. And this is in a period which covers the brief flowering (1972–75) of Soviet-US commercial relations.

By the late 1970s, therefore, Soviet-US commercial relations had been only partially 'normalised'. Western European and Japanese companies still dominated Soviet non-agricultural transactions with the West; the Japanese and West European governments still offered MFN tariff treatment to Soviet exports and competed with one another to offer cheap official credit to Moscow, while the US had once more opted out of this 'normality'. Soviet-US commercial relations further deteriorated after the Soviet invasion of Afghanistan and after the Polish *coup*.

It might be argued that this was not too important to Soviet policy-makers. With so many West European and Japanese capitalists competing to sell the rope with which they would be hung, why worry about the absence of American competitors? It is likely, however, that the proponents in Moscow of closer commercial relations with the West pinned their hopes on the United States. If Kissingeresque arguments about trade creating 'a vested interest in mutual restraint' were deployed in the Kremlin, they must have referred to Washington rather than to Paris or Rome. And the attention devoted by the Soviet authorities to the paraphernalia of Soviet-US trade relations (joint commissions, representation, accommodation and so on) in 1972–77 was enormously disproportionate to the importance of the US in the Soviet Union's non-agricultural trade with the West, implying a belief in the pre-eminent role of the US, at least potentially, in Soviet dealings with the West. The United States was almost certainly seen as the crucial western trade partner for the political symbolism involved, for the sake of US influence on other western countries, for US government influence over the foreign subsidiaries of US corporations, for reasons of 'linkage', and because of a whole tangle of feelings about actual and potential complementarities and similarities between the two giant powers.[21] I suggest, therefore, that the deterioration in Soviet-US relations in the late 1970s was a major setback for proponents in Moscow of greater Soviet-western trade generally; and this despite the minor direct role of the US in Soviet non-agricultural trade.

Paradoxically, the role of the US as a source of rescue from agricultural difficulties continued to be important throughout the period. Rough, preliminary calculations indicate that net grain imports from all sources in 1976–80 were equivalent to about 12 per cent of total, usable domestic grain supply, and that the US supplied about half of the (gross) imports.[22] (US soya bean exports were a further contribution to the maintenance of Soviet livestock herds after poor grain harvests.) Agricultural trade developed in a way that was scarcely consistent with US foreign policy because it proved to be difficult for the US Administration to regulate. The difficulty seems to result from the anonymity of agricultural products and their numerous channels of supply – and the pressure exerted by the US farm lobby. The aim of the post-Afghanistan grain embargo was to reduce Soviet grain imports by as much as 17 million tonnes in 1979–80; in the event the shortfall seems to have been of the order of 5–8 million tonnes, though with an addition of perhaps $1000 million to the Soviet grain import bill in 1980 because prices were enhanced by the embargo. Agricultural trade, in short, was only rather moderately affected by the cooling of relations between Washington and Moscow.

So far as technology imports are concerned, however, the deterioration of political relations seems *prima facie* to have led Soviet policy-makers to turn away from the West. After the sanctions following the Polish *coup*, this consideration must have strengthened.

Table 3.8 Reported Soviet Equipment Orders from
Western Firms, 1970–81
(millions of US dollars)

1970	500	1976	5,990[a]
1971	850	1977	3,800
1972	1,700	1978	2,800
1973	2,600	1979	2,600
1974	4,300	1980	2,400[b]
1975	4,650	1981	4,120[b]

[a] Includes about $1000 million ordered for the CMEA joint Orenburg gas pipeline project.
[b] Author's compilations of $1664 million (1980) and $2854 million (1981), scaled up in the ratio of CIA 1979: author's 1979 figures, and rounded to three significant digits.
Source: Ericson and Miller, op.cit., 1976, Appendix I; CIA op.cit., ER 80–10328; author's compilations for Economist Intelligence Unit, *Quarterly Economic Review of the USSR*, 1981, no. 1, 21.

It is in 1977, after the first deterioration in Soviet-US relations, that Soviet orders for western machinery fell sharply (see Table 3.8). The volume of machinery imports has indeed fallen, and their role as

Table 3.9 Soviet Imports of Machinery and Transport Equipment from the West, 1955–79

Year	Value in current prices (US$ mn.) (1)	Price index (1964=100) (2)	Estimated in Soviet 1969 prices (mn domestic roubles) (3)	Imports as percentage of Soviet domestic equip. investment of following year (4)
1955	104	81	148	2.0
1956	139	85	188	2.4
1957	128	89	166	1.8
1958	123	90	158	1.6
1959	177	90	227	2.2
1960	310	91	393	3.4
1961	390	95	472	3.6
1962	436	98	510	3.6
1963	402	99	467	2.8
1964	489	100	561	3.2
1965	366	100	421	2.2
1966	395	104	436	2.2
1967	457	105	499	2.4
1968	639	102	721	3.2
1969	889	106	966	3.8
1970	905	114	913	3.4
1971	840	122	792	2.8
1972	1126	133	979	3.1
1973	1574	155	1166	3.4
1974	2094	174	1378	3.6
1975	4184	194	2476	6.1
1976	4259	199	2462	5.7
1977	4571	219	2393	5.1
1978	4994	254	2254	4.6
1979	4851	273	2037	4.1

Source: Column (1) Exports, f.o.b., of SITC 7 goods, from the 14 major OECD countries to the USSR (the only OECD exporter of machinery on more than a negligible scale to the USSR that is omitted is Finland; (see text) from OECD, *Statistics of Foreign Trade,* Series B and C.
Column (2) Weighted average of various national prices series, with adjustments for parity changes; weights (altered as between four subperiods) reflect country shares in SITC 7 sales to USSR. For 1970–78, the index is based on the export price index series for machinery and transport equipment for Japan, FRG, US and Sweden only, from *UN Monthly Bulletin of Statistics,* May 1979, p. xxx, weighted by 1975 share.
Column (3) Conversion rates pivot on a modified 'Boretsky' rouble–dollar

Table 3.9—continued

conversion rate for 1964, adjusted annually in line with Column (2).
Column (4) Column (3) as a percentage of a 1969-rouble-estimate series
derived from *Narkhoz* (various years) for total gross investment in machinery
and equipment. For the 1970s this series incorporates adjustments to
wholesale machinery prices of 1 January 1973. (*Narkhoz 1977*, pp. 341, 349).
The differences between 1969 and 1973 valuation appear to be small.

ingredients in the Soviet investment programme has dwindled (Table
3.9). It is my contention, however, that this turning away from the
West has been the result of a conjuncture of several economic and
political circumstances in the mid-to-late 1970s, and that explanation
in terms of one crucial determining factor would be misleading. It
seems to me that an explanation of this development must be sought
amongst the following (or some combination of them).

(1) The deterioration of political relations with the US in 1975,
already discussed, leading the Politburo to return to a suspicious
semi-isolation in matters of trade. (Kosygin's retirement in 1980
comes too late to be a cause of this shift, but his frequent and
lengthy absences through illness in the period may have played a
part.)

(2) Long-range strategic planning in 1976–77, in the expectation
that Soviet activities in the Third World (such as subsequently
took place in Angola and Afghanistan) would lead the West to
try to exert economic pressure; potential Soviet vulnerability to
such pressures was therefore deliberately reduced.

(3) Long-run economic planning in the expectation that there would
be – as the CIA was predicting in 1977 – a fall in Soviet oil
production sufficient to enforce a sharp cut in Soviet hard-
currency earnings in the early 1980s, so that rates of non-grain
imports (in volume) would have to be cut; it might have been
argued that technology-assimilation problems and financial
pressures would be eased if the hardware imports were tapered
off gradually, outstanding debt was reduced and gold and hard-
currency reserves built up.

(4) The need to maintain the faith of western banks and governments in the 'umbrella theory' (that the USSR will in the last
resort bail out financially ailing CMEA partners) by signalling
loud and clear that Soviet hard-currency finances, alone in the
CMEA, were healthy; if this theory lost credibility and western
banks and governments cut their losses and ran from the weakest

CMEA countries, the financial burden of propping up Eastern Europe could in fact fall on the USSR.[23]

(5) Extreme financial conservatism amounting to an irrational belief that the absolute size of Soviet net external debt was a measure of Soviet weakness and dependence, to be reduced at all costs; this would interact with consideration (1).

(6) A more pragmatic set of financial calculations, according to which further increases in indebtedness and the debt-service ratio threatened in 1976–77 to be large unless drastic action was taken; in this case the USSR might lose its high credit rating, have to pay more for hard-currency loans, and become more vulnerable to western pressure.

(7) A reaction among domestic economic policy-makers against a strong emphasis on technology imports. Initial assimilation of the imported technology was generally slow, further domestic diffusion extremely limited, and the overall effect on productivity was probably much less than the advocates of larger commercial technology imports had projected. In this situation, the disgruntled do-it-yourself advocates in Soviet research and industrial management and in the Party apparatus would have been gathering ammunition for their more isolationist strategy.

Explanation (1) is likely to have played some part in the cutback in technology imports. It is true that the deterioration in Soviet-US relations did not directly engender western-imposed restrictions sufficient to reduce the rate of West–East technology flows. The US was a small direct contributor to these flows, and other western countries did not withdraw official export credit, MFN and the like. But the cooling-off in political relations, I suggest, strengthened the arguments of those in Moscow who were opposed to, or extremely cautious about, a strong 'turn to the West'. The cutbacks were initiated in Moscow not in the West. Explanation (2) will appeal to those who credit the makers of Soviet foreign policy with a guile and foresight worthy of the Bene Gesserit in Frank Herbert's *Dune* trilogy. It seems a bit far-fetched to me. Explanation (3) is also, on the face of it, not very plausible. The 1985 plan target of 630 million tonnes of crude oil represents a planned growth of 0.9 per cent per annum from the 1980 level of 603 million tonnes.[24] This is very slow, but it is still rather better than the CIA's most 'optimistic' scenario for Soviet crude oil output in this period: the so-called 'flat oil' scenario.[25] It is conceivable that the Soviet planners do not really think that even this modest growth is feasible. But a strong element in the case against the CIA's doom-and-gloom view of Soviet oil production is precisely the observation that the Soviet authorities have not been taking steps in domestic energy policy which imply a belief that oil output will fall. Articles have appeared in Soviet publications, it is true, that expressed a fear of declining petroleum output.[26] But they are couched in the form of terrible warnings about what could happen if such-and-such steps are not taken. They have not propounded the iron logic according to which CIA analysts have virtually ruled out an increase in output after 1980 and have made even stagnation appear a generous scenario. In short, the evidence such as it is suggests that Gosplan does not expect Soviet oil output to fall. (Whether the Soviet planners might be wrong in this respect is a separate issue which need not concern us here.) Let us suppose that the true state of opinion among Soviet policy-makers was nonetheless more sceptical than the plan indicates, and favoured a constant rate of oil production at around 605 million tonnes p.a. for 1981–85. What would follow for the planning of hard-currency trade?

This would correspond to oil production 'scenario C' in Bond and Levine's exploration of possible developments in Soviet hard-currency trade in the 1980s.[27] On their assumptions about Soviet production of other energy sources and domestic energy usage, that in turn would facilitate some 70 million tonnes of oil exports to the rest of the CMEA in 1985 and a very small export for hard currency, at that date, of 3 million tonnes. They assume that world oil prices will pass the $180 per ton mark only in 1983–84 (whereas in fact that mark had been reached by the end of the year in which their paper was published). If Soviet planners in the late 1970s had shared something like the Bond–Levine assumptions about future oil prices, they would have expected hard-currency earnings from oil exports to decline from $8–9 thousand million in 1980 to about $600 million in 1985 and total hard-currency fuel export earnings from about $10,000 million to about $3800 million.

This would perhaps suffice to persuade financially conservative policy-makers in the late 1970s of the need for some preparatory belt-tightening in hard-currency trade. But the Soviet planners would not have been contemplating a disastrous turnaround in hard-currency trade of anything like the order suggested by the CIA: a shift to a hard-currency fuel-trade *deficit* of $7–17 thousand million by 1985. So we may tentatively conclude that there could have been sufficient concern about prospects for hard-currency fuel trade to induce some caution in late-1970s ordering of machinery for hard currency (or the product-payback equivalent of hard currency); but that Soviet planners are most unlikely to have envisaged hard-currency problems on the scale suggested by the CIA: where the CIA projected a $27 thousand million deterioration in the hard-currency fuel account between 1980 and 1985, Gosplan might more plausibly have foreseen a deterioration of at most about $6 thousand million (in current prices).

Explanation (4) also cannot be ruled out as a contributory factor, despite recent explicit Soviet denials of the validity of the umbrella theory. There are good reasons for western banks and governments to assume that the external finances of the CMEA countries are strongly linked together. The smaller CMEA countries are more closely controlled in most respects by the CMEA and Warsaw Pact super-power than is the case of the smaller NATO/OECD countries vis-à-vis the US; the appointment of political leaders is believed to be *de facto* subject to Moscow's veto. They share, broadly, the same arrangements for managing trade and payments; their energy dependence on the USSR is high; and they engage in a certain amount of joint financial activity on world money markets through the two CMEA banks. The extent to which the creditworthiness of one CMEA country depends on that of other CMEA countries is therefore unusually high. (Here the umbrella theory generates a self-fulfilling prophecy: if western bankers and governments believe it, CMEA governments are to some extent forced to take account of that belief in their external financial policies.)

None of this requires that there should exist a secret formal commitment on Moscow's part to come to the financial aid of the other ruling communist parties. But in the 1970s Moscow happened to be generally well able to do so; and in the late 1970s almost all the East European countries looked as if they might soon be in need of such aid. In the case of Poland, some hard-currency assistance from the Soviet Union was actually reported in 1980.[28] And in the April 1981 negotiations over the rescheduling of Polish debt, western creditors naturally tried (unsuccessfully) to co-ordinate their actions with the Soviet Union as a fellow-creditor.

If the doubt which was raised in the West in 1975–76 about Soviet debt repayment had continued to gain force, the flow of additional western credit to the entire CMEA group could have been severely restricted. That could have forced the East European countries with the most severe liquidity problems to seek Soviet hard-currency aid; that in turn would have had to be provided for the sake of the continuing creditworthiness of the whole bloc; so any Soviet financial difficulties would have been sharpened. It is therefore reasonable to suppose that East Europe's growing financial problems in the late 1970s were another factor contributing to Soviet decisions in 1977–80 to stabilise and then reduce the level of Soviet net outstanding hard-currency debt. A cutback in machinery ordering was clearly the most direct way of achieving this. In the light of this (hypothesised) development, the cutback need not be explained in terms of a Soviet financial conservatism that was simply irrational (explanation (5)). But explanation (6), in conjunction with (4), begins to look quite plausible.

To assess Soviet external financial policy in 1975–80 as a whole, we need to return to the observation that drastic changes affecting Soviet trade and finances were concentrated in 1975–76. The adoption of intra-CMEA pricing rules less unfavourable to Moscow, the renewed emphasis on CMEA co-operation, a mild reform of Soviet foreign trade organisation and the first deterioration in bilateral relations with the US all occur in this period.

The external financial changes at this time are also striking. The Soviet hard-currency current account balance deteriorated sharply in 1975 (Table 3.4). A combination of large grain imports and the early 1970s upsurge in machinery acquisition (Tables 3.8 and 3.9) generated an enormously increased import bill (Table 3.4). The recession in western economic activity contributed to a levelling-off of hard-currency export earnings after the large post-1973 energy-price gains (Tables 3.3 and 3.4). To add to the difficulties, gold sales, hard-currency arms sales and net invisibles all dipped from their 1973–74 levels (Table 3.4). Large new hard-currency borrowings were unavoidable. Soviet policy-makers, traditionally extremely cautious financially, were suddenly confronted with a four-and-a-half-fold jump in end-year outstanding net debt and a $4700 million current account deficit (Table 3.4).

In addition, world gold prices levelled out between 1974 and 1975. The value of Soviet gold reserves, somewhat speculatively estimated (see Table 3.4 and note to table), almost ceased rising after a rapid increase from 1970 to 1974. The admittedly rather notional measure of the ratio of value of gold reserves to net hard-currency debt fell from about 5.8 to about 1.3.

One immediate effect of this dramatic development, I suggest, was that Soviet policy-makers embarked on a cutback in machinery ordering. At the same time personnel and minor organisational changes in foreign trade were initiated primarily (I suggest) to boost hard-currency export performance, and some shift of policy-makers' attention towards closer CMEA integration probably also occurred. All these developments would seem to follow quite logically from a startling loss of Soviet international liquidity. That the Soviet position was basically a great deal stronger even in 1975 than that of many other socialist and Third World countries does not, I think, make the reaction of Soviet policy-makers foolish and unjustified. The suddenness of the change must be borne in mind; so must the fact of its occurring at a time of deteriorating political relations with the US and of worsening East European external finances – our explanations (1) and (4).

There was some improvement in 1976, so far as the current account was concerned (Tables 3.3 and 3.4). But substantial gold sales during 1976 and a falling gold market (the average annual London gold market price per fine ounce fell from $161 to $125) meant that at the end of the year the hypothetical value of Soviet gold reserves had fallen well below the 1974–75 levels (Table 3.4). Soviet liquidity, crudely measured by the ratio of gold reserves to debt, fell further.

From 1977 onwards, however, the external financial position improved markedly. The current account went back into surplus, the absolute level of outstanding net debt was contained and then reduced, and the value of gold reserves began to climb again (Table 3.4). The question that now arises, therefore, is why Soviet ordering of western machinery was further reduced in 1978 and 1979 (Table 3.8); the western 'Afghanistan' response could have been a sufficient explanation of the low level of reported contracts in 1980. The increase in 1981 is fully accounted for by the Urengoi pipeline deals on a self-financing basis.

Table 3.10 suggests that the holding-down of technology importation in 1978–79 cannot easily be attributed simply to the Soviet Union's own financial position: it contains an extrapolation of a crude 'rule of thumb' explanation of the rate of Soviet importation of western machinery that I found quite effective for the period 1955–72.[29] It was shown that there was a strong statistical relationship between machinery imports in a given year (the outcome, on average, of orders placed in the previous year) on the one hand and the level of Soviet exports to the West in the previous year (a positive relationship) and the level of Soviet imports of grain from the West in the previous year (a negative relationship) on the other. But since there were very strong time trends (upwards) in both exports to the West and machinery imports this relationship could have been in part a spurious one. The time trends were therefore eliminated and the statistical association was explored between deviation from trend in machinery on the one side and deviations from trend in exports to the West and grain imports; the association was found to be significant (still with a one-year time lag).

The notion that Soviet policy-makers would still act as though guided by such a crude rule of thumb in the 1970s seemed implausible. The sharply increased role of borrowing, the rapid increase in the value of hard-currency arms sales and the value of Soviet gold reserves all seemed likely to influence decisions on the rate of technology importation. Surprisingly, however, an extrapolation of the 1955–72 relationship works tolerably well in 'predicting' Soviet machinery imports in 1974–77 (though not for the disorderly year 1973). This is indicated by the last column in Table 3.10. So it could with some plausibility be contended that the rate of Soviet commercial acquisition of western technology continued to be set by Soviet policy-makers on the basis of some rule of thumb that was not too far from the one implied by the regressions for 1955–72: a rule of thumb in which the two salient considerations in each year's ordering were the concurrent level of exports to the West and of grain purchasing from the West.

Table 3.10 Actual and 'Predicted' Soviet Imports of
Western Machinery 1973–79
(millions of US dollars)

	Actual	*Predicted*	*Error as percentage of Actual*
1973	1574	1036	34.2
1974	2094	2415	15.3
1975	4184	4821	15.2
1976	4259	4664	9.5
1977	4571	4703	2.9
1978	4994	7444	49.1
1979	4851	7703	48.8

Source: Actual, Table 3.9; Predicted, by: (a) extrapolating the 1955–71 trend growth (10.3 per cent p.a.) to 1979; (b) predicting each year's deviation from the extrapolated 1955–72 trend of machinery imports: by applying the coefficients estimated for 1955–72 to the previous year's deviation from trend and previous year's actual imports; and (c) adding the predicted deviation of imports to the extrapolated trend series.

Any such relationship, however, disappeared in 1978–79, as Table 3.10 shows; perhaps its appearance of validity in 1974–77 is fortuitous.

But an attempt to relate the rates of machinery ordering to two quite different financial measures – net debt and gold reserves – also seems to break down around this time. In Chart 3.1 the 'machinery-import propensity' is defined as the value of imports of western machinery in any year divided by an amount equal to the value of all hard-currency

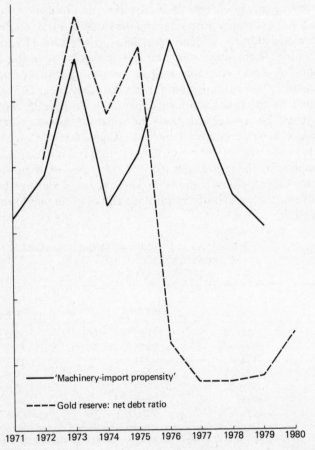

'Machinery-import propensity'

--- Gold reserve: net debt ratio

1971 1972 1973 1974 1975 1976 1977 1978 1979 1980

Chart 3.1 Soviet 'machinery-import propensity' and hard-currency liquidity, 1971–80

exports of the previous year less the value of grain imports of the previous year (for visual convenience it is multiplied by 10 to facilitate comparison with the 'liquidity ratio'). In this case hard-currency exports include not only reported merchandise exports to the West but also hard-currency exports to the Third World, gold sales, arms sales for hard-currency and net invisibles (that is, they are the total of rows 2–4 in Table 3.4). The 'liquidity ratio' in Chart 3.1 is simply the value of end-year gold reserves divided by that of net outstanding hard currency debt; it is assumed that the evolution of debt and gold reserve values during any year towards their values at the end of that year influences decisions on machinery ordering which show up (roughly) in recorded machinery imports in the ensuing year. They fit together quite nicely until 1975. The sharp deterioration in the former during that year then affects the latter only with a rather greater time-lag than before in 1976. But when liquidity improves in 1978 and 1979 the propensity to use current hard-currency earnings (net of the grain bill) on western machinery continues to decline. Such calculations are crude and somewhat speculative as indicators of actual influences on Soviet external financial policies. But they tend to strengthen the view that the continued turn away from western technology imports in 1978–79 cannot be attributed simply to immediate Soviet hard-currency constraints. Manifestly, the USSR could in 1978–79 have borrowed more (net) and imported substantially more western technology without facing balance-of-payments difficulties of the sort encountered by most of its CMEA partners. And Soviet policy seemed to depart at that time from its past proclivity for importing western machinery and know-how up to (or very close to) some 'rule of thumb' limit of hard-currency finance. Why?

It is reasonable at this point to refer again to explanations (1) and (4). Both Angola and US pressure over human rights precipitated a further deterioration in political relations with the US in 1978. And at the same time Soviet concern over the finances of the East European countries must have increased. At the end of 1979, Afghanistan added greatly to the political tension, and in the course of 1980 Poland's financial and other problems reinforced the tendency to play down Soviet resort to western technology *via* trade.

In addition, there is some evidence that explanation (7), a reaction in domestic economic policy against technology imports, may also have come into play at that time. I am inclined to see this as the surfacing of arguments against large-scale technology imports that had been present but concealed earlier in domestic policy-making but which gained ground when external circumstances threw doubt on the so-called 'import-led growth' strategy. It is safe to assume that there have always been some domestic sources of pressure against the idea of expanded imports of western machinery and know-how. Apart from resistance on diplomatic and strategic grounds at high levels of policy-formation, there is likely to have been resistance from at least some industrial research and design institutions, anxious that their monopoly as suppliers of expertise in a particular field should not be threatened. Such anxiety may in some cases have been heightened by fear that the plagiarism of western innovation in work passed off as their own would be revealed.[30] It would not be surprising if such 'grass-roots' objectors to intensified technology imports gained access on occasion to patronage and encouragement from individuals and groups quite highly placed in the party hierarchy.

Criticisms of particular technology-import deals, however, rarely appeared in the Soviet press before the very end of the decade. In the summer of 1979 two such attacks appeared in the newspaper *Sotsialisticheskaya industriya*.[31] Both referred to chemicals and petro-chemicals (the sector which had absorbed about a quarter of all imports of western machinery since the late 1950s). In the first article the author drew attention to a fiasco involving an imported ionol unit, which had not been put into operation while an adequate – indeed superior – unit of indigenous origin had been brought on stream instead. Selyunin went on to claim that in 1973–78 stocks of uninstalled foreign machinery had risen much faster than stocks of uninstalled domestically-manufactured machinery (not surprisingly, since foreign suppliers almost certainly keep closer to scheduled delivery times than Soviet machine-building enterprises). In 1976–77, Selyunin wrote, the central planners had instructed the ministry of petrochemicals to change this situation. (Whether they were to do this by lowering the rate of importation, by concentration on the installation of foreign machinery, or both, was not specified.)

The second article was more melodramatic. It virtually accused the head of an industrial association responsible for paints and varnishes of accepting bribes from foreign firms: his Volga car was sprayed a beautiful shade of (foreign) gold. The story in this case concerned a long-running argument between the managers of the paint and varnish association, who favoured the purchasing of foreign licences, and the director of the industry's Research and Project Institute, who favoured paints and varnishes developed by his own researchers. The former had been winning for some time, but the local (*raion*) Party Committee responsible for the Moscow *raion* where the Institute was located had begun in 1978 to press Kostandov, the (then) Minister for the Chemical Industry, to investigate the dispute. The article purported to show that the 'importers' were technically mistaken as well as corrupt, and implicitly criticised Kostandov for taking no action. (Kostandov has been one of the most conspicuous travellers in the West among Soviet branch ministers, and had become an inveterate purchaser of western plant since the start of Khrushchev's 'chemicalisation' drive in 1958.) In the November Plenum of that year, Kostandov was criticised by the most authoritative voice of all in the USSR.[32] It is true that several other branch ministers were also criticised by name, and that Kostandov was not criticised specifically for overindulgence in western hardware. But he was criticised (along with USSR Gosplan) for putting up large numbers of mineral fertiliser plants which, when opened, had insufficient oil and gas feedstocks to go on stream.[33] At the June 1980 Plenum Secretary General Brezhnev added 'the import of equipment' to his usual late 1970s short list of key economic problem areas: energy, steel and transport.

Technological chauvinism seemed by then to be coming back into style in the Soviet press. An article in *Pravda* on powder metallurgy referred to a British firm requesting more than three million roubles in gold (*sic*) for a licence; a Soviet institute instead came up with something better.[34] At the XXVI Party Congress Brezhnev returned to this issue: 'We must go into the reasons why we sometimes lose our lead [in a technology], and spend large sums of money on purchasing abroad equipment or technology which we are fully able to make for ourselves, often indeed at a higher quality level'.[35] This reads very much like a reversal of the late Premier Kosygin's call for more technology trade at the XXIII Congress in 1966, in which he said, 'The purchase of patent rights from abroad will allow us in our new Five-Year Plan to save hundreds of millions of roubles in scientific-technical work'.

There are signs that the advocates of large-scale technology imports have not been totally silenced. A call for continued extensive use of negotiable international technology transfer was made by Dzherman Gvishiani, who wrote in *Pravda* in March 1981 as though his father-in-law were still alive and in office and the State Committee for Science and Technology were still riding high.[36] He criticised the existing organisation of major research, development and innovation programmes in the USSR. He produced the latest figure for the total number of co-operation agreements between his Committee and foreign (nearly all western) firms and research institutes (290 on 1 October 1980). And he drew attention to the importance of such co-operation and of trade. 'Any artificial hindrances', he went on to say 'to [that] trade which serves as a means of transfer of the latest technology inevitably inflict damage on this [Soviet research-development-and-innovation] effectiveness'. This could be read as an attack on western 'cold warriors', but there is nothing in the immediate context to indicate a precise addressee. It is an observation that appears to be made To Whom It May Concern. It may not be too fanciful to suggest that it is addressed (*inter alios*) to some members of the Soviet leadership.

Evidence of this sort is circumstantial and slippery. But tentatively, at least, we may conclude that there has been something resembling a backlash, among Soviet domestic policy-makers, against the notion that major benefits for Soviet economic growth would flow from enlarged inflows of western machinery and know-how. It is also likely that this strategy still has its advocates; it would be strange if it did not. Such a reaction is not surprising. The unreformed economic system has in my judgement performed relatively poorly in commercially acquiring, assimilating and diffusing western technology. There have been substantial benefits, but they have very likely not lived up to the expectations of the more enthusiastic advocates of import-led growth. Explanation (7) has therefore probably contributed, along with foreign policy and financial considerations, to the apparent turn away from the West in the late 1970s.

CONCLUSIONS

It would be unwise to make too much of this turn away from the West, just as it was unwise to project enormous consequences from the earlier commercial turn to the West. It is nonetheless a significant development in Soviet relations with the outside world.

It has been suggested here that a combination of circumstances operated to limit the development of Soviet trade – especially technology trade – with the West in the late 1970s. Western stagflation and the lack of dynamism in Soviet exports of manufactures contributed to a sharp deterioration in Soviet hard-currency finances in the mid-1970s, after a particularly rapid growth of grain and technology imports. At this time political relations with the US were also deteriorating. A cautious cutting-back of technology imports followed, perhaps prompted at first mainly by Soviet hard-currency constraints. But when a return to higher levels of technology trade appeared financially possible in 1978–79, despite further large grain imports, other influences made themselves felt. There were increased worries about East European finances; possibly fears about early 1980s Soviet hard-currency earnings from oil, and a further sharp deterioration in political relations with the West. In those circumstances, opposition to large technology imports on other grounds was able to make itself felt as well.

It does not follow that the present 'turn away' from the West will necessarily be very prolonged. I do not consider that the earlier turn to the West was ever a long-term grand strategy conceived as such by Soviet policy-makers in 1958 or 1968 or 1970. The logic of greater participation in international commercial flows of technology – which is only a special case of comparative advantage – is a powerful logic that is valid for the long run (with some qualification, perhaps, about the dangers of atrophy for domestic research and development in certain circumstances). This logic was, I think, conceded by Soviet leaders somewhat gradually between the mid-1950s and the early 1970s. But this occurred, I suggest, as a series of medium-term expedients with no very clear long-run strategy.

By the same token, Soviet policy-makers may return to a somewhat greater degree of autarky for a period, without consciously devising a long-term strategy for so doing. The logic of engaging more extensively in international technology transfer remains strong, and institutional changes and personal experience amongst the élite seem likely to maintain at least a modest level of technology importation in the near future. Return to higher rates might come sooner or later, but would probably require above all an improvement in East–West political relations. (At the time of writing, these have deteriorated once more, following the introduction of martial law in Poland.)

Meanwhile the turn away from the West entails a heightened importance for intra-CMEA trade only in a rather limited sense. The percentage shares of the West and CMEA in Soviet trade have an obvious arithmetical relationship. And Eastern Europe can to some extent serve as a substitute market or source of supply for a number of items. But it has been argued that the dynamic contribution of East–West trade to the development of CMEA production and trade has been considerable. A more inward-looking development of CMEA is therefore likely to be, to that extent, a rather limited development. In any case, increased Soviet economic control of Eastern Europe is a mixed blessing for Moscow: at present it still comes at a high economic cost, and further increases in such control may be surplus to requirements.

There is therefore quite a strong case for greater cultivation by Moscow of trade with the group of countries that has been left out of the preceding discussion, the Third World. Much of this trade is on a commercial basis, without the disadvantage of low cost-effectiveness which the USSR encounters in CMEA trade or the danger of political disruption which exists in trade with the West. Since a good part of such trade is settled in hard currency, moreover, it provides an opportunity of earning surpluses to cover deficits in trade with the West.

NOTES

1. I am indebted to participants in the St Antony's seminar for comments on a first draft of this chapter and to Michael Kaser and Colin Lawson for comments on a second draft. I have tried to trace the development of Soviet official attitudes and policies, with special reference to technology imports, in Chapters 5 and 6 of my *Trade and Technology in Soviet-Western Relations* (London, 1981).
2. Bulgaria, Czechoslovakia, the German Democratic Republic, Hungary, Poland and Romania are the East European members of the CMEA; other members are Cuba, Mongolia and Vietnam.
3. P. G. Ericson and R. S. Miller, 'Soviet Foreign Economic Behaviour in a Balance of Payments Perspective' in US Congress Joint Economic Committee (JEC), *Soviet Economy in a Time of Change* (Washington DC, 1979), Vol. 2, pp. 208–44; CIA, *The Soviet Economy in 1978–79 and Prospects for 1980*, ER 80-10328, June 1980; CIA, *Estimating East European Hard Currency Debt*, ER 80-10327, 1980; H. Stephen Gardner, *Soviet International Economic Relations: Recent Trends in Policy and Performance*, Santa Monica, California Seminar on International Security and Foreign Policy, Discussion Paper No. 90, February 1981; Scott Bozek, 'The USSR: Intensifying the Development of its Foreign Trade Structure, US Congress JEC, op. cit., pp. 506–26.
4. *Vneshnyaya torgovlya SSSR v 1980 g.* (Moscow, 1981), pp. 6, 16.
5. Jewish emigration in the 1970s fluctuated widely according (mainly) to the state of Soviet-US relations, peaking at about 51,000 in 1979; in the mid-1970s, though, it was at an annual rate of around 15,000 (*Radio Liberty Research Bulletin*, RL 468/80, 9 December 1980). The Soviet population at the end of the decade was 265 million.
6. C. H. McMillan, 'Soviet Investment in the Industrialized Western Economics and in the Developing Economies of the Third World' in US Congress JEC, op. cit., 1979, pp. 625–48, at pp. 629–30.
7. One of the best accounts of the system is by Franklyn D. Holzman: *International Trade Under Communism: Politics and Economics* (New York, 1976).
8. Ericson and Miller, op. cit., Appendix B, contains a list for 1970–78.
9. Marie Lavigne, 'L'URSS dans le Comecon face à l'Ouest' in Centre d'Economie Internationale des Pays Socialistes, *Stratégies des pays socialistes dans l'échange international* (Paris, 1980), pp. 37–68, at pp. 42–43.

10. 'Terms of trade' here refers to the net barter terms of trade (ratio of unit value index for exports to that for imports). Reference will also be made later on to the gross barter terms of trade (ratio of index of import volume to that of export volume).

11. The scale of Soviet gold production is a state secret. Western estimates differ considerably. See M. C. Kaser, 'Soviet Gold Production' in US Congress JEC, op. cit., pp. 290–7. There has recently been some narrowing of the range of western estimates, which is now of the order of 280–350 tons a year for 1979 (personal communication from Michael Kaser, whose revised estimates, based upon a fresh field-by-field analysis, are forthcoming in R. Jensen, T. Shabad and A. Wright (eds), *Soviet Natural Resources in the World Economy* (Chicago University Press), Chapter 24).

12. OECD, *Statistics of Foreign Trade*, Series A. The real GDP growth rates of these countries were much higher (8–10 per cent a year) than that of the USSR.

13. Machinery and transport equipment, large-diameter pipe and instruments as a percentage of exports to the USSR of the 14 leading OECD countries. See *Trade and Technology . . .*, Chapter 8.

14. P. Gutman, 'Cooperation industrielle Est-Ouest dans l'automobile et modalités d' insertion des pays de l'Est dans la division internationale du travail occidentale', *Revue d'études comparatives est-ouest*, 11 Nos 2 and 3 (June and September 1980), 99–154 and 57–100.

15. Hanson, *Soviet Strategies and Policy Implementation in the Import of Western Chemical Technology, 1958–1978*, Santa Monica: California Seminar on International Security and Foreign Policy, Discussion Paper No. 92, 1981.

16. For input-output studies of the factor content of Soviet trade, see C. H. McMillan, 'Factor Proportions and the Structure of Soviet Foreign Trade' *ACES Bulletin*, Spring 1973, 57–81 and H. S. Gardner, 'The Factor Content of Soviet Foreign Trade: A Synthesis', *ACES Bulletin*, Summer 1979, 1–14. There are, as these authors acknowledge, methodological problems in these studies which are sufficient to make conclusions about 'gains' and 'losses' from trade somewhat precarious.

17. It is impossible, of course, to be sure of the true annual balances of payments between the USSR and each of its CMEA partners, since non-merchandise transactions are not reported. The change in the merchandise trade balances, however, is striking: it looks as though credits in 1976–77 began to be repaid in 1978 but that credits were again extended in 1979–80 when energy prices again rose sharply.

18. C. H. McMillan and J. B. Hannigan, *The Energy Factor in Soviet-East European Relations*, Ottawa: Carleton University Institute of Soviet and East European Studies East–West Commercial Relations Series, Research Report No. 18, 1981. See also Table 8.5.

19. The 1972 agreement covered a number of other matters, including Soviet-US maritime arrangements, commercial representation of each country, arbitration arrangements, scientific and technological co-operation, Soviet repayment of Lend-Lease debt, double taxation, etc. See H. W. Heiss, A. J. Lenz and J. Brougher, 'United States–Soviet Commercial Relations since 1972' in US Congress JEC, op. cit., pp. 189–208.

20. See *An Assessment of the Afghanistan Sanctions: Implications for Trade and Diplomacy in the 1980s*, report prepared for the Sub-Committee on Europe and the Middle East of the Committee on Foreign Affairs, US House of Representatives (Washington DC, April 1981) and Thane Gustafson, *Selling the Russians the Rope? Soviet Technology Policy and US Export Controls*, Santa Monica, Calif.: RAND Report R-2649-ARPA, April 1981. The US sanctions in response to the imposition of martial law in Poland were listed in *The Times*, 30 December 1981 and the CoCom agenda in the *Financial Times*, 19 January 1982.

21. On the last of these considerations see US International Communications Agency, Office of Research, *Soviet Perceptions of the US. Results of a Surrogate Interview Project*, mimeo Washington, June 1980.

22. Derived from *Narkhoz 1979*, p. 220; *Pravda*, 24 January 1981; CIA, *The Soviet Economy in 1978–79 and Prospects for 1980, ER 80–10328*, June 1980; J. D. Goldrich, 'USSR Grain and Oilseed Trade in the seventies' in US Congress JEC, op. cit., 1979, pp. 122–65; M. D. Zahn, 'Soviet Livestock Feed in Perspective', ibid., pp. 165–89 and oral communication about Soviet 1980 grain imports from W. A. Root, Director, Office of East–West Trade, US Department of State. From these sources I get 1976–80 totals in millions of tonnes: officially reported grain output 1025; dockage and wastage about 125; imports about 120; exports about 12; imports from US about 60.

23. Soviet officials are reported to have warned western bankers on 24 April 1981 that the umbrella theory was not valid, and that the USSR would not feel obliged to bail out Poland if the latter could not repay the $24 thousand million it owed to the West (*Financial Times* 25 April 1981). This is an important communication but it should be noted that it was part of tactical manoeuvring vis-à-vis both the West and the Polish government over the rescheduling of Polish debt. And it stresses the absence of an *obligation* (implying a formal commitment which the umbrella theory does not require). By the end of 1981 the Polish authorities had failed to meet the conditions set by the 501 western banks involved for a rescheduling of commercial debt, and the Soviet government had, indeed, not stepped in to support the necessary payments. An exercise in brinkmanship was nevertheless under way; Soviet specialists may well have judged that the western banks would not, under all the circumstances, declare Poland to be in default.

24. Derived from *Pravda*, 24 January and 18 November 1981.

25. The CIA 'best guess' scenario in 1979 was a fall in production; the 'flat oil' projected output stagnating at about 550 million tonnes a year to 1985 (CIA, *Simulations of Soviet Growth Options to 1985*, ER 79-10131). In fact in 1981, output was 609 million tonnes (see Table 8.4).

26. For example, A. P. Krylov, 'O tempakh razrabotki neftyanikh mestorozhdenii', *EKO* 1980, no. 1, 66–75.

27. D. I. Bond and H. S. Levine, 'Energy and Grain in Soviet Hard Currency Trade', in US Congress JEC, op. cit., pp. 244–90; the references in the calculation are to their Tables A-5, A-7 and A-8 respectively.

28. For a summary see Yakov Samoilov, 'Soviet Economic Aid to Poland', *Radio Liberty Research* RL 49/81 (2 February 1981). For a valuable

discussion of Polish debt problems and the potential links between the West and the USSR as creditors of Poland, see Richard Portes, *The Polish Crisis: Western Economic Policy Options*, London: Royal Institute of International Affairs, February 1981.

29. *Trade and Technology* . . . , Chapter 7.
30. For testimony to this effect by an emigré scientist, see M. Perakh, 'Utilization of Western Technological Advances in Soviet Industry' in NATO, *East–West Technological Cooperation* (Brussels, 1976), pp. 177–97. Western executives involved in technology deals frequently comment on the stern opposition put up to the deal by a branch research or design institute.
31. V. Selyunin, 'Podpis' pod kontraktom' on 7 June 1979, p. 2, and K. Ikramov 'Dvoinaya igra', 6 July 1979, p. 3.
32. Brezhnev speech, *Pravda*, 28 November 1979, at page 2.
33. A grossly unfair criticism of Kostandov since oil production was well below its five-year plan target in 1979, and transport problems in that year were particularly severe.
34. A. Batygin, 'Kopeika million berezhet', *Pravda*, 14 June 1980, p.3.
35. Brezhnev report to Congress, *Pravda*, 24 February 1981, at p. 5.
36. Dzh. Gvishiani, 'Glavnyi put' povysheniya effektivnosti proizvodstva' *Pravda*, 27 March 1981, pp. 2–3. Gvishiani is married to a daughter of A. N. Kosygin and is a deputy chairman of the State Committee for Science and Technology (GKNT), with particular responsibility for foreign technological co-operation.

4 Legal Trends

John N. Hazard

'Comrades, we have enacted quite a few good laws. Now it is chiefly a matter of their precise and steadfast implementation. Any law lives only when everybody complies with it.'[1] This was Secretary General L. I. Brezhnev's way of telling his colleagues at the XXVI Communist Party Congress of 1981 that the primary post-Stalin legislative task had been completed. The task of the future is consolidation to create the basis for a stable society, a society officially heralded as a society of 'developed socialism'.

For Brezhnev's septuagenarian Politburo colleagues the battles of their youth have been won. There remain today no hostile classes to be suppressed. The 'dictatorship of the proletariat' has been declared at an end, and in its place there has been installed 'a state of all the people'. Brezhnev reaffirmed the 1977 Constitution's declaration to this effect to put an end to any doubt concerning the definition of the nature of the state which Nikita Khrushchev had written into the Communist Party programme of 1961.[2] Although Brezhnev told the XXVI Congress that the old programme needed updating, he concluded that the 1961 programme 'correctly mirrors the laws of social development'.[3]

For the future of law in the 1980s the doctrinal position reflected in the slogan 'state of all the people' is of critical importance. It means that there is to be only one system of law for everybody; not one for the masses and another for those who are scions of the private enterprise classes of the past. Equality before the law is to be the norm. The task of the supreme legal institutions, the Supreme Courts of the federation and of its republics, the Ministry of Justice of the USSR with its republic counterparts and the Procurator General of the USSR, is to ferret out and set aside the departures from this rule by lower echelons.

Although Brezhnev was talking in generalities when he established the overall goal, he had been specific a moment earlier by indicating priority areas for what he called 'renewal of Soviet legislation on the basis of the constitution'. These were management of the national economy, assuring citizens and public organisations that they will in fact be able to exercise their constitutional rights, and completion of the publication of the Code of Laws of the USSR.[4] This last task had been set five years earlier at the XXV Communist Party Congress,[5] but its completion had not yet been achieved.

For those who have followed the legislative record since Stalin's death in 1953 there can be no doubt that Brezhnev had reason to exult over what had been achieved. Although it was his predecessor, Khrushchev, who had taken the initial bold and courageous step to repudiate Stalin, most of the legislation to which Brezhnev referred had been enacted during his own term as Secretary General of the Party. Khrushchev's step had been important for the future of law. In denouncing Stalin he had singled out as the base for personal dictatorship Stalin's declaration of 1930[6] that the state as an instrument of compulsion must remain the strongest state the world has ever known before it could wither away on completion of its task of creating the base for a new classless society. Khrushchev argued that the state must begin withering by degrees,[7] and he instructed his jurists to draft laws appropriate to the process. He had them begin with federal fundamental principles on court structure, criminal law and criminal procedure.

The first group of three 'fundamentals' to be used as guides by republic draftsmen in preparing their own new codes was enacted on 25 December 1958.[8] In most of their language they restated what had been established by the constitution of 1936, from which Stalin had so often departed in practice. In so doing, the 'fundamentals' reaffirmed the faith of Stalin's successors in those principles and their determination to adhere to them in the post-Stalin era. But the new drafts were not entirely restatements; they introduced some novelties as well. These novelties became even more apparent when the republics enacted new codes based upon the guidelines.[9]

The contribution of the 'fundamentals' to the new era was varied, depending upon the subject with which each was concerned. The 'fundamentals' on court structure reaffirmed the principles of equality of all citizens before the law, the right to defence, and the right to open trial. This latter principle had been restricted in the event that the court found state secrets in need of protection or to exclude the curious from trials concerning sex offences, intimate aspects of the lives of persons participating in the case, or offences of minors.[10] Stalin had used the exception for secrets to close not only trials but to create a structure of

Special Boards within the Ministry of Internal Affairs to 'purge' society of his enemies through secret hearings in which the accused had no counsel.[11] The 1958 reform was designed by the new leaders to put the final stamp of disapproval on secrecy, although the same exceptions to publicity of the trial were repeated with one difference. The old codes' inclusion of 'diplomatic secrets' among the reasons for closing the trial was omitted, perhaps because it was believed to be subsumed under the general term 'state secrets'.[12]

The companion 'fundamentals' of criminal law and criminal procedure developed further the principles of stability and publicity. The major change was removal of the 'analogy' article of the old codes. This meant that judges could no longer convict a citizen merely by arguing that his act was socially dangerous even if not specifically defined as such by the code, and that social danger was evident because the act was analogous to some other act defined as such by the code. This flexible principle of analogy had grown out of the first decree on the courts of 1917 when courts were authorised to find law in their socialist consciousness,[13] and it had been codified in the first republican criminal codes of 1922[14] and 1926.[15] The principle which had been established for the general courts became the foundation of all activity of the Special Boards when they condemned their victims to the noted GULag camps, for they needed to cite no articles of the code as the basis for their action.

In the procedural field the new 'fundamentals' incorporated the post-Stalin amendments to the code of criminal procedure which had restored in 1956 the right to appeal against all sentences by trial courts. This reaffirmation confirmed the determination of the new leaders to undo Stalin's net of the purge era of the 1930s when he had amended the then existing code to exclude from appeal all sentences for the crimes of 'terrorism', 'counter-revolutionary wrecking' and 'diversion'. Again, equality of procedural rights was to be the rule regardless of the type of offence alleged.

Although changes in the 'fundamentals' of civil law and civil procedure were seen to be less dramatic when they emerged from the draftsmen in 1961, they were heralded as contributions to the policy of stabilisation of law. Even these, however, retained some openings for backsliding to flexibility. The most noted such opening was the rule that judges might depart from the provisions of the civil code if a party before the court seemed to be attempting to exercise his legally defined right 'in a manner which would be inconsistent with the purpose of such rights in a socialist society during the period of the establishment of communism'.[16]

The impact of this exception was enhanced over the provision of Article 1 of the old code, as a noted commentator has said,[17] because it now applied to all civil rights, not solely to property rights, and it was now extended to organisations as well as individuals. On the other hand, the new formula was to be applied sparingly, for it was limited to circumstances in which a judge found elsewhere within the code a spirit that had been violated. He could not make a decision based upon some subjective whim as to what he or she thought was socially desirable.[18] Further, the Article is to be applied, as in Romano-Germanic systems generally, to cases of *abus de droit*, that is when a party seeks to assert a right for the sole purpose of causing harm to another party.[19]

Khrushchev's ouster in 1964 resulted in no turning back by Brezhnev and his colleagues from the recodification process. Although Khrushchev's restructuring of the Communist Party, the local soviets, and the system of industrial management was abandoned as 'hare-brained', his 'fundamentals' of law and and the republic codes enacted in accordance with them were kept in place. Draftsmen continued to prepare drafts on additional topics. There were enacted 'fundamentals' and republic codes in the fields of family law, labour law, corrective labour law, land and water conservation law, health care law, public education law, mineral resources and forest law,[20] and in 1980 administrative law.[21] Some of the new legislation was solely federal, such as air law, merchant shipping law and customs law, since the Constitution reserved jurisdiction in these fields to the federal Supreme Soviet.[22]

Not only have laws relating to substantive and procedural matters been revised, but new statutes have restructured institutions.[23] Statutes have redefined the structure of the USSR Council of Ministers, the Supreme Court, the Military Tribunals, the Ministry of Justice, the Procuracy, the Advocates, the Notariat, the Civil Registries, the Comrades' Courts, the Voluntary People's Guards, State Arbitration, People's Control, administrative commissions, the collective farm, the provincial, county and city soviets, the status of a deputy to a soviet, the state enterprise, the industrial and production associations, and the agro-industrial complexes.

This is the record to which Brezhnev referred when he praised the enactment of 'quite a few good laws'. There is now reason to believe that the 1980s will see the end of flexibility which had its start with 'war communism' (1917–21) and which continued to be a rule of application even during the period of codification prepared to support the New

Economic Policy (1921–28) as well as in the Stalinist period (1929–53). Of course, it can be anticipated that circumstances will continue to arise when opportunities to apply law flexibly emerge. It can also be foreseen that these opportunities will not always be resisted, for the codes still retain openings for flexibility. There are still some vague definitions of crime in the codes, notably those in the chapter on state crimes. Also the closing of courtrooms when secrets are concerned may occur under expansive interpretation of the word. Finally, even if courtrooms are ostensibly open, there may be circumstances in the 1980s, as there were in the previous decade during trials of political dissidents, when courtrooms are crowded with supporters of the charges so that opponents cannot gain admission. Time will tell whether these openings are used often or infrequently. Soviet jurists seem to want to reduce the number of these 'exceptional' cases, but passions can run high among the generalists, and it is still the generalists who make policy.

Evidence of the desire of Soviet jurists to introduce a quantitative reduction in exceptions to a point that it becomes qualitative abounds in the legal textbooks. Authors are pressing for stability, and they have been supported by the courts. Perhaps the most notable example of the jurists' pressure for stability is their campaign for recognition of the 'presumption of innocence' by Soviet courts, in spite of the reluctance of the generalists to permit draftsmen to include it *expressis verbis* in the 'fundamentals' and the codes of criminal procedure. The issue is much debated among western scholars, some of whom find no such presumption in Soviet law.[24] In spite of this position, Soviet official texts conclude that the presumption has been recognised by Soviet judges as a necessary interpretation of the code's rule that the burden of proof in criminal prosecutions is on the prosecutor.[25]

Law-trained Soviet scholars evidently want to close the door on ignorance of law, on violation of it, and on flexible application of it through questionable interpretation. They want the Stalin past outlawed and eventually forgotten. They now think their hands strengthened by the elevation during 1980 to full membership in the Communist Party's current Politburo of its first law-trained communist.[26] While the meaning of this elevation is unclear since it occurred ostensibly because the man is an expert on agriculture, the fact that he received his education at the Faculty of Law of Moscow University is taken by jurists to be significant. They seem to sense that they now have an advocate at the very top.

So far as the specifics of Brezhnev's recommendations to the XXVI

Communist Party Congress are concerned, the topic to which he gave priority was 'management of the national economy'. This has long been a topic of concern both to economists and jurists, for communism needs abundance if it is ever to be realised. Productivity of labour is a prime consideration for those who devise and for those who implement policy. Various aspects of economic policy are considered elsewhere in this book, but there may be something more to say by a lawyer concerned with the institutional structures required to achieve the goal of abundance and also to assure social stability. It is clear that contemporary social planners hope to avoid in the future the incessant structural innovation of Khrushchev as he sought to grapple with the problem of productivity. It was those frequent structural changes that earned him the characterisation of having been 'hare-brained'.

While sudden and frequent structural change is not to be anticipated in the 1980s, there is no evident desire among the reformers to avoid all structural innovation in economic management. The revised form of the 1977 constitution makes this clear, for it departs from the 1936 formula by omitting from its provisions the membership in the Council of Ministers. This omission has been explained as desirable to permit structural change without need of frequent constitutional amendment. The list of ministries is now relegated to a statute on the Council of Ministers,[27] and in this form it is easily amendable. Indeed new ministries have been created since enactment of the statute and, presumably, more will follow as the economy expands. The changes now envisaged will be incremental rather than revolutionary. That seems to be the message for the 1980s.

The promise of limited incremental change in economic structures does not mean that all interest to outsiders will vanish in the 1980s. Much is being said of the need to revise structures to meet the needs of an increasingly complex economy and to introduce the benefits of what is called the 'scientific and technological revolution'.[28] Already there is indication in the law of what can be expected. The major need is to provide institutions which can function effectively even though ministerial lines of command have to be crossed to provide co-ordination. The current answer is the 'association' (*ob'edinenie*), and statutes define its structure.[29] In a measure the changes suggest that managerial specialists have rethought their criticism of Khrushchev's regional economic councils (the *sovnarkhozy*) and are seeking a form that will combine both branch direction through the ministries and regional co-ordination. A special division of the State Planning Commission has been created to plan in these terms. One might characterise the policy as one of 'neo-sovnarkhozism'.

From the political point of view, the generalists have decided that local communities require a larger share in the policy decisions of economic management if they are not to become restless with the leadership of the country. The 1977 constitution signalled the new attitude by authorising in its Article 147 local soviets

> to ensure the comprehensive, all-round economic and social development of their area: exercise control over the observance of legislation by enterprises, institutions and organizations subordinate to higher authorities and located in their area; and co-ordinate and supervise their activity as regards land use, nature conservation, building, employment, production of consumer goods, and social, cultural, communal and other services and amenities for the public.

Reports of jurists indicate that this right of intervention by local authorities in the planning of enterprises (even those of federal importance) is being taken seriously. Gone are the days when an electric utility, responsible solely to the centre, can cut down boulevard trees standing in the way of transmission lines. Urban infrastructure must also be considered in the placing of buildings so that urban soviets are not faced with unbearable financial burdens and undesirable concentration of population, when new enterprises wish to enter the community or to expand.

What has been said of legislation on the administration of industry applies also to agricultural administration. During 1980 and 1981 incremental change was introduced to retard, if not reverse, the long-term trend introduced by Stalin in his 1952 political testament shortly prior to his death.[30] At that time he had anticipated a speedy transition from collective to state farming. Khrushchev had proceeded to implement Stalin's programme and many collective farms were transformed, especially those encircling cities. Khrushchev even pressed further in a direction which he thought would implement Marx's expectation that the city and village would be brought closer together under socialism as village work was mechanised. Khrushchev's method was to merge small collective farms into large ones, to house the farmers in multistorey apartment houses, and to remove the farmers from immediate access to their private garden plots. With this enlargement of the farms, it became necessary to abandon the old rule that farms would be governed by a general meeting of all members. In its place a representative assembly was to be elected.

Today, all of this has been retarded. The new model charter for collective farms adopted under Brezhnev in 1969[31] indicates that the collective model is still seen to be of value, although the legal status of members now resembles that of state farmers in some respects, namely in that their wages are guaranteed and they are included within the state social security system. The construction of the *agrogorod* (the city-type centre) will not be speeded, although inefficient farms will be merged with others, and some villages will still be marked as 'lacking a future' which means that no new construction will be licensed. Finally, private farming on family plots is to be encouraged, even to the extent of directing collective farm executive committees to render assistance to farmers in improving production on their plots. Brezhnev reported to the XXVI Congress that the Central Committee of the Party wanted to establish conditions 'both material and moral – that would make citizens more interested in subsidiary farming and, above all, in raising livestock and poultry'.[32] He called for the giving of aid to private families in providing them with both young stock and fodder.

In keeping with this recent policy emphasis, private plot legislation multiplied during the year prior to the XXVI Congress: farm directors were instructed to assist in the provision of means for ploughing the plots, of seeds, cattle feed and other necessities.[33] In a sense there has emerged a neo-NEP[34], although it does not return farming to private farmers as was the case in the 1920s. Collectivisation and state farming remain the dominant forms of agricultural production, but the supplementary plots of the farmers are given a prominent part to play in meeting the pressing demands of the population for meat, dairy products and vegetables and fruits.

Farming has also been restructured on a territorial basis to provide an institution to bring the processing of products into direct relationship with the growers. This has been done by a statute creating the agro-industrial enterprise which provides for the association of canning factories, cattle-fattening lots, orchards and specialised processing enterprises in a single legal entity.[35] Since the lines of economic command are varied, a single legal unit was thought necessary to co-ordinate operations. The new enterprise might be called a 'stock corporation', because the various co-operating entities provide direction through a stockholders' meeting in which representatives of each contributor to the enterprise sit to choose management and to establish overall policy.

Brezhnev's attention to productivity was not limited to revision of the managerial system. He turned his ire against the individual workmen as well when he said, after praising the Constitution's incorporation of the 'right to work':

> However, on the recommendation of many people the Constitution also records that shirking socially useful work is incompatible with the principles of socialism. This implies that all organization, fiscal, and juridical levers should be used to close once and for all every opening for parasitism, bribery, profiteering, unearned incomes and infringements of socialist property.[36]

Judging from the frequent accounts both from Soviet authors who have remained at home and from those who have emigrated, bribery and theft of state-owned property are indeed two crimes that have upset the rationality of the state economy and lowered morale. Even the Central Committee of the Communist Party found it necessary in 1979 to order local Party committees to strengthen their audits of state institutions and to remind Communists that they must be models of morality and clean living.[37]

Much of the state-owned property is resold after theft, giving rise to the conditions which Brezhnev calls 'profiteering and obtaining unearned incomes'. Court reports abound with convictions of this type of activity, and it seems high today even though the Supreme Court reports that there has been a general reduction in criminality since 1940.[38] This being the fact, it can be presumed that during the 1980s policy will focus on punishment for theft, although there will be continuing efforts through education in socialist morality to reduce the incidence of such crime.

The obsession of Soviet leaders with the problems created by economic crime was reflected in the passing of the decree of 25 July 1962 during Khrushchev's First Secretaryship. It introduced the death penalty for theft of state or social property on an especially large scale or for the acceptance of a bribe by a responsible official under especially aggravating circumstances.[39] Stalin had evidenced in the 1930s during the campaign for collectivisation of agriculture his belief that a death penalty acted as a deterrent to crime. At that time his decree of 7 August 1932 authorised the penalty of death for theft from state or collective farms.[40] In subsequent years, as thievery increased, the 1932 decree was extended by the courts on the 'analogy' principle to all thefts of importance which violated the sanctity of state property.[41]

With repeal of the 1932 decree on 4 June 1947, the policy of terrorising the public was changed by reducing the penalty for theft striking at the heart of the economy to 25 years imprisonment.[42] A second reduction in penalty occurred in 1960 after Stalin's death, for the new 'fundamentals' of criminal law established a general reduction of maximum prison sentences from 25 to 15 years. This brought lesser penalties for theft of state and social property in its various forms.

The spirit of moderation was not to last, however, for Khrushchev evidently became frustrated in his efforts to create a new Soviet man. He arranged for the amendment of the codes to reintroduce the death penalty in 1962, as has been indicated. Nothing suggests that Brezhnev's regime will in the 1980s reduce the penalties for theft of state and social property, nor will he be lenient when officials accept bribes. The running attack on these offences which has been mounted in the Party press over the past few years, and Brezhnev's interpolation in his XXVI Congress report of strictures on the topic indicate no reduction in severity of law on this score.[43]

Brezhnev's concern with the problem of productivity was manifest not only in his attack upon thieves and bribe-takers, but it extended to parasites as well. These people are not criminals, but those who loaf on the job, or take no jobs at all. To his listeners at the XXVI Congress he said: 'People who work conscientiously should be given every encouragement, while idlers and slackers should be left no loophole for living high on slipshod work'.[44]

This theme of improved labour discipline had been taken up by the Supreme Court in an Order of 1979 instructing courts to improve their educational work by eliminating drunkenness, absenteeism and failure of workers to perform their tasks.[45] The wartime decree of 1940 establishing penalties for 20 minutes' tardiness in arriving for work[46] has long since been repealed, but there is no less interest in persuading workers to give full value for what they receive. Enforcement today is through the code of labour law's provisions on right of dismissal.[47] Management is authorised to oust workers for 'systematic non-fulfilment by the manual or office worker, without good reasons, of the responsibilities placed upon him by the labour contract or internal work regulations'. Dismissal is also permitted for absence without good reasons. The effectiveness of these provisions has been somewhat dulled by two other code provisions, those requiring that the trade union give its consent to dismissals [48] and authorising courts to reinstate workers who have been dismissed without acceptable reasons.[49] Presumably, the 1979 order of the Supreme Court is to induce trial courts to be less ready to order reinstatement on the job than they have been. If this proves to be a correct interpretation of present trends, the difficulty which managers have met in dismissing workers, a difficulty reported by many former factory managers and legal advisers who have emigrated, will be lessened during the 1980s. It is clear that Soviet leadership has lost patience with those who fail to meet productivity standards.

The emphasis upon court responsibility for improving labour discipline probably does not mean that they will succeed the trade unions as the first line of defence against low productivity. Those who follow Soviet labour law know that the trade unions have long since become an arm of the state to aid in stimulating production. Although they have by law some duties which are popular with workers, such as conducting cultural activities, providing legal services to those who need to go to court on labour matters, resisting management claims that are unfounded, and administering social insurance during temporary absence because of illness and injury, their task has long been stimulation of production. Trade unions in the West have ceased to co-operate with Soviet trade unions in many cases because of this fact, and have gone to the length of creating the International Federation of Free Trade Unions to compete with the World Federation of Trade Unions, which has become an instrument of trade unions in Eastern Europe.

The relationship of trade unions to the state has recently been the focal point of unrest in Poland, and even the USSR has not entirely escaped the impact of rebellious union members. Dissident trade union members who have sought to establish independent trade unions in the USSR have been detained, interrogated and even interned. Brezhnev reflected leadership concern when he told the XXVI Congress that trade unions have shown lack of initiative in protecting workers' rights to labour safety, to performance of obligations by management, to prevention of bureaucratic practices and violations of labour legislation.[50] In view of this situation, the progress of labour law in the 1980s can be expected to be along existing lines, with an effort to increase the protective services the unions give their individual members, but without any extension to unions of the right to strike to respond to the demands of a collective nature which workers may wish to present to management. The Communist Party of the Soviet Union is in no way prepared to allow emergence of a force in Soviet society that can challenge its leading role in policy-making, a position most recently reaffirmed by Article 6 of the USSR constitution.

Turning now to Brezhnev's second priority in 'renewal of Soviet legislation on the basis of the Constitution', namely assurance to citizens and public organisations that they will in fact be able to exercise their constitutional rights, the following may be said. Unquestionably, the definition and protection of constitutional rights have become major topics of discussion since Stalin's death.[51] Out of this discussion came the 1977 constitution, and much was made of the fact that the bill of rights was advanced in the chapters of the document from a place near the end of the 1936 constitution to a place near the beginning of the new basic law.

The topic of a bill of rights is not new on the Soviet jurists' agenda, for there has been a constitutional bill of rights in effect ever since the first Russian Republic constitution of 1918. All of these bills of rights have included clauses that expressed the Marxist emphasis upon the community as the environment within which the individual lives. All have reflected in their way the Marxist admonition that 'personal freedom is possible only in the collective'. All have provided that rights will not be recognised that do not contribute to the achievement of socialism. Article 39 of the 1977 constitution says bluntly: 'In exercising their rights and freedoms, citizens may not injure the interests of society or the state or the rights of other citizens'. Since those interests are throughout the document defined as the building of socialism, there can be no doubt what Article 39 means. The point is further elaborated in Article 50's guarantee of the right of expression, for it declares that the right is granted: 'In accordance with the interests of the people and in order to strengthen and develop the socialist system'.

This having been said, it has become evident since Stalin's death that jurists have been pressing for procedures that will assure the orderly conduct of trials and conviction only of those guilty of violation of defined crime. This development has been elaborated upon at the outset of this chapter. There is also, however, a new note that is being sounded in legal literature and which has become codified in the 'fundamentals on administrative law' which was enacted in 1980. It is a note that relates to the individual's rights against the ever-increasing bureaucracy of the USSR, built upon a long-standing tradition of bureaucracy in the Russian Empire.

Prior to the 1977 constitution, the solution to bureaucratic violation of constitutional and statutory provisions conferring rights upon the citizen was intervention by the Procurator General of the USSR and his subordinates in republics. Much has been written by westerners on the practice of the Procurator in performing his duties of 'protest' against violation of law by the bureaucracy.[52] In generalising upon the

impact of his intervention scholars have found that political conditions
at the time greatly influence his activity. During the great purges of the
late 1930s, the Procurator General did little, even when the police
turned on his own subordinates. On other occasions also his right of
protest did little to help the individual, but Soviet leaders could accept
no other procedure for enforcing constitutional provisions. Sugges-
tions that individuals might protect themselves directly by taking their
problem to a court, as is often permitted in western countries, fell on
deaf ears.

The entering wedge for the reformers has been the insertion in the
1977 constitution of Article 58, which reads:

> Citizens of the USSR have the right to lodge a complaint against
> the actions of officials, state bodies and public bodies. Complaints
> shall be examined according to the procedure and within the time
> limit established by law.
> Actions by officials that contravene the law or exceed their
> powers, and infringe the rights of citizens, may be appealed against
> in court in the manner prescribed by law.

It is this last clause that has stimulated legal scholars to discuss
appropriate procedures to be followed in presenting complaints. An
émigré who worked on the staff of the constitutional drafting committee has reported that during the winter of 1976–77 specialists
argued that individuals ought to be given the right to direct access to
courts rather than having to proceed through the office of the Procurator.[53] This argument failed in the face of opposition from the
generalists who preferred to leave the wording of Article 58 vague, and
in a vague form the Article went to the Supreme Soviet for adoption in
the constitution.

The legal specialists seem not to have resigned themselves to defeat,
if one may judge from what has transpired since 1977. The USSR
Supreme Court has instructed the inferior courts to strengthen
attention to complaints under Article 58, and to show tact in relation to
complainants.[54] Finally in 1980 the Supreme Soviet enacted a set of
federal 'fundamentals' on administrative offences and procedures for
their rectification. While its draftsmen appear to have been cautious
on an issue involving judicial review of administrative acts, the new
'fundamentals' undoubtedly make an inroad into what had been the
almost impregnable castle of the administrative official.

Under the new 'fundamentals', which will need to be incorporated as always into detailed codes by the republics, administrative acts by state officials exacting penalties against individuals and associations may be appealed against to higher administrative authority, and if satisfaction is not obtained, to a court. The court is not to make a final determination in the matter, for it is authorised only to ask the administrative agency responsible for exacting the penalty to review their action in the light of the court's findings.

The question remains whether the remand should be to a superior administrative agency which has already reviewed the case and found it justified, or to the original actor. The 'fundamentals' are silent on this point, but two highly-placed authors from the Ministry of Justice of the USSR and the USSR Academy of Sciences' Institute of State and Law respectively suggest that the original actor should receive the court's order for review rather than the affirming agency.[55]

The 'fundamentals' permit detention of a violator in what is called 'administrative arrest' for a period of 15 days, but only in exceptional circumstances. Authority for detention must be granted by the people's court of first instance. No arrest may occur of pregnant women, women with children under 12 years of age, minors under the age of 18 or invalids of the first or second group. Circumstances to be considered in exacting a less severe penalty than the law prescribes for administrative offences are set forth.

These 'fundamentals' and the discussion continuing on court review of administrative acts suggest that during the 1980s there will be inroads upon the arbitrary acts committed by bureaucrats. This does not mean that direct action by an individual to set aside an administrative order can be expected. Complaints of constitutional violation must still pass through the office of Procurator. Also, development of any procedure for challenging the constitutionality of legislation of the Supreme Soviet of the USSR is not to be expected. Under long-established legal doctrine within the USSR, there is no recognition of the separation of powers between legislative, executive and judicial branches of government. The Supreme Soviet is the repository of the general will, and when it speaks it alone is the judge of the constitutionality of what it says. It would also be unrealistic not to remind readers at this point that the Communist Party in exercise of its leading policy-making role guides the legislative process and the judicial process. Conflict between the two branches at the highest policy level is today unthinkable. In light of this attitude, the current trend toward court review of administrative acts is remarkable, for it indicates willingness to recognise some division of interest between the executive and judicial agencies, the latter ranking higher than the former in assuring observance of the Constitution, but it is a cautious first step. There is no hint that the judiciary might be authorised to review the work of the legislature.

In spite of the subordinate position of the judiciary to the legislature, there may eventually be a call upon the judiciary to decide just what civil rights exist in law in the USSR. The problem was raised by ratification on 18 September 1973 by the USSR of the United Nations Covenant on Civil and Political Rights.[56] Some of the rights set forth in the Covenant were not incorporated in the USSR constitution in 1977. These are the right to strike, the right to freedom of religious education, and the right to freedom of movement.[57] Soviet legislation restricting strikes, religious education and freedom of movement remains on the statute books.

The issue of priority of the Constitution over the Covenant seems unclear, at least from the West's distance. Soviet doctrine supports the view that ratification of a treaty by the Supreme Soviet makes it the law of the land. This being so, it is hard to understand why the Constitution of 1977 did not include the three Covenant rights indicated. It is known that Ministry of Foreign Affairs lawyers made a study of international obligations of the USSR prior to the drafting of the Constitution. Presumably, their report indicated what the Covenant required: yet the two documents were not made to correspond. The outsider can but wonder how to reconcile the Covenant's obligations with those of the Constitution.

The issue has been treated in discussion of the 'presumption of innocence' to which attention has already been directed. Two prominent Soviet authors have justified the conclusion that the presumption exists in Soviet law, in spite of its absence in the constitution *expressis verbis* by arguing in part that it must be Soviet law since it was established as an obligation on ratification of the Covenant.[58] The question for outsiders is whether the argument can be generalised to refer to all obligations established by the Covenant, or whether it was no more than a lawyer's brief for recognition of the presumption in which several impelling reasons for its recognition were thought to exist. Although the basis for concluding that an argument relating to one obligation of the Covenant must relate to all seems sound, the exclusion of the three rights indicated cannot have been because of ignorance. There must have been a decision on policy at the highest levels, and that being so, it is unlikely that the three Covenant rights will be recognised in practice within the foreseeable future.

Finally, there remains Brezhnev's third priority item, namely completion of the Collection of Law begun after the XXV Congress in accordance with a resolution on the topic. In some measure the legislation of the USSR has been in as much confusion as was that of the Russian Empire when Alexander I ordered Michael Speransky to gather and publish chronologically the Imperial Rescripts, and then to assemble a topically organised Collection of Laws. Indeed, an historian has examined the possibility of such comparison.[59]

Work has begun on the Collection, even extending to the purchase abroad of machines to produce a loose-leaf series of legal publications. The collection has been announced as filling many volumes, but it will not be sold abroad. It is not to include all laws in spite of the evident purpose of providing a comprehensive source for use by courts. Some laws will be distributed only to agencies which have a need to know. This will continue a long-standing practice of secrecy both within the Russian Empire and the USSR.[60]

In the light of this review of current legislative history and Brezhnev's statements of policy it seems safe to predict that the 1980s will witness no massive change in the attitude of Communist Party leaders toward law or in the laws themselves. The system that has moved from flexibility to relative stability over six decades will be preserved. Soviet law will remain formally within the Romanist tradition, but in its political underpinning it will implement a philosophy enunciated by V. I. Lenin on the basis of the Marxist heritage.

The element that is new since Stalin's death, namely the effort of leaders to avoid the excesses of his period, will be developed incrementally through definitions of the rights and duties of citizens, public organisations, state institutions and officials and through legislation which will establish procedures designed to enforce conformance to the law. Within these procedures there will be evidence of increasing reliance upon the judicial process to determine fact and to hold administrative agencies and officials to their obligations when dealing with citizens.

Perhaps most importantly, individuals trained in the law and practising as judges, procurators, attorneys at the bar and scholars on the law faculties and in the Academies of Science will demonstrate their determination to prevent backsliding by the generalists to the vagueness and flexibility characterising law in the Stalin period. The legally trained group working within the Communist Party may strengthen the position of the defenders of what they choose to call 'socialist legality'.

This legally trained group of Communists can hardly be called an 'interest group', in the meaning of western political scientists,[61] but they have been seen to be pressing with increasing vigour and courage for adoption of their point of view as to what 'justice' requires. The lawyers cannot be expected to challenge the Communist Party's monopoly of policy-making authority, but they are likely to become the watchdogs restraining the administrators on the state side from losing sight of the individual through arbitrary application of bureaucratic procedures. In a sense, they may be seeking a cure for what Marshal Tito once called the 'cancer of socialism', namely bureaucratic ossification.

If this reform in attitudes and legislation and practice can be achieved, the 1980s will emerge in Soviet history as a memorable decade, not only for Soviet law, but for the entire Soviet system.

NOTES

1. Brezhnev, 'Report to the CPSU Central Committee', part III (3), *Reprints from the Soviet Press*, 32 (New York, 1981), nos. 5-6-7, p. 92.
2. For relevant portions, see J. Hazard, *The Soviet System of Government* (Chicago, 5th edn, 1980), p. 288
3. Brezhnev, op. cit., no. 1, part IV (3), p. 112.
4. Ibid., part III (3), p. 92.
5. Brezhnev, 'Report to XXV Communist Party Congress, Feb. 24, 1976', part III (3), *Current Digest of the Soviet Press*, 28, No. 8 (1976), 30.
6. For relevant portion, see J. Hazard and H. Babb, *Soviet Legal Philosophy* (Cambridge, Mass., 1951).
7. N. Khrushchev, *The Crimes of the Stalin Era. Special Report to the 20th Congress of the Communist Party of the Soviet Union.* Annotated especially for this edition by Boris Nikolaevsky (New York, 1956).
8. For an English translation of 'fundamentals', see W. Butler, *The Soviet Legal System: Legislation and Documentation* (New York, 1978).
9. For an English translation of Russian Republic Codes of Law, see W. Simons, *The Soviet Codes of Law* (Law in Eastern Europe Series, v. 26), (Alphen aan den Rijn, 1980).
10. Russian Republic Code of Criminal Procedure, Art. 18.
11. Decree of 10 July 1934 [1934] I. *Sobranie zakonov SSSR*, item 283 and decree of 5 November 1934 [1935], ibid., item 84.
12. Russian Republic Code of Criminal Procedure. Revised edn of 1923, Art. 19. [1923], I *Sobranie Uzakonov RSFSR*, item 106.
13. Decree no. 1 on the courts, sec. 5, 27 November 1917. [1917], I ibid., item 50.
14. Russian Republic Criminal Code, 1922. Art. 10. I ibid., item 153.
15. Russian Republic Criminal Code, Revision of 1926, Art. 16. [1926], I *Sob*.

Uzak. RSFSR, item 60.

16. USSR Fundamental Principles of Civil Law, 1961. Butler, op. cit., n. 8, p. 393.
17. E. Fleyshits (ed.), *Nauchno-prakticheskie komentarii k G.K. RSFSR* (Moscow, 1966), pp. 16–18.
18. Ibid.
19. Ibid.
20. For English translation, see W. Simons, op. cit., n. 9.
21. Law of 23 October 1980 (effective 1 March 1981). *Vedomosti Verkhovnogo Soveta SSSR*, 1980, item 909.
22. For an English translation of the three federal codes, see W. Simons, op. cit., n. 9.
23. For an English translation of many of these statutes, see W. Butler (ed.), *Collected Legislation of the USSR and Constituent Republics* (New York, 1978–80).
24. For a review of the literature, see H. Berman, *Soviet Criminal Law and Procedure: the RSFSR Codes* (Cambridge, Mass., 2nd edn, 1972), pp. 57–62. For a debate as to what presumption of innocence means in Soviet law, see J. Gorgone, 'Soviet Criminal Procedure Legislation: A Dissenting Perspective', and Berman's reply, *American Journal of Comparative Law* 28 (1980), 577–623.
25. M. Bassiouni and V. Savitski (eds), *The Criminal Justice System of the USSR* (Springfield, Illinois, 1979) pp. 47–8. The USSR Supreme Court Order no. 5, 16 June 1978, par. 2, reads: 'In order to secure for the accused (defendant) rights to defence, courts must hold strictly to the constitutional principle, under which the accused (defendant) is considered innocent until his guilt is proved in the manner provided by law and established by a sentence of the court which has entered into force'. *Byulleten' Verkhovnogo Suda SSSR*, no. 4 (1948), 9.
26. M. S. Gorbachev was named a candidate member of the Politburo of the CPSU Central Committee in November 1979 and a full member on 21 October 1980. He is a graduate of the Law Faculty of Moscow University. For the communiqué and a biography, see *Pravda*, 22 October 1980, p. 1.
27. For relevant articles, see Hazard, op. cit. n. 2, p. 285.
28. Brezhnev, op. cit., n. 1, part II (2), p. 74.
29. See S. Pomorski, 'The Soviet Economic Associations: Some Problems of Legal Status after the 1973 Reform', *Review of Socialist Law* 2 (1976), 129–72.
30. J. Stalin, *Economic Problems of Socialism in the USSR* (New York, 1952).
31. Text in *Pravda*, 30 November 1969, pp. 1–2. English translation in Butler, op. cit., n. 8. pp. 197–213.
32. Brezhnev, op. cit., n. 1, p 84.
33. Resolution of CPSU Central Committee and USSR Council of Ministers 'on personal auxiliary farming operations', 17 September 1977. *Izvestiya*, 18 September 1977, p. 1.
34. Lenin's 'New Economic Policy' was introduced in 1921 to overcome shortages created by peasant resistance to a policy of requisitioning farm produce and compulsion to enter agricultural co-operatives. It restored a policy of permitting peasants to farm state land on a private family basis

and to sell their produce on the open market. The policy was terminated through heavy taxation and ultimately by the campaign of 1929 to force peasants to enter collective farms.

35. For an English translation see Butler, op. cit., n. 23, vol. II, part 4-5.
36. Brezhnev, op. cit., n. 1 part III (2), p. 85. See USSR Supreme Court's order no. 16 of 23 September 1977 on 'Court practice in cases concerning bribery'. *Byulleten' Verkhovnogo Suda SSSR,* no. 6 (1977), 10.
37. Order of Central Committee CPSU on improving and on protecting law and order and strengthening the struggle with violations of law. *Byulleten' Verkhovnogo Suda SSSR,* no. 5 (1979), 3.
38. For a review by the President of the Court, see ibid. n. 5 (1977), 3–15.
39. Russian Republic Criminal Code, Art. 93 (1), added to code by amendment 25 July 1962.
40. [1932] I *Sob. Zak. SSSR,* item 360.
41. Karnitsky and Roginsky, *Ugolovnyy Kodeks RSFSR Posobie* (Moscow, 1935) p. 67.
42. *Vedomosti Verkhovnogo Soveta SSSR,* no. 19 (1947), 1.
43. Brezhnev, op. cit., n. 1, p. 36.
44. Ibid., p. 84.
45. See Order no. 2, 29 June 1979. *Byulleten' Verkhovnogo Suda SSSR,* no. 4 (1979), 15.
46. *Ved. Verkh. Sov. SSSR,* no. 20 (1940), 1.
47. Russian Republic Code of Labour Law, Art. 33.
48. Ibid., Art. 35.
49. Ibid., Art. 213.
50. Brezhnev, op. cit., n. 1, p. 95.
51. For current thinking on a Marxist approach to human rights, see leading article, *Sovetskoe gosudarstvo i pravo,* no. 7 (1980), 3–12.
52. G. Smith, *The Soviet Procuracy and the Supervision of Administration* (Alphen aan den Rijn, 1978).
53. K. Simis, 'The Making of the New Soviet Constitution: Conflict over Administrative Justice', *Soviet Union/Union Soviétique,* 6 (1979), part 2, 203–7.
54. Order no. 1 of 3 February 1978 on the new constitution of the USSR and the tasks of further implementation in court activity. *Byulleten' Verkhovnogo Suda SSSR* (1978), no. 2, 9.
55. Nikolaev and Kudryashova, 'Osnovy zakonodatel'stva ob administrativnykh pravonarusheniyakh i voprosy grazhdanskogo sudoproizvodstva', *Sovetskaya yustitsiya* (1981), no. 6, 3.
56. See *United Nations Monthly Chronicle,* 1973, no. 10, p. 36.
57. See Uibopuu, 'The Human Rights Covenants of the United Nations and the Constitutional Law of the USSR', in L. Lipson and V. Chalidze (eds), *Papers on Soviet Law* (New York, 1977), p. 14.
58. See Bassiouni and Savitski, op. cit., n. 25, p. 47.
59. Marc Raeff of Columbia University made the comparison at the annual meeting of the American Association for the Advancement of Slavic Studies, Washington DC, 1978. See M. Raeff, 'Codification et droite en Russie Impériale', *Cahiers du Monde russe et soviétique,* 20, no. 1 (1979), 5–13.

60. For the Regulation on preparation and publication of the Code of Laws USSR, of 2 September 1976, see *Vedomosti Verkhovnogo Soveta SSSR* (1976), item 515. A report on progress appears in *Sovetskoe gosudarstvo i pravo* (1980), no. 3, 3–12.

61. The book that stimulated discussion of 'interest groups' in Soviet political life is H. G. Skilling and F. Griffiths, *Interest Groups in Soviet Politics* (Princeton, N.J., 1971).

5 Demographic Policy

Ann Helgeson

Uneasiness about the possible consequences to the Soviet economy and society of decreasing rates of labour force growth underlies the increased interest in demographic matters in the USSR. The economy has survived many crises, but never that of a labour shortage. Throughout Soviet history there has always been a huge pool of potential labourers to draw upon; the impressive achievements of the Soviet economy have been effected, to a very large degree, by the attraction into state employment of this labour pool. Now, in the 1980s, the rural reserve has been depleted by decades of out-migration. The other source of growth in the labouring population, natural increase, shows signs of a decided slowing as the post-War fertility decreases begin to manifest themselves in smaller labour-age cohorts.

The 10th Five-year Plan was referred to at the XXV Party Congress in 1976 as the plan of quality and productivity. By that time looming labour shortages were clear to everyone and the solution to the problem was seen, at least in the short term, in the intensive use of labour. It was announced that labour productivity in industry was to increase by 30–34 per cent from 1976 to 1980.[1] In February of 1981 at the XXVI Party Congress, the Chairman of the Council of Ministers, Nikolai Tikhonov, in summing up the achievements of the previous five years, referred to the lack of success in achieving this labour productivity growth as the single most disappointing result of the 10th Five-year Plan. Only a 17 per cent increase, half that planned, was achieved. He, and the Party General Secretary, Brezhnev, in his speech at the Congress, blamed this failure on forces of inertia, tradition, the habits of industrial managers and, implicitly, on the tremendous difficulties of the shift in attitudes and practices necessary to use industrial resources efficiently.[2]

One might have expected a stronger commitment to stimulating population growth – the long-term solution and one much more amenable to Soviet industrial habits – as well as the push for improvements in labour productivity. But there was really only one reference in the materials of the XXV Congress to demographic policy. Hundreds of demographic works written since 1976 have cited this passage, which seems to have been taken by the Soviet demographic establishment as their reason for existence in the second half of the 1970s.

> Environmental and population problems which have become more pressing in recent years, should not escape the view of Soviet scholars. The improvement of socialist natural resource use and the development of an effective demographic policy are important tasks for physical and social scientists[3]

Note in particular that the brief is the development (*razrabotka*) of a demographic policy and not the implementation of one.

Judging from the statements made at the most recent Party Congress the collective labours called for in 1976 bore fruit, because they now talk about the implementation of an effective demographic policy and not simply its development. Labour productivity, on the other hand, was not nearly so prominent a catchphrase as in 1976 and the goals for growth in this indicator are significantly more modest. It appears that the long-term solution to labour shortages has been given renewed importance.

The second half of this chapter examines the new demographic policy designated for implementation between 1981 and 1985 and tries to isolate its essence, which is still obscure despite the volume of academic research referred to above. The first half of the chapter will review demographic trends in recent years in three important areas: fertility, mortality and migration.

FERTILITY

The current Soviet manpower crisis that scholars East and West are talking about is most directly due to the fact that in the 1960s birth cohorts were smaller than at any time in Soviet post-War history. This can be seen in Table 5.1. The lowest number of Soviet births was recorded in 1969 and there has been a small, but steady, increase since then.

The 10th Five-year Plan period saw a large growth in the labour force because the young generation coming into the working ages was

Table 5.1 Demographic Movement in the USSR 1959–81

Year	Births	Births per 1000	Deaths	Deaths per 1000	Natural increase	Increase per 1000	Total popula-tion (thous)
1959	5,264,501	25.0	1,604,400	7.6	3,660,100	17.4	208,827
1960	5,340,975	24.9	1,528,600	7.1	3,812,400	17.8	212,372
1961	5,191,915	23.8	1,563,000	7.2	3,628,900	16.6	216,286
1962	4,959,092	22.4	1,666,740	7.5	3,292,352	14.9	220,003
1963	4,757,744	21.1	1,626,927	7.2	3,130,817	13.9	223,457
1964	4,456,787	19.5	1,581,311	6.9	2,875,476	12.6	226,669
1965	4,253,096	18.4	1,689,834	7.3	2,563,262	11.1	229,628
1966	4,241,624	18.2	1,710,951	7.3	2,530,673	10.9	232,243
1967	4,093,100	17.3	1,799,000	7.6	2,294,100	9.7	234,823
1968	4,087,900	17.2	1,833,500	7.7	2,254,400	9.5	237,165
1969	4,087,000	17.0	1,957,300	8.1	2,129,700	8.9	239,468
1970	4,225,600	17.4	1,996,200	8.2	2,229,400	9.2	241,720
1971	4,371,500	17.8	2,015,400	8.2	2,356,100	9.6	243,873
1972	4,404,000	17.8	2,105,400	8.5	2,298,600	9.3	246,293
1973	4,386,200	17.6	2,164,200	8.7	2,222,000	8.9	248,625
1974	4,546,100	18.0	2,191,400	8.7	2,354,700	9.3	250,869
1975	4,611,500	18.1	2,363,400	9.3	2,248,100	8.8	253,261
1976	4,719,700	18.4	2,426,500	9.5	2,293,200	8.9	255,524
1977	4,693,400	18.1	2,494,700	9.6	2,198,700	8.5	257,824
1978	4,763,400	18.2	2,545,600	9.7	2,217,800	8.5	260,020
1979	4,807,100	18.2	2,665,900	10.1	2,141,200	8.1	262,436
1980	4,851,368	18.3	2,743,805	10.3	2,107,563	8.0	264,486[a]

[a]Population in millions on 1 January 1981: 266.6; 1982: 268.8.
Note: The crude birth rate, crude death rate and natural increase rate are per 1000 total population at mid-year. The total population is that on 1 January; but the Census population is used for 1959, 1970 and 1979.
Source: Vestnik statistiki, various issues 1967–81; *Naselenie SSSR, statisticheskiy sbornik* (Moscow, 1975).

a large one comprising those born in the late 1950s while the retiring generation was small, consisting of men and women born during the difficult years of the First World War, Revolution and Civil War who then had to make it through the Second World War. Exactly the opposite situation will prevail in the latter half of the 1980s. The generation coming into the working ages is a very small one born in the late 1960s when fertility rates were an all-time low and the retiring cohort is a numerous one born in the reconstruction period of the early 1920s. Table 5.2 shows the size of these entering and leaving generations as they were at the time of the 1970 census.

There are at least two major factors in explaining the small birth cohorts of the 1960s: the relatively small number of mothers in prime child-bearing ages and a decline in fertility rates among these women. The second factor, the smaller number of children born to each woman, has persisted; the increase in the number of births since 1969 is mostly due to the simple fact that the number of mothers (born in the post-War baby boom) has been greater. (We can think of the numbers of births in Table 5.1 as potential parents, say twenty years later, and predict the grosser effects of age structure on future fertility.) Because relatively low fertility rates seem to have established themselves more or less permanently, the successive waves of large cohorts of mothers will eventually flatten out, and the low fertility rates will mean relatively small numbers of births.

An additional element in the labour crisis, if not in the nationwide demographic situation, has to do with the regional and ethnic distribution of these births. The Turkic share of the Soviet population, in the Central Asian republics and parts of the Caucasus, has increased from 11 to 17 per cent and will almost certainly reach 25 per cent by the

Table 5.2 Age Groups Projected as Entering and Leaving Labour-age during the 12th Five Year Plan (1986–90)

Republic	Size of age group in 1970 census 0–4 thousands 40–44		0–4 as percentage of 40–44
	0–4	40–44	
RSFSR	9,318.6	10,940.3	85
Latvia	160.2	181.7	88
Ukraine	3,442.0	3,881.3	89
Estonia	96.1	103.8	93
Belorussia	742.1	687.5	108
Georgia	432.5	364.5	119
Lithuania	267.5	225.6	119
Moldavia	337.6	239.1	141
Armenia	288.0	168.8	171
Kazakhstan	1,545.3	849.1	182
Kirghizia	413.0	180.7	229
Azerbaydzhan	743.7	289.6	257
Turkmenia	348.0	115.5	301
Uzbekistan	1,882.0	622.7	302
Tadzhikistan	493.2	153.0	322
USSR	20,509.0	19,003.1	108

Source: V. I. Perevedentsev, 'Sotsial'no-demograficheskaya situatsiya i vstuplenie molodezhi v trudovuyu zhizn'', *Rabochiy klass i sovremenniy mir*, No. 2, 1980, p. 90.

end of the century. So, much of the labour force growth will occur outside the regions where the bulk of industrial production takes place and where the most important new industrial enterprises are to be located. The breakdown by republic in Table 5.2 shows the regional contours of future labour force growth and decline.

As the oscillations in the number of mothers die out, increasingly fertility rates and their levels take on pivotal importance. The most often used fertility rate is the Crude Birth Rate (CBR) which is shown in Table 5.1. I have included this for reference only; there are better measures which do not mask the distorting effect of age structure. Table 5.3 shows age-specific fertility rates, the general fertility rate and the total fertility rate for the USSR as a whole and for four of the fifteen Soviet republics which are selected as representative of specific patterns of fertility. The three periods are selected to correspond as closely as possible to the three most recent census years 1959, 1970 and 1979. The general fertility rate, which expresses the number of births during a specified period in relation to the number of women of child-bearing ages, shows a decline in the USSR as a whole during the decade of the 1960s and a small recovery since then up to approximately the same level as it was in 1965. The pattern in the republics differs, with no significant change in either the high levels of Uzbekistan or the low levels of Estonia, a similar pattern to the all-Union one in RSFSR, and quite dramatic decline in Azerbaydzhan. The latter republic is often cited in the Soviet literature as being in a transitional stage between the high fertility of the traditional rural Islamic society to an urban industrial one (for example Uzbekistan and Estonia or the RSFSR respectively).

The pattern of age-specific fertility rates differs considerably among the republics. It can readily be seen in Table 5.3 that the high fertility of the Central Asian republics, exemplified here by Uzbekistan, is attributable not only to higher age-specific rates, but to the effective lengthening of the reproductive period, with fertility rates among women in their 40s at levels approaching those for much younger women in the Russian Republic. Looking at the change over time in age-specific rates for the USSR as a whole, one can see that decline has come about by a tendency for women to have children at younger ages and for fertility to drop off sharply after the age of 30. Again, the extremes can be seen in the Uzbek and Estonian cases.

The total fertility rate (TFR) is one not often used by Soviet demographers. It is a hypothetical rate and can be thought of as the number of children each thousand women would bear in a reproductive lifetime given the current age-specific fertility schedule. So, a TFR of less than 2000 (in fact 2000 plus if we are to take mortality into account) indicates a fertility schedule which would not reproduce the parent population. As can be seen in Table 5.3, this is characteristic of Estonia and the RSFSR. It also indicates that the GFR 'improvement'

Table 5.3 Age-specific Fertility Rates in USSR and Selected Republics

	15–19	20–24	25–29	30–34	35–39	40–44	45–49	15–49 GFR	TFR
USSR									
1958–59	29.2	162.2	164.8	110.1	66.6	24.1	5.0	88.7	2810
1969–70	30.4	163.9	128.7	88.1	48.5	15.3	2.9	65.7	2389
1978–79	39.4	174.6	125.6	72.1	31.9	11.7	1.6	69.9	2285
RSFSR									
1958–59	28.4	157.9	156.4	101.9	57.7	19.9	3.0	82.9	2626
1969–70	28.3	146.9	107.4	69.3	32.2	9.0	1.1	53.4	1971
1978–79	40.8	155.0	103.1	55.6	19.6	5.9	0.4	59.0	1902
Uzbek SSR									
1958–59	38.3	209.9	240.7	206.0	178.6	96.8	38.4	158.8	5044
1969–70	41.7	261.3	265.2	245.6	194.9	91.5	27.0	158.5	5636
1978–79	35.4	277.3	281.7	210.7	134.7	66.9	12.5	149.6	5096
Azerbaydzhan SSR									
1958–59	43.0	209.6	266.5	216.1	162.7	73.5	29.6	163.3	5005
1969–70	40.8	228.4	233.1	210.0	146.9	53.3	14.1	134.6	4633
1978–79	17.5	196.7	222.6	143.7	78.3	33.4	4.6	98.6	3484
Estonian SSR									
1958–59	20.1	122.3	119.1	72.9	41.9	12.0	0.9	59.9	1946
1969–70	30.1	157.1	130.6	73.0	29.9	7.4	0.5	59.3	2143
1978–79	41.0	165.2	111.6	55.8	23.4	5.5	0.3	58.6	2014

Note: The age-specific fertility rate (ASFR) is expressed as the number of births per 1000 women of the given age group. Soviet practice uses the mean number of births to women of the relevant age group for the two years shown as the numerator, and the mid-period population of women in the age group as the denominator in calculating this rate.

The general fertility rate (GFR) in Soviet practice includes births to women over the age of 49 in addition to births to women 15–49.

The total fertility rate (TFR), not usually shown in Soviet practice, is the sum of the ASFRs each weighted by 5 and can be thought of as the number of children each woman would bear in a reproductive lifetime given the current fertility schedule.

Source: Naselenie SSSR, statisticheskiy sbornik (Moscow, 1975), pp. 137–8; *Vestnik statistiki*, No. 11, 1980, p. 76.

observed for the USSR as a whole during the 1960s was an artifact of the age structure of women in the reproductive ages.

It is not the place in a short treatment of this sort to go into an exhaustive catalogue of the social explanations of declining fertility. Many of the explanations in the USSR are similar to those in other urban industrial populations. Similarly much of the explanation for high fertility in the Central Asian region is not specific to the Soviet Union, Central Asia or even the Muslim cultural realm. Some light will be shed on these questions in the section dealing with the formulation of demographic policy.

MORTALITY

At the same time as fertility seems to be settling down at fairly low levels in the western parts of the country at least, mortality levels are increasing. This is visible in the Crude Death Rate (CDR) (see Table 5.1) which has moved steadily upwards from an extremely low level of around 7 per 1000 in 1960 to somewhat over 10 per 1000 at the present time. It is still fairly low by the standards of most industrial countries (1979 United Kingdom – 12; USA – 9).

Much, but by no means all, of this increase is attributable to the ageing of the Soviet population which puts a larger proportion of the population in the older ages more at risk of death. But there are two other elements which have assumed great importance in rising mortality levels in the late 1970s: a rising infant mortality rate and increases in male mortality in the adult ages between 30 and 60. These two elements are treated briefly below.

A good deal of concern has been expressed in the Soviet demographic literature about the rising adult male mortality levels, and the volume of published data has been curtailed. Table 5.4 presents age- and sex-specific mortality levels for the most recent period available in print. The increases are overwhelmingly concentrated among the adult male population, although there are some smallish rises for the female population over 40. If one examines age-specific death rates in other industrialised countries of the world shown in the *UN Demographic Yearbook* over the last two decades, this Soviet development can be seen to be very unusual and deserving of serious study. But in the Soviet demographic literature we are given only clues to possible explanations and few, if any, data.

Soviet demographic works cite the following in explanation of the

Table 5.4 Age-specific Mortality Rates

Age	1958–59	1964–65 Male	1964–65 Female	1973–74 Male	1973–74 Female	Percentage change 1964–74 Male	Percentage change 1964–74 Female	1975–76	Percentage change 1958–76
0–4	11.9	7.7	6.5	8.5	6.8	+10	+5	8.7	−27
5–9	1.1	0.9	0.7	0.8	0.5	−11	−29	0.7	−36
10–14	0.8	0.7	0.5	0.6	0.4	−14	−20	0.5	−38
15–19	1.3	1.3	0.6	1.4	0.6	+8	—	1.0	−23
20–24	1.8	2.1	1.0	2.5	0.8	+19	−20	1.7	−6
25–29	2.2	2.8	1.1	3.1	0.9	+11	−18	2.1	−5
30–34	2.6	3.7	1.4	4.4	1.4	+19	—	3.0	+15
35–39	3.1	4.6	1.9	5.4	1.8	+17	−5	3.8	+23
40–44	4.0	5.7	2.5	7.4	2.6	+30	+4	5.3	+33
45–49	5.4	7.5	3.5	9.7	3.7	+29	+6	6.9	+28
50–54	7.9	11.9	5.4	13.9	5.8	+17	+7	9.3	+18
55–59	11.2	16.5	7.4	19.5	8.2	+18	+11	13.4	+20
60–64	17.1	26.2	12.6	28.7	12.6	+10	—	18.9	+11
65–69	25.2							28.0	+11

Source: Naselenie SSSR, statisticheskiy sbornik (Moscow, 1975), p. 141; *Vestnik statistiki,* No. 11, 1967; No. 12, 1975; No. 11, 1977.

increases. First, rises in the rate of heart disease among adult males: causal factors cited in the increase of heart disease include nervous tension, insufficient physical exercise, smoking, irrational eating and misuse of alcohol. Secondly, an increase in the rate of cancer in men over 40. Accidents are a third and very large category. Accidental death is the third largest general cause of death in the official classification. The growth in fatal accidents recently has been attributed to increased automation and mechanisation in industry, an increase in the use of private automobiles, the home use of technical equipment and chemicals and the use of chemicals in agriculture. Four out of five deaths to men in the ages 20–24 are accidental. The fatal accident rate is, incidentally, much higher in the rural areas than in urban, almost as if safety is not moving into the countryside as fast as the scientific-technical revolution. Finally, a factor is the generally weaker constitutions of those who survived their younger years during the deprivations of the Second World War. What we may be seeing in the USSR is the transition to 'affluent' mortality patterns, which in the West have tended to affect men more than women. The transition may, as with the urban and industrial transition in the Soviet Union, be taking place at a more rapid rate than in those countries experiencing it earlier.

The other contributing element to increasing mortality levels in the USSR in recent years is the rate of infant mortality. These rises are the source of great concern in the Soviet Union as the infant mortality rate is generally recognised as one of the basic indicators of levels of health care and social progress in any society. The increase in infant mortality by more than a third in the period between 1971 and 1976 has been the subject of extensive research by Christopher Davis and Murray Feshbach and their findings may briefly be summarised.[4] As they report, the USSR is the first among the developed nations of the world to experience a sustained reversal of the normal downward trend in infant mortality. The index has gone up from a level of 22.9 per 1000 live births in 1971 to an estimated 31.1 per 1000 in 1976. The data are no longer published and even the death rates among 0–4 year-olds, upon which a reasonable estimate can be based, have ceased to be published. Among their considered explanations for the rises are: influenza epidemics, growing levels of pollution, the use of abortion as a primary form of birth control, underutilisation of pre-natal medical services due to the pressures on working women, the instability of the family leading to a deterioration in child care, the shift from breast-feeding to formula milk, the quality of which may not yet be adequate, and the growing reliance on institutional child-care.

MIGRATION

In this all-important demographic category during a period of labour shortages, which have very distinct regional dimensions, the data problems are now almost overwhelming. The three major sources of information about interregional migration have all dried up in the second half of the 1970s. Annual data from the migration registration system, based on residence permits stamped in internal passports, ceased to be published in 1974. Regional (*oblast'*) level CBRs and CDRs, allowing an imperfect residual calculation of net migration, also ceased publication in 1974. The age-structure data for Soviet regions from the 1979 census, upon which a rather more reliable residual net migration could be calculated, have not yet been published.

Considerably more can be said about migration during the 1960s. An analysis of population and industrial labour force dynamics in the 1959–70 intercensal period, as summarised below, shows that inter-regional migration, far from alleviating some of the regional labour

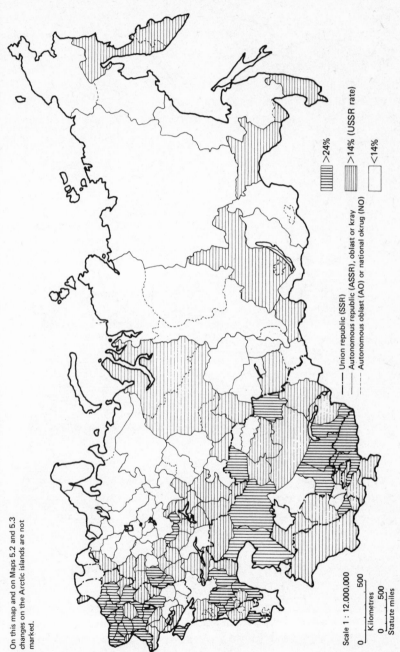

On this map and on Maps 5.2 and 5.3 changes on the Arctic islands are not marked.

>24%

>14% (USSR rate)

<14%

Union republic (SSR)
Autonomous republic (ASSR), oblast or kray
Autonomous oblast (AO) or national okrug (NO)

Scale 1 : 12,000,000

0   500
Kilometres
0   500
Statute miles

Map 5.1 Industrial labour force growth, 1965–70

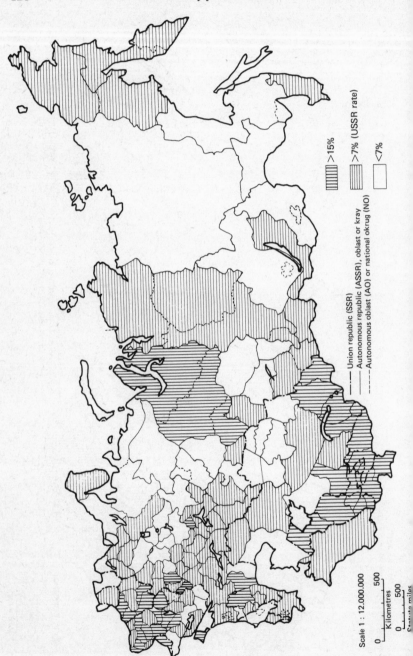

Map 5.2 Industrial labour force growth, 1970–75

imbalances in the country, has tended to exacerbate the problems.

Elsewhere I have calculated net inter-*oblast'* migration for the 1959–70 period, using a census survival rate method.[5] The results give net migration rates for 10-year age groups for each of 168 regions and their urban and rural components. As a whole the estimates show a total net population redistribution on the order of 7 million, much of which the economic planners would probably have preferred not to have happened at all. There was a southward redistribution of about 3 million, much of which resulted in accumulations of working-age population in already labour-surplus regions like the North Caucasus and Southern Ukraine. The RSFSR, where the largest part of industry is concentrated, lost about 2 million persons. There was a very small East–West exchange, especially modest in the light of efforts to get workers to relocate to the developing regions of Siberia and the Far East. The 1960s was a period of relaxation of control over individual movement and the patterns on the map of net migration indicate that many took advantage of the opportunity to move to regions of residential amenity that were not necessarily the locus of jobs.

The examination of growth in the industrial labour force lends support to the notion that the population movements of the 1960s were irrational from the point of view of labour needs (see Maps 5.1 and 5.2). The data shown on the maps were derived from published data on gross industrial production and industrial labour productivity at the *oblast'* level, which also ceased publication in the late 1970s. During this period of developing regional labour deficits and surpluses I could find no statistically significant relations between any of the following, on the *oblast'* level: labour-age population, urban labour-age population, net migration, net urban migration, growth in the industrial labour force, or expected (that is in the absence of migration) growth in labour-age population, urban and total, There seems hence to have been little enough accomplished in matching labour growth and labour supply in the 1960s. People went where they pleased and industry muddled through with what labour it could attract. It would be useful to do similar calculations for the 1970s but none of the necessary data are being published.

Nonetheless, we can see at least the basic patterns of population growth by *oblast'* in the 1970–79 period (see Map 5.3), but the patterns are complicated by large regional differences in natural increase and migration) growth in labour-age population, urban and total. There observed during the 1959–70 period we observe on Map 5.3 that the main belt of settlement, forming an attenuated triangle with its base

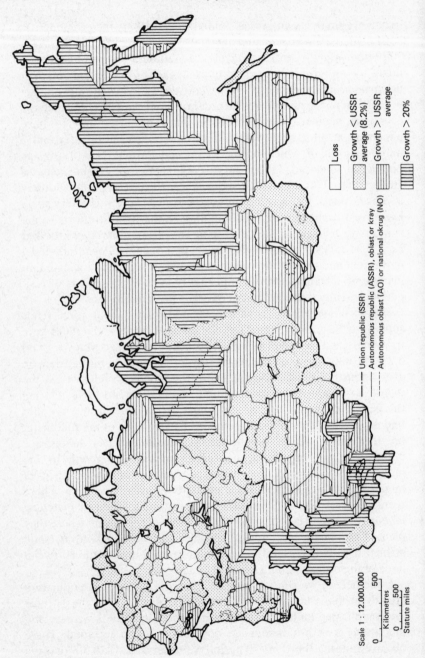

Map 5.3 Regional growth rates, 1970–79

against the western border and its apex strung out along the Trans-Siberian railway, is characterised by slower than average growth. Although natural increase rates are not high in central European Russia, much of this slow growth is probably attributable to out-migration as it was during 1959–70. There is a slackening off of growth in the southwestern regions. The southern Ukrainian economic region, which was a growth area in the 1960s, is still growing at rates far above the national average, but this cannot be said of the Donets–Dniepr or the North Caucasian-Krasnodar regions. The above-average growth in Central Asia is nearly wholly attributable to natural increase. As noted above, fertility rates among the traditionally Islamic nationalities remain high. There is no sign yet of a massive migration from labour-surplus Central Asia into the industrial regions.[6] Although the population bases in Northern Siberia and the Far East are small and we should not overestimate the numerical importance of the above average growth rates here, it should be noted that there has been some success in the 1970s in getting people to relocate to the East. There has been a particularly noteworthy movement of labour to the oil-rich northern regions of Tyumen *oblast'* in northwestern Siberia.

THE DEVELOPMENT OF DEMOGRAPHIC POLICY

It is difficult to differentiate clearly the concept 'demographic policy' from social or welfare policy now that a demographic policy has been adopted for the period beginning with the 11th Five-year Plan. At the 1974 World Population conference in Bucharest the definition used was that of policy with the explicit objective of influencing the size or composition of a population. The size or composition objective would seem to be an intermediate one and begs the question of the ultimate goal. Why larger? Why smaller? Why an older population, or a younger? this seems to me to underlie a distinction which Soviet demographers use frequently now between population policy (*politika narodonaseleniya*) and demographic policy (*demograficheskaya politika*).[7] To confuse matters the terms have sometimes been used the other way round, but in general population policy seems to operate on theoretically measurable things like population size and composition, while demographic policy is aimed at a much wider range of targets with fuzzy names like population quality, the Communist population, etc. Although the 11th Five-year Plan calls for the implementation of a demographic policy, it would seem to be, on the whole, of the more limited variety.

There has been much published work on the development of demographic policy since the call for it at the XXV Party Congress, and in the course of the ensuing five years its objects have become broader as Soviet scholars emphasise the complex and interrelated system that is involved in human demographic behaviour. There has been a transition in thinking from the 'bigger family allowance/better housing' school of pro-natalist thinking to a realisation that if larger families are required, then something more than material compensation for the cost of having children is necessary. Undoubtedly there are still material conditions which discourage large families, or indeed more than one child; and there are many other carrots to be held in front of potential parents. But a major conclusion to be drawn from the work of Soviet demographers in recent years is that the coming of the good life to the USSR has altered the 'demand' for children,[8] in comparison with the demand for other uses of time and money.

A 1980 monograph which has come out of the Leningrad University Laboratory for Social Psychology serves as a useful illustration of this point. It is called *The Small Family* and it is an attempt to explain the drop in family size in large cities at a time when the Soviet population has never had it so good.

> The reproductive behaviour of most people cannot always be explained by the obvious. Living conditions have improved sharply. . . . Yet against the background of colossal human achievements, the age-old tradition of large families had toppled. More often a family has one or two children. There is a paradox in this which can be explained only by human psychology.[9]

This kind of work has its source in the early 1970s in the work of Belova, Darsky and others at the demography section of the Scientific Research Institute of the Central Statistical Administration on desired and expected family size,[10] which discovered all sorts of non-economic, seemingly irrational, reasons for wanting and expecting small numbers of children. This particular research institute is now doing a lot of work on divorce and expectations of duration of marriage. This may be because a crisis in the Soviet family seems to play a very important role in low fertility levels. Indeed, at the XXVI Party Congress there was a striking number of references to measures to strengthen the family, which might seem to be a less than direct approach to the objective of raising fertility rates. Moreover, the recent spate of books with titles like *Marriage and the Family* and *Marriage and Divorce in the USSR*[11] might seem like less than the concentration on issues directly related to the formulation of practicable policy called for after the XXV Congress.

The increased attention to the family may reflect a real crisis of confidence on the part of potential mothers, which may in turn be a fundamental explanation of the small family.[12] The new literature in the social-psychology vein is full of descriptions of the heavy dual burden of Soviet women as workers and mothers, the depressingly unequal time-budgets of husbands and wives, of amazingly Victorian sexual attitudes, and of drunkenness and regular wife-beating. It is as if the family has remained in its unchanged Russian patriarchal mould while the society outside was busy building atomic power stations and conquering the cosmos. The divorce rate is high (ironically, as the housing shortage is eased, divorce becomes more practicable) and much the larger number of Soviet divorces are initiated by women. Many women are choosing not to remarry, judging from recently published results from the 1979 census which indicate that 66 per 1000 women aged 16 and above are divorced or separated while only 32 per 1000 men are in this category.[13] In the Russian republic and three others from 16 to 18 per cent of families have only one parent.[14]

About a month before the XXVI Party Congress a major decree 'On measures to Strengthen Government Help to Families with Children' was promulgated.[15] Some progress has been made towards the realisation of measures which have been proposed, although the decree, on the whole, represents a modest amount of resources to be transferred to families with children. The intention of the measures is clearly stated as the encouragement of growth of the population as well as the raising of general well-being.

The major innovations in the 1981 decree are: the institution of a system of partially paid leave to working mothers until the first birthday of their new-born child; an increase in the monthly allowance for single mothers; and the establishment of one-time grants to be paid at the birth of first, second and third children.

INSTRUMENTS OF DEMOGRAPHIC POLICY

The advocacy of paid leave for mothers of small children is perhaps most closely associated with the Moscow demographer A. Ya.

Kvasha.[16] A survey conducted by the Centre for the Study of Population Problems in the Economics Faculty of Moscow University has been used by Kvasha to demonstrate the potential of this kind of demographic policy. Only 57 per cent of the 5200 Moscow women surveyed sent their young children to nursery schools, while 85 per cent of them sent their older children to kindergartens. And he demonstrates that the reason for the smaller number enrolled in the nurseries was not the unavailability of places (only 5 per cent of the respondents said they were unable to enrol their children in the nurseries), but rather a desire to remain at home with very young children. (60–80 per cent of the women said they would take advantage of partially paid leave for a year after the birth of their children.)

Paid leave for mothers to spend the early years with their children had been advocated as early as the 1920s by Alexandra Kollontay,[17] but the 1981 decree is the first practical measure in the Soviet Union to begin such a programme. Up until then women had been allowed to retain their right to employment and their seniority (*stazh*) in their jobs while not being paid for six months after the end of paid maternity leave, but the recent measure is said to be the beginning of a period of part-paid leave for child-raising that will eventually be extended to two years and perhaps more. Urlanis estimates that, assuming that women do not postpone the birth of their second (or third) children, the average period spent out of the work force will be five or six years if half of Soviet women choose to have two children and the other half choose to have three (Kvasha's 'optimal reproduction').[18] The experience of the Eastern European states, particularly Hungary and Czechoslovakia, with programmes of this sort has clearly been taken into account in the decision on this measure.[19]

It should be noted that payment will be made only to women who were working for at least one year before the birth of the child (or who were taking time off from work to further their education). The programme began in November 1981 in regions of the Far East, Siberia and northern European Russia, where the monthly payment was 50 roubles. Implementation will occur for other European areas of the USSR in November 1982 and in Kazakhstan, Central Asia and the Caucasian republics in November 1983. In the latter two groups of republics the payment will be 35 roubles per month. The two-year delay before implementation in Central Asia will, intentionally or not, allow Central Asian women who would not ordinarily work before their child-bearing begins, to acquire the work experience necessary for eligibility for the monthly payments and could signal an increase in female labour participation rates. The January 1981 decree makes a commitment to the further extension of this programme of leave for child-raising to be introduced during the period of the 12th Five-year Plan (1986–90).[20]

The single parent, female-headed family has been a part of the Soviet social structure since the Second World War left a substantial male deficit in the prime child-raising ages. The discrepancy in sex ratios has by now disappeared in younger cohorts, but the single mother is still a phenomenon of great numerical significance, largely as a result of divorce. As many as one in six families is headed by a single female,[21] or somewhat over 9 million.

The considerable increase in government monthly payments to single mothers will lighten the load for many, if not all, these female-headed families. The allowances are not paid for children of previous marriages (alimony or social security exists for these children), but only for those born out of wedlock and without the voluntary acknowledgement of the father. From 1981 20 roubles per month per child is being paid to these mothers. This is not only a generous improvement on the previous allowances (5 roubles for one child, 7½ for two and 10 roubles for three), but the period for payment is extended from the child's twelfth birthday to the sixteenth (eighteenth if still studying and not receiving a stipend). Female-headed families are a large proportion of low-income families in the USSR[22] and therefore many of them would be eligible for the Family Income Supplement of 12 roubles per child per month instituted in 1974.[23] With the introduction of these two measures, it becomes a lesser hardship for a single woman to have children.

Nearly 42 per cent of Soviet women over the age of 16 in 1979 were unmarried (16 per cent never married, 19 per cent widowed and 7 per cent divorced or separated.)[24] Not all of these women are in the child-bearing ages (widows in particular, but note the comments on adult male mortality above) and many of the younger women will marry before they begin their child-bearing. But there are at least 6 or 7 million women who could conceivably benefit from the new provisions for single mothers. The evidence is building up to show that divorced women are much less likely to remarry than men. In 1978–79 re-marriage rates among Moscow men were three times higher than among women;[25] we should perhaps look at these increased allowances for children born out of wedlock as facilitating the possibility of more children born out of wedlock. Desfosses[26] points to an increasing tendency to view illegitimacy as a demographic good.

She notes that 'beginning in the late 1970s, Soviet women were asked to consider whether being an unwed mother was better than being unwed'. And Boris Urlanis, an extremely authoritative source among demographers, notes that 'we should make the role of single mothers more attractive, and we should consider giving them material assistance, various services, preferences for housing, and so on'.

The previously existing system of birth grants and of monthly child allowances was applicable only to mothers with large families (*mnogodetnye*). The announcement of the introduction of grants for all births may herald a change of orientation. Although mothers of fewer than four children are not yet entitled to monthly allowances, birth grants for first, second and third children announced in 1981 are considerably more generous than existing grants for higher order children (see Table 5.5). The grants announced in the January 1981 decree of 50 roubles for the first child and 100 roubles for the second

Table 5.5 Birth Grants, Child Allowances and Single Mother's Allowances

Paid to:	*Birth grants* *All mothers* *(at birth)*	*Monthly* *allowance* *All mothers* *(monthly from* *1st to 5th* *birthday)*	*Single Mother's* *allowance* *Single mothers* *of children* *born out of* *wedlock* *(monthly from* *1st to 16th* *birthday)*
1 child	50/30[a] (before 1981=0)	0	20[b]
2 children	100/30 (before 1981=0)	0	20[b]
3 children	100/30 (before 1981=20)	0	20[b]
4 children	65	4	20
5 children	85	6	20
6 children	100	7	20
7 children	125	10	20
8 children	125	10	20
9 children	175	12.50	20
10 children	175	12.50	20
11 children+	250	15	20

[a] 50 and 100 roubles paid to working women; 30 roubles paid to non-working women. (See source in note 20.)
[b] Prior to 1981 the allowance was 5 for one child, 7.50 for two and 10 for three children.
Source: Allowance before 1981, see source in note 22, pp. 306–18; after 1981, see source in note 15.

and third are to be paid to working women only – the same women who are eligible for part-paid leave. But the September 1981 decree establishes 30-rouble grants for first, second and third children born to non-working mothers.[27] One of the components of the further development of the system to come in the 1986–90 period may well be the extension of monthly allowances to mothers of small families.

Soviet demographic research has pointed to the necessity of facilitating the appearance of second and third children in the Soviet urban family. Numerous surveys[28] have shown the discrepancies between ideal and actual family size. Some four out of five women surveyed considered two or three children ideal, but the majority of Soviet families consist of one or two children. At the same time the births necessary to assure replacement of the population and modest growth, Kvasha's 'optimal reproduction',[29] are roughly equal to those births considered ideal by the majority of women.

It is questionable whether simply offering financial compensation for second and third children is enough. But leaving aside this question for a moment, let us examine the possibility of a new orientation for demographic policy – from the propagandising in favour of and financial compensation for *large* families to the same for two–three-child families. Such a policy could even include disincentives or lesser incentives for larger families. As can be seen in Table 5.3, the Soviet Union faces excess fertility in some regions and a deficit in others. The orientation towards the two–three-child family in policy measures is a reasonable way to get round the charge of ethnic discrimination that might easily result from a regionally differentiated demographic policy. There are economic reasons for wanting to slow population growth in Central Asia, where due to increase rates comparable to those in some developing countries the dependency ratio is high and accumulation must be sacrificed to current consumption. At the same time an increase in the proportion of the working-age population of 'European' origin would result from increased fertility in the western regions of the country, which so far account for a disproportionate share of highly skilled industrial workers.

In keeping with the new emphasis on the complex scope of demographic policy, the 1981 family decree contains a variety of other measures. They can be grouped provisionally under three categories: easing the double burden of Soviet women, material incentives for young newly-weds, and various health measures.

An article in *Voprosy filosofii* by Yu. B. Ryurikov in 1977 introduces the concept of the changing 'demand' for children as their 'costs' change. He proposes that the root of the current high 'cost' of a child lies in excess burdens (*peregruzka*) on mothers. Engels envisioned two structural changes which would emancipate women: the introduction of women into social production and the socialisation of private domestic work.[30] Only half of this transformation has taken place. Soviet women put in a double shift every day – at work and at home. The low level of mechanisation in Soviet households, the inconveniences of shopping in an economic system characterised by shortages of consumer goods, and the attitudes of Soviet men towards 'woman's work' in the home make the burden of housework even greater for Soviet women than for their western counterparts.

The 1981 decree provides some help in this area. An extra three days paid holiday for women with two or more children under 12 is profferred as well as an extra two weeks without pay. The amount of paid time-off to tend sick children is extended to 14 days, the extra days (4 for single mothers, 7 for married women) to be paid at a rate of 50 per cent of wages. There is a vague commitment to increasing the production of prepared or partially prepared foods, the extension and improvement of public dining facilities, home delivery services and special shops for mothers and children. Some would see the three-month deadline for the preparation of plans for the introduction of part-time work for women as an effort to ease the double burden. But it, of course, entails a cut in wages and may, in fact, lead to a considerable decrease in the number of woman-hours of work in the national economy, which is a heavy price to pay in a nation suffering from labour shortage and in which women make up over half of the labour force. It is not altogether fanciful to suggest that a law making it obligatory for men to help with the housework and child-raising would do more to ease the double burden than the likely effects of the measures noted above.

Considerable resource reallocation and administrative rearrangements will occur during the 11th Five-year Plan to make child-bearing more attractive for young couples. This is particularly true in the area of housing, one of the keystones of the Soviet good life. All young people entering upon their first marriage before the age of 30 are to be guaranteed one room at the minimum. Those who have a child within three years of marriage are to be assigned a one-room flat at minimum. These guarantees are to be realised first in the Far East, Siberia, the North and the Non-Chernozem agricultural development zone. Young families are to be given first options to join housing co-operatives and the down payments are to be reduced to 20 per cent of the cost in Siberia, the Far East, the North and the Non-Chernozem zone and 30 per cent elsewhere. Interest-free loans are to be provided by enterprises and collective farms to young families with at least one child for the purpose of improving their housing conditions, the principal to be diminished with the birth of further children. The small-family tax (roughly 6 per cent of income) is to be cancelled for one year from the date of marriage for young people.

Finally, in the interests of the health of pregnant women and children further improvements are to be made in the health services for these groups, a three-day period of paid leave is to be introduced for abortions and the paid-maternity leave is to be extended from 56 to 70 days.

The 1981 decree on government help to the family is a comprehensive demographic policy statement. It deals with a variety of policy objects and is not a mere extension of the family allowance system or any other previous demographic measures. It reflects the realisation that influencing demographic behaviour necessitates a complex and integrated approach. However, its comprehensiveness may also be a measure of policy compromises. We see a slight preference established, for example, for encouraging fertility by allowing women to stay at home with their children at the expense of active participation in the labour force rather than providing comprehensive pre-school child care facilities, which would allow women to continue in full-time work. The question of regionally-differentiated fertility levels is not addressed directly, although the establishment of generous birth grants for first, second and third children and the retention of old levels for higher order births, along with a suggestion that monthly allowances may be introduced for small families in the same manner at some time in the near future are indirectly concerned with this thorny political problem.

As Ryurikov and many others see it, the root of the recent fertility decline is women's double burden and, more generally, their desire to take their places with male colleagues as equals in the larger social sphere, while sharing the rewards and responsibilities of child-rearing with their men. Very little in the 1981 decree deals with this issue.

POPULATION DISTRIBUTION POLICY

There has been no major policy statement on population distribution to compare with the 1981 family decree. But the regional maldistribution of labour is frequently acknowledged. At the XXVI Party Congress and in the 11th Five-year Plan there were indications of more attention being given to labour resources in the siting of new industry, although the commitment to the development of mineral and energy resources in the (labour-deficient) eastern regions remains unchanged. Brezhnev and his colleagues showed full understanding of the unattractiveness of Siberian living conditions and demonstrated that they understood that high wages were not enough to attract the needed manpower. Brezhnev also mentioned the necessity of drawing the Central Asian rural surplus into the developing regions. Such statements do not amount to the full articulation of a migration policy, but two developments from which such a policy can tentatively be inferred should be mentioned, as well as, first, some comments on past policies.

Stalinist migration policy had two major objectives: the restriction of unplanned and individually motivated movement; and the channelling of migration to those regions and construction projects where labour was needed. The first objective called into play such measures as the introduction of the internal passport system, the tying of social security benefits to length of service in a single place and the gradual curtailment of a worker's ability to quit his job and move on which ended in the measure of 1940 which made job-changing illegal without official permission. The second objective is manifested in the establishment in the 1930s of several organised migration channels which still exist today.

In the post-Stalin period many of the barriers to unplanned personal mobility came down. Since 1956 (according to decree) and apparently since the early 1950s in practice, there have been no penalties for quitting a job and moving elsewhere. Since 1960 a person's record of uninterrupted work (*nepereryvnyi stazh*), upon which the level of social security benefits depends, is unaffected if a person gets another job within a month. The internal passport system still limits choice of residence through the system of residence permits, but there is argument over the continuation of these controls in their present form. Passport reform in 1974, at any rate, led to the removal of special mobility restriction on collective farmers.[31] The organised migration channels remain. In the 1960s, however, in numerical terms they were mere shadows of Stalinist mobilisations. 'Unorganised' personal mobility was increasing – a result not only of the expected mobility transition experienced by an urbanising and industrialising population, but also a result of relaxation in government authority over personal mobility.

Two recent measures signal a possible return to the principles, if not always the practice, of earlier years. The 1979 labour discipline decree established a new system of benefits tied to long service in one enterprise and the creation of the State Committee on Labour and Social Questions in 1977 has resulted in, among other things, new life for the organised migration channels. The 1979 decree 'On the Further Strengthening of Labour Discipline and the Reducing of Labour Turnover in the National Economy'[32] points to time losses in industry as a result of slack discipline and frequent job-changing. It stops short of introducing new penalties for frequent job-changing and accurately reflects the current preference for incentive measures to encourage the labour force to do the right things. The measures introduced by the decree comprise a list of new benefits to be associated with long service in one enterprise. They include: credits for house-building or joining a co-operative (to be repaid if the recipient leaves his job of his own volition or is fired for infringement of labour discipline); extra holidays; an extra addition to the old age pension; and new medals and awards. The decree inspired much discussion in the press and scholarly journals. There is even evidence of pressure from some quarters for making job-changing without official permission illegal, which would be a giant step backwards to the situation prevailing in the post-1940 Stalin period.[33]

High labour turnover is characteristic of the younger generation of workers. A director of a factory in Vladivostok revealed that 80 per cent of those leaving jobs at the factory for employment elsewhere were under the age of 30, and that management and older workers were suggesting that job-changing without official permission be made illegal.[34] Clearly there is a small population group, largely young, which can be said to be hypermobile. Probably many of the members of this group are the much maligned 'flitters' (*letuny*) of the popular press. However, there is a great danger that measures taken to discourage 'flitters' will result in a general discouragement of mobility, which is clearly necessary if the regional economic plans are to be fulfilled. Khorev has explicitly pointed to this problem on a number of occasions, stressing that the struggle against the flitters should not lead to the administrative restriction of migration.[35] The 1979 labour discipline decree stops short of imposing administrative restriction to migration, but it is also questionable if the carrots held out will appeal to the small group of *letuny*. At the same time the measures will serve as a disincentive to unplanned migration by other workers, especially those who have been given housing credits which would become subject to repayment if they moved elsewhere.

So, if staying put is now to be rewarded, how is the required re-distribution of the labour force to be accomplished? This is by no means clear, but the recent reorganisation of the organised migration programmes under the new national umbrella of the State Committee on Labour and Social Questions should be scrutinised with this in mind. The State Committee (Goskomtrud), created in 1977, now provides a nationwide planning organ for labour and has taken over the responsibilities of planning Orgnabor as well as the (largely agricultural) resettlement programmes.[36] In April of 1978 a conference on improving labour utilisation was attended by over 1000 academics and government spokesmen and there were numerous calls for the reorganisation of Orgnabor reflected in the speeches at the conference.[37] Goskomtrud is also to have an oversight of the distribution of graduates of higher education institutions, and the Komsomol-organised appeals.

The proportion of labour that is hired through one of the organised channels (Orgnabor, the Komsomol appeals, transfers, the resettlement programme and the new employment bureaux) has risen rapidly in the last decade. From 1967 to 1978 the percentage of industrial workers hired in this way has gone up from 6.1 to 25.6 per cent.[38] Most of this increase is attributable to the increased use of the employment bureaux attached to local soviets, but Orgnabor alone more than doubled the number of its placements during 1967–76. The major function of Orgnabor today seems to be the provision of unskilled labour for construction projects and extractive industries (especially seasonal ones) in newly-developing and/or unattractive regions.[39] The responsibility for mobilising specialists, a field Orgnabor had had some responsibility in from 1958 to 1978, has now been placed on the employment bureaux.[40] Even as late as 1974 fewer than 20 per cent of Orgnabor recruits were sent as specialists, reflecting the popular attitude towards Orgnabor as a channel for unskilled labour, left over from the pre-1953 days when two-thirds or more of Orgnabor recruits were from the villages. Many of the jobs Orgnabor recruits do are those in the sectors of greatest labour shortage in the current situation of overall shortage. Although much has been made of the the declining proportion of rural Orgnabor recruits since the mid-1950s,[41] the ratios show a sign of beginning to shift again. This should come as no surprise, because new industrial workers in the 1980s will have to come to a much greater extent from the agricultural sector because of the depletion of other sources. Research in the last two decades into employment of manpower on collective farms in particular has shown much of what has been called 'excess labour', particularly in Central Asia, the North Caucasus and the Caucasian republics.[42] To be sure, there are serious agricultural labour deficits, particularly in the European regions of the USSR, but, overall, the surpluses exceed the deficits. There are signs, although still uncertain ones, that transfers of 'surplus' agricultural labour from Central Asia to deficit regions is being considered as a partial answer to the regional maldistribution of labour resources.[43]

A new all-Union Orgnabor statute was published in 1980.[44] In it the rights and responsibilities of the hiring enterprises and the Orgnabor middlemen within the Goskomtrol structure are laid out. Quarterly plans are to deal with groups of no fewer than twenty-five recruits for each enterprise. Recruits are to be accompanied by a representative of sending organ and control is to be exercised over the provision of promised working and living conditions for the recruits. It is explicitly stated in the decree that this type of organised recruitment is intended to fill labour deficits in newly developing regions and nationally important enterprises. Although Orgnabor contracts are still for a fixed term, the desire that these temporary workers will become permanent underlies much that is provided for in the decree, particularly the references to the recruitment of married persons with accompanying family.

The other organised migration channels are also receiving increased attention. A new statute on the distribution of graduates of higher and secondary specialised educational institutions has recently been published.[45] As in the Orgnabor statute, it is explicitly laid down that the distribution of graduates is to be concentrated in newly-developing regions. There has also been a recent statute on the graduates of professional-technical educational institutions (PTU), in which for the first time it is clearly specified that they, too, are subject to compulsory placement.[46] There is as yet no general statute regulating the Komsomol appeals, which also place young workers in the developing regions.

The radical alternatives in the field of demographic policy have not been taken. Population, its growth rates and redistribution are still seen as things to be manipulated. There is little sign of a change to the adjustment of the economy to likely prospects in population growth and distribution. No-one has questioned the ultimate 'good' of population growth or the state's right to determine where people will live. The old established pro-natal, anti-mobility positions remain unchallenged. But policy mechanisms are designed with their incentive value in mind, and coercive administrative measures (such as an abortion ban, a ban on job-changing or a less-than-voluntary Orgnabor) have not been employed. The signs point to a continuation of tried if not so true methods. Experience seems to indicate that the level of material incentives likely to be provided to potential parents and migrants will remain insufficient.

NOTES

1. *Materialy XXV S"ezda KPSS* (Moscow, 1976), p. 175.
2. *Trud*, 24, 28 February 1981.
3. *Materialy . . .*, p. 75.
4. Christopher Davis and Murray Feshbach, *Rising Infant Mortality in the USSR in the 1970s*, US Dept. of Commerce, Bureau of the Census, Series P-95, No. 74, 1980.
5. Ann Helgeson, 'Soviet Internal Migration and its Regulation Since Stalin', unpublished PhD thesis, University of California, Berkeley, 1978.
6. Murray Feshbach, 'Prospects for Out-migration From Central Asia and Kazakhstan in the Next Decade', in *Soviet Economy in a Time of Change*, US Congress, Joint Economic Committee, 1979.
7. See Chapter 1 in A. Ya. Kvasha, *Upravlenie rasvitiem narodonaseleniya v SSSR* (Moscow, 1977).
8. Yu. B. Ryurikov, 'Deti i Obshchestvo', *Voprosy filosofii*, No. 4, 1977, 111–21.
9. V. V. Boiko, *Malodetnaya sem'ya: Sotsial'no-psikhologicheskoe issledovanie* (Moscow, 1980).
10. V. A. Belova and L. Ye. Darsky, *Statistika mneniy v izuchenii rozhdaemosti* (Moscow, 1972); V. A. Belova, *Chislo detey v sem'e* (Moscow, 1975); *Izuchenie mneniy o velichinye sem'i* (Moscow, 1971).
11. See also the newly issued 'marriage handbooks' as V. Zatsepin, *O zhizni supruzhekoy* (Moscow, 1978).
12. Kvasha op. cit., pp. 118–30.
13. *Vestnik statistiki*, No. 12, 1980, p. 58.
14. *Sem'ya segodnya*, Moscow, 1979, p. 41.
15. *Sobranie postanovlenii i rasporyazhenii pravitel'stva SSSR*, no. 13, 1981. See also *Pravda*, 30 March 1981.
16. Kvasha, op. cit., p. 99.
17. A. Kollontay, *Obshchestvo i materinstvo* (Moscow, 1922); cited in Boris Urlanis, *Narodonaselenie – issledovaniya publitsistika* (Moscow, 1976), p. 297.
18. Urlanis, op. cit., p. 73.
19. Boris Urlanis, Problemy dinamiki naseleniya SSSR (Moscow, 1974), pp. 297–8.
20. *Sobranie postanovlenii*, no. 24, articles 139 and 141.

21. A. Meliksyetyan, 'Ot lyubvi do razvoda', *Zhurnalist*, No. 1, 1978, p. 50.
22. See Alastair McAuley, *Women's Work and Wages in the Soviet Union* (London, 1981), Chapter 2.
23. Details of the family income supplement can be found in *Sotsial'noe obespechenie i strakhovanie v SSSR – Sbornik normativnykh aktov* (Moscow, 1979), pp. 286–306. As a result of the 1981 family decree the level of per capita income to qualify has been raised to 75 roubles in Siberia, the Far East and the North, while it remains at 50 roubles for the rest of the country.
24. *Vestnik statistiki*, No. 12, 1980, p. 58.
25. A. G. Volkov, 'Sem'ya kak faktor izmeneniya demograficheskoy situatsii', *Sotsiologicheskoe issledovanie*, No. 1, 1981, p. 39.
26. Helen Desfosses (ed.), *Soviet Population Policy: Conflicts and Constraints* (New York, 1981), p. 110.
27. See note 20.
28. See note 10.
29. Kvasha, op. cit. p. 141.
30. For a good exposition of Engels's position and of the Soviet woman's dual burden see Alena Heitlinger, *Women and State Socialism* (London, 1979).
31. See Ann Helgeson, 'The Soviet Internal Passport System', Discussion Paper No. 126, Department of Economics, University of Essex, 1979.
32. *Sobranie postanovlenii . . .*, No. 3, 1980.
33. *Radio Liberty Research Bulletin*, No. 22, 3 June 1981.
34. See *Ekonomika i organizatsiya promyshlennogo proizvodstva*, No. 10, 1980, pp. 31–7.
35. B. S. Khorev, *Problemy gorodov* (Moscow, 1975), p. 261.
36. *Sobranie postanovlenii . . .*, No. 26, 1977.
37. *Sotsialisticheskiy trud*, No. 9, 1978; L. A. Kostin (ed.), *Trudovyye resursy SSSR* (Moscow, 1979).
38. Kostin 1979 op. cit., p. 239.
39. I. S. Maslova, *Ekonomicheskiy voprosy pereraspredelenie rabochey sily pri sotsializme* (Moscow, 1976), pp. 157–9.
40. E. V. Magnitskaya and A. S. Pashkov, *Raspredelenie trudovykh resursov – pravovyye voprosy* (Moscow, 1980), p. 83.
41. See Maslova 1976, p. 155.
42. V. I. Perevedentsev 'Sotsial'no-demograficheskaya situatsiya i vstuplenie molodezhi trudovuyu zhizn' ', *Rabochiy klass i sovremenniy mir*, No. 2, 1980, pp. 88–9.
43. See S. Enders Wimbush and Dmitry Ponomareff, 'Alternatives for Mobilizing Soviet Central Asian Labor: Outmigration and Regional Development', Rand Corporation, Santa Monica, Calif., 1979.
44. *Byuleten' gosudarstvennogo komiteta SSSR po trudu i Sotsial'nym Voprosam* No. 4, 1980.
45. *Byulleten' Ministerstva Vysshego i Srednego Spetsial'nogo Obrazovaniya SSSR*, No. 10, 1980, pp. 25–36.
46. *Sobranie postanovlenii . . .*, No. 18, 1980.

6 Social Policy

Alastair McAuley

Social policy can mean different things to different people and I must specify how I shall be using the term in this chapter. At the risk of some oversimplification one can identify three determinants of living standards in the USSR: wages (together with earnings from private agricultural or other second-economy activities), transfer payments (pensions, etc.) and the value of services such as education provided free of charge (or at subsidised prices) by the state. The same three components determine the living standards of most families in all modern industrial economies. Soviet economists categorise the resources committed to transfers and to 'free' services as social consumption funds. By social policy I mean policies concerned with the character, composition and allocation of these social consumption funds – and with the ways in which they are financed.

Social policy in the sense that I use it here is the resultant of three factors: social attitudes, economic potential and demographic constraints. Hence, attempts to predict the course of social policy in the 1980s involve the need to forecast its determinants. Also, since discontinuities in economic potential or demographic constraints do not occur, sudden changes in social policy are unlikely; evolutionary development is much more characteristic. This means that a study of the past can tell us much about the future.

An examination of Soviet social policy over the past fifty years or so does in fact reveal that the policies pursued under Khrushchev and Brezhnev differed from those of the Stalin period; these in turn differed from the socialist policies advocated by the Russian Social Democratic Party (bolshevik) and pursued in the 1920s. But change has been gradual rather than abrupt. Social policy will continue to evolve in the 1980s, but there is little in present trends to suggest that the authorities are likely to pursue egalitarian policies or become committed to a programme of radical social justice as these terms are usually understood in Western Europe.

146

To be more specific: growth in social consumption expenditures on Soviet definitions in the next decade will be modest in comparison with the past. Open social consumption expenditures are being squeezed between a weakening in the growth of the economy on the one hand and increases in commitments to unacknowledged social programmes (notably food subsidies) on the other. In the next quinquennium (and probably for the rest of the decade) the erosion of public consumption narrowly conceived in favour of a relative expansion in cash transfers will continue. Even so, this relative expansion will be the result of piecemeal improvements to particular programmes rather than any wholesale reformulation of the social security system. Thus, social policy will do little to generate a new dynamic for Soviet society; it is unlikely to recreate a sense of ideological commitment to the goals of equality or social progress.

These are the conclusions that emerge from the analysis of Soviet social policy that follows. To establish them I first look at the evolution of attitudes towards inequality and redistribution over the past forty years; this is followed by an analysis of the growth and composition of social consumption over the same period. The material in these two sections highlights the evolution of cash transfer programmes and these are then examined in greater depth. The chapter concludes with an attempt to project expenditures for the rest of the decade.

EVOLUTION OF ATTITUDES TOWARDS INEQUALITY AND REDISTRIBUTION

As pointed out above, the social policy pursued in the USSR (or in any other country for that matter) results from the interaction between what the authorities want to do and what the state of the economy permits. Both of these elements have changed in the past half-century or so and here I describe the ways in which official attitudes towards the role of the state have changed. Discussion of these questions is inevitably superficial but I have dealt with some of them at greater length elsewhere.[1]

Arguably the best-known phrase that Marx ever wrote was 'from each according to his ability, to each according to his need'. The phrase and the vision of an egalitarian society that it conjured up exercised an enormous political appeal in Russia in the years immediately before and just after the 1917 revolution. It also exercised some influence on the conduct of Bolshevik social policy in the early 1920s. But, by 1931 at the latest, it had been abandoned as a principle of government policy. Rather, acceptance of the doctrine of 'socialism in one country' and commitment to rapid industrialisation through central planning entailed what has subsequently become known as the socialist principle of distribution: from each according to his ability, to each according to his labour. Implicit in this formulation and in the Stalinist approach to social policy of which it was originally a part, is the belief that economic development requires labour discipline and an emphasis on the acquisition of skills and, secondly, the conviction that these must be predicated upon a substantial differentiation in wages. Further, such a belief implies that cash-transfers should be modest in amount and inegalitarian in structure if they are not to subvert the material incentives built into the wage system. In allocating resources assigned to social consumption, preference should be given to public consumption – and in particular to education – rather than to the alleviation of private distress. (Although it must be pointed out that official unwillingness to commit resources to the relief of poverty was accompanied by effective action to eliminate unemployment and to provide a job of some kind for all who were willing to work.)

The introduction of policies that embodied this Puritan work-ethic, however, was accompanied (either as a result of woolly thinking or deliberate obfuscation) by claims that, in the field of social consumption, distribution was already in accordance with Communist principles, 'according to need'. In effect, distribution according to need was identified with the absence of a rouble price for particular goods and services – irrespective of the alternative rationing mechanisms employed. This resulted in the belief that as the USSR gradually approached the phase of full communism, social consumption would expand relative to personal consumption, that more and more goods and services would be made available to the population 'without charge'. These attitudes are embodied, for example, in the 1961 Party Programme where it is suggested that by 1980 the Soviet population will enjoy free bread and free urban transport.[2]

Since the death of Stalin, lip-service has continued to be paid to the slogans set out in the preceding paragraphs, but their content has been changed to a greater or less extent. Officially, the desirability of earnings differentiation continues to be stressed:

[Socialist] forms of payment for labour are in no case compatible with egalitarianism, (*uravnilovka*). All such tendencies are harmful, in conflict with the rapid development of productive forces and the creation of conditions necessary for the continuing growth of workers' welfare. Egalitarianism undermines material incentives and, in the last analysis, causes irreparable harm to the building of communism.[3]

And, it is suggested, cash transfers should reinforce rather than alleviate the distribution of earnings. But a desire to ensure continuing growth in the living standards of all sections of the community, and the need to cope with certain social problems has led to the growth, both relative and absolute, of cash transfers.

Because resources for social consumption have been limited, increased importance attached to the alleviation of poverty has resulted in reduced priority for public consumption narrowly conceived. This has been accompanied by an attack on the claim that any part of social consumption funds have ever been allocated 'according to need'. It has been pointed out that one of the defining characteristics of the socialist phase of development is the scarcity of goods and services; consequently, if services are scarce, access to them must be rationed so they cannot have been made available according to need. Thus, it is wrong to see public consumption as the 'first shoots' of communism that will ultimately expand to absorb the whole of personal consumption. On the contrary, public consumption, narrowly conceived, has the limited role of imposing the state's preferences over the allocation of resources upon the population. It is intended to ensure that what western economists refer to as 'merit wants' are satisfied at the expense of other elements of personal consumption. In this analysis, the objective of public policy is explicitly limited to the attainment of equality of opportunity and the share of social consumption in total consumption is expected to remain limited throughout the socialist phase of development. The arguments outlined here have been put most cogently, I believe, by B. Rakitsky[4] and clearly, in so far as they characterise current official attitudes, imply the abandonment of a substantial part of the social policy enunciated in the 1961 Programme.

The views set out in preceding paragraphs may be characterised as official; that is, they represent the majority view among policy-makers. That minority views exist – both among policy-makers and in the society at large – is virtually certain. What is not clear is what those minority views are and how widely they are held. The fact that official analyses of social policy continue to criticise egalitarianism some fifty years after Stalin's initial attack, suggests that, in some circles at least, there continues to be a desire for greater equality. Also, in the specialist academic literature one can find arguments for a more purposive social policy, for the adoption of programmes that do more to alleviate the problems of particular disadvantaged groups. But the *samizdat* literature contains no coherent alternative policy. And I suspect that there is no such alternative capable of commanding sufficient support to replace the official policy in the near future.

Thus, the formulation of social policy in the USSR is dominated by a set of attitudes that accepts the necessity if not the desirability of inequality, that has abandoned the millenial goals of distribution according to need associated with early bolshevism. On the one hand, it is argued that policy should aim at the creation of equality of opportunity; this is the role, for example, of the state's educational programmes. Alternatively or additionally, resources should be committed to the alleviation or elimination of particular problems. But such an approach should be piecemeal and gradualist in conception. It does not appear to be determined by any wider vision of a just and equal society.

THE COMPOSITION OF SOCIAL CONSUMPTION EXPENDITURE, 1940–79

The evolution in social philosophy from chiliastic egalitarianism to a somewhat conservative meritocracy, described above, has been accompanied by a parallel evolution in the composition of social consumpton expenditures and their sources of finance. In this section I attempt to illuminate these shifts. Unfortunately, consistent statistics of social consumption expenditure covering the whole period of Communist Party government – or even the period since the end of NEP – are not available. Therefore in this chapter I restrict attention to the period since 1940, at which date the Stalinist transformation had been substantially completed. Also, information on the sources of finance for the Soviet social consumption is not nearly as complete as that relating to the composition of expenditure. This is unfortunate as it means that the whole issue of the incidence of the Soviet welfare state can receive only the most cursory analysis. I take up the issue of finance first, before going on to the discussion of the character and composition of spending programmes.

Analysis of the methods by which particular social programmes are financed (taken either in isolation or in conjunction with patterns of expenditure) can cast light on attitudes to equity and inequality held by policy-makers. In fact, our knowledge of methods of finance employed in the USSR is so limited that only heuristic judgements are possible. Under Stalin, social consumption expenditure consisted primarily of programmes such as health and education. As Table 6.1 shows, these were financed largely out of the state budget – that is by means of regressive turnover tax on such items as bread. The Social Insurance Fund, financed by means of a more or less proportional payroll tax, accounted for less than one-sixth of total expenditure. Thus, in 1950 as in 1940 there is little sign of a commitment to progressive redistribution in the methods chosen to finance social consumption.

Table 6.1 The Financing of Social Consumption: USSR, 1940–80
(percentages of total expenditure)

	1940	*1950*	*1960*	*1970*	*1980*
Social insurance fund	15.2	14.3	25.8	26.8	30.0
Social organisations	18.9	12.6	21.2	23.7	22.5
Trade unions	—	—	18.1	18.0	—
Collective farms	—	—	1.5	3.8	—
Enterprises, etc.	—	—	1.6	1.9	—
State budget	65.9	73.1	53.0	49.5	47.2

Source: Row (1) *Narodnoe khozyaystvo SSSR* (hereafter: *Narkhoz*), *1969*, p. 773, *1980*, p. 580; Row (6) calculated as the sum of budgetary expenditure on education, medical care, social security (as not covered by social insurance) child allowances and transfers to the central kolkhoz pension fund, *Narkhoz 1969*, p. 772–3, *1980*, pp. 525–6; Row (2) residual; Rows (3)–(5) A. McAuley, *Economic Welfare in the Soviet Union* (London, 1979), p. 264, adjusted.

Under Khrushchev and again under Brezhnev, the trend in social consumption expenditure has been towards cash transfers. These have been financed from social insurance funds and from the resources of enterprises, etc.; at the same time, the dependence of budgetary revenue on the turnover tax has diminished and the regressive nature of that tax has also decreased. Thus, the figures in Table 6.1 suggest that in the past thirty years or so there has been a shift from an extremely regressive structure of finance towards a more neutral proportional one. But there is little evidence of progression. There is no reason to believe that in the USSR the obligations to provide for social consumption are shouldered by those best able to meet them.

Analysis of the composition of expenditures, both in terms of the relative importance of specific categories within the total and of levels of expenditure on social consumption vis-à-vis other components of national income, can also cast light on the attitudes of policy-makers. This is the issue that is taken up next. Table 6.2 contains data on total and per capita expenditures on social consumption as well as information about its compositon for a number of years since 1940. Before turning to an analysis of the figures in the body of table, there are two general points to be made: first, the table refers to social consumption on Soviet definitions and these differ from those employed in most western countries. Second, the table reports expenditure in nominal terms; in so far as the USSR has suffered from inflation, the figures in Table 6.2 will overstate the increase in real resources committed to social consumption. Each of these issues is discussed further below.

Table 6.2 Social Consumption Expenditures: USSR, 1940–80
(thousand million roubles and percentages)

	1940	1950	1960	1970	1980
Total expenditure (th. mn. roubles) of which (per cent)	4.6	13.0	27.3	63.9	116.5
Pensions	6.5	18.5	26.0	25.2	28.3
Allowances	10.9	9.2	9.5	9.6	9.4
Stipends	4.3	3.8	2.2	2.0	2.2
Holiday pay[a]	12.1	13.1	11.7	14.2	14.0
Total cash transfers	33.8	44.6	49.4	51.2	53.9
Education	39.1	33.8	26.7	27.1	24.9
Medical care, etc.	21.7	16.9	18.3	15.5	14.8
Social security	2.2	0.8	1.1	0.8	1.4
Housing subsidies	2.2	3.8	4.4	5.5	5.9
Expenditure per head (roubles)	24	73	128	263	438

[a]Holiday pay is included as a social consumption expenditure according to Soviet convention; for 1940, holiday pay was calculated as the product of annual average employment and half the average monthly wage.
Source: McAuley, op. cit., p. 262; *Vestnik statistiki*, No. 2, 1970; p. 88; *Narkhoz 1980*, p. 381.

It is clear that a proper appreciation of the growth in social consumption expenditures in the USSR requires that they be expressed at constant prices. But this poses difficulties. The Soviet authorities do not publish a cost-of-living index (even if they calculate one.) And since much of social consumption is excluded from net material product on Soviet definitions, there is no implicit deflator that one can use either. The best that one can do is to fall back on the unofficial Schroeder-Severin cost-of-living index. But it must be recognised that this index is supposed to apply only to personal consumption and, in any case, has been calculated only for the period since 1950. (In the calculations reported below I used the official retail price index to cover the period 1940–50; in so far as Soviet consumers substituted away from goods whose prices rose most rapidly, this will overstate the increase in the cost of living. But I do not think that the overstatement was substantial.)[5]

If the Schroeder-Severin index is used to deflate the entries in the last row of Table 6.2, one obtains the following estimates of annual average rates of growth of real per capita social consumption expenditure (in per cent):

	Nominal	Real
1940–50	11.7	4.9
1950–60	5.8	7.2
1960–70	7.5	6.1
1970–80	5.2	3.6

Thus, in so far as we have correctly allowed for the impact of inflation, it can be seen that the figures in Table 6.2 give a misleading impression of the growth in real expenditure. First, much of the apparent increase in expenditures in the late Stalin period was no more than compensation for a rise in the cost of living. It is the Khrushchev years, particularly the early ones, that stand out as the period of most rapid growth. Finally, there has been a particularly sharp decline in the real rate of growth of social consumption in the latter part of the Brezhnev period.

Turning now to the body of the table: the most striking change has surely been the growth in the relative importance of pensions – indeed of all cash transfers – in the twenty years to 1960. As shown below, this was occasioned by an interaction between changes in attitudes and changes in population structure. The relative growth in cash transfers has inevitably meant a relative decline in expenditure on public consumption: education has fallen from two-fifths of the total in 1940 to a quarter in 1980; over the same period the share of health has fallen from one-fifth to one-seventh of the total. Only housing subsidies have increased in relative importance. This reflects the growth in the housing stock as well as the progressive obsolescence of the structure of housing rentals.

Before leaving Table 6.2, there is one further point to be made. The figures cited above indicate that in the thirty years from 1950 to 1980 there was a fivefold increase in real per capita expenditure on social consumption. This is a substantial achievement for which the Soviet authorities should be given due credit. But it is something of a statistical artefact. The figures in Table 6.2 do not identify the social status of recipients. Yet in 1960 as in 1950 and still more in 1940, the rural population was largely excluded from protection under the state's social security system; it also derived fewer benefits from other components of public consumption. What has happened since 1965 is that the collective farm population has been progressively enfranchised under various social security schemes. For collective farmers growth in real per capita social consumption has been considerably more than fivefold since 1950; for the rest of the population it has been less.

The figures in Table 6.2 refer to social consumption expenditures on Soviet definitions; these differ from those commonly used in the West. The principal differences are the inclusion of holiday pay and the exclusion of the vast majority of consumer-good subsidies. It is my belief that social consumption on western definitions allows a more precise assessment of the impact of policy upon popular living standards but absence of data does not allow recomputation to be made in full for the whole period since 1940. However, in the last decade, the cost of subsidies on meat and dairy products has grown to such a level that some attempt must be made to include it in the discussion.

As pointed out above, under Stalin the Soviet government derived a significant portion of its budgetary revenue from the sale of agricultural products to the population at prices substantially in excess of those it paid to producers. That is, it levied an indirect tax on food. In his attempts to solve the agricultural problem after Stalin's death, Khrushchev raised the prices that the state paid for its procurements. This resulted in an erosion of tax revenues in the 1950s. In an attempt to avoid the payment of food subsidies the Soviet government raised retail prices in 1962 and this, it is reported, led to civil disturbances in Rostov and Novocherkassk. At all events, there have been no further increases in retail prices for meat and dairy products despite several further increases in prices paid to producers. As a result, since 1965 the Soviet authorities have effectively subsidised the purchase of meat and dairy products in state stores; and by 1979 these subsidies were large both as a proportion of the retail price of meat and as a share of total budgetary expenditure.

Some indication of the scale of these subsidies can be derived from the following figures: in 1979 the average price of a kilogram of beef in state stores in the USSR was 1.65 roubles; the average price paid to producers was 3.21 roubles. Subsidies on meat, milk and dairy products amounted to 48.2 per cent of total retail expenditure on these items. In other terms, they amounted to 9.08 per cent of total budgetary expenditure – almost one and a half times the acknowledged defence budget.

The Soviet government subsidises the purchase of other food items and of such things as books and children's clothes but the cost of such policies is thought to be moderate. Also, if allowances are made for subsidies, logically one should include those indirect taxes that raise retail prices as well. Data on all of these are not available. But allowing for the two adjustments mentioned above, one obtains the following series for social consumption expenditure in the 1970s (thousand million roubles):

	1970	1975	1979
Social consumption (Soviet definition)	63.9	90.1	110.2
less Holiday pay	9.1	12.3	15.3
add Estimated food subsidies	14.3	17.2	25.2
Social consumption (revised definition)	69.1	95.0	120.1

If one divides the entries in the last row by the relevant population figure and deflates the quotient by the Schroeder-Severin cost-of-living index then one obtains the following estimates of the growth in real per capita social consumption (in per cent per year):

	1970–75	1975–79	1970–79
Social consumption (Soviet definition)	4.2	2.2	3.6
Social consumption (revised definition)	3.7	3.6	3.7

Thus, it appears that the growing cost of subsidies and particularly those on meat, milk and milk products is a drain on resources that might otherwise be devoted to improving the position of the poor and the poorest in the Soviet Union.

The changes in attitude towards inequality and redistribution, sketched in the previous section, can be seen reflected in both the composition of expenditures and the ways in which they have been financed. The USSR remains a meritocratic society in which social policy is committed more to equality of opportunity than to any radical egalitarian programme. The extensive system of cash transfers that has been developed in the past quarter-century has been designed to alleviate particular problems; so long as the 'symptoms' remain, resources will continue to be committed to these purposes and will not therefore be available for alternative programmes. These problems are compounded when one moves outside the framework of Soviet conventions; the subsidy programme, although not an acknowledged part of social consumption expenditure, constitutes a substantial drain on budgetary resources. But, unless the Soviet authorities are prepared to face the political problems implicit in a reform of retail prices, these resources will not become available for other more pressing social welfare purposes.

To appreciate the constraints under which social policy is formulated in the USSR one needs to understand what I have called the social 'problems' that have resulted in the expansion of cash transfers. This is taken up in the next section.

EXPANSION OF CASH TRANSFERS, 1940–79

In 1940 cash transfers accounted for about one-third of total social consumption expenditure; by 1970 this had increased to more than half. The relative importance of cash transfers increased further in the decade 1970–80 and it will continue to increase until 1985 if not 1990. This growth in the relative importance of transfers is the most significant change in social policy to have occurred in the post-war period. Examination of Table 6.2 shows it to have been due almost exclusively to a growth in pension payments and this topic is considered first. At the end of the section, however, the changes in composition of other transfer programmes that have taken place in the 1970s are traced.

In Table 6.3 estimates are reported of the number of pensioners of various sorts for a sequence of years since 1940. It should be stressed that the categories are determined by the laws under which the pension payments were made rather than the social status of the recipient (and thus, many of the 6 million or so war-disabled who were receiving pensions in 1950 will have been collective farmers). For old age pensioners, however, the correspondence between administrative scheme and social status was close until the widespread conversions of the 1960s; thus very few of those recorded as receiving old age pensions

Table 6.3 Number of Pensioners: USSR, 1940–81
(thousands on 1 January)

| | State pensioners | | | Under collective farm law | | Population of pension-able age |
	Old age	War veterans	Other	Old age	Other	
1940	225	3,413		—	—	16,536[a]
1950	846	18,983		—	—	
1960	4,531	6,264	9,811	—	—	25,501
1970	13,185	4,419	10,449	10,530	1,532	36,254
1975	18,241	3,647	10,399	10,594	1,529	38,423[b]
1979	22,000	14,200		9,900	1,500	—
1980	23,100	14,200		10,000	1,400	40,344[b]
1981	24,200	14,800		9,800	1,400	—

[a]Calculated on the assumption that 60 per cent of those aged 55–59 were female.
[b]Derived from projections rather than censuses.
Source: Cols (1)–(5) 1940–50 *Vestnik statistiki,* No. 2, 1979, p. 79; 1960–75 *Vestnik statistiki,* No. 7, 1976, p. 85; 1979, *Narkhoz, 1980,* p. 411. Col (6) 1940–60 (in fact 1939, 1959) *Itogi vsesoyuznoy perepisi SSSR,* vol. SSSR, 1970, Tables 12 and 13; *Itogi vsesoyuznoy perepisi, 1970g,* vol. II, Table 3; 1975–80 G. Baldwin, *Population Projections by Age and Sex for the Republics of the USSR, 1970–2000,* US Bureau of the Census, International Population Report P-91, No. 26, Washington, DC, 1979, Table 3.

in 1960 or before will have been rank-and-file collective farmers.

Although old age pensions were one of the first benefits to be intro-duced by the Bolsheviks after the 1917 revolution (in an attempt to realise Lenin's 1912 Programme), it is clear from the figures in Table 6.3 that this scheme must have remained very much a dead letter. In 1940, some twenty or more years after the scheme was introduced, there were only 225,000 old age pensioners out of a population of 16.5 million persons of pensionable age. Thus, a mere 1.4 per cent of those entitled by age to receive a pension were in fact in receipt of one. This is a far lower proportion than that of the elderly in the working-class or the urban population. The fact that the number of pensioners was so small must cast doubt on the claim that the Stalinist pension scheme took account of work undertaken before 1917. This apparent under-provision of old age pensions continues into the post-war period. Even in 1960, some forty-three years after the revolution and more than thirty years after the introduction of central planning, there were only 4.5 million old age pensioners in the Soviet Union – less than one-sixth of those of pensionable age. It is not until after 1965 when pensions were accorded to collective farmers that a majority of those of pensionable age in fact received pensions. But, as the figures in Table 6.3 show, since 1965 the spread of old age pensions has been rapid: in 1970 some two-thirds of the relevant age cohort was in receipt of an old age pension; by 1980 the proportion was about 85 per cent.

An examination of Table 6.3 shows that for all of the Stalin period and for several years thereafter pensioners were primarily those in receipt of disability payments (or survivor benefits); although the figures do not show this explicitly, collective farmers were not even insured against many of these disabilities until 1965. There were some 3–3.5 million persons in receipt of disability pensions in 1940 – a majority of whom would have been incapacitated as a result of industrial accidents in the preceding ten years; at this date, such pensioners were fifteen times as numerous as old age beneficiaries. By 1960 there were some 9–10 million such pensioners; they were still much more common than old age pensioners. Between 1960 and 1980, despite some extension in coverage, the number of disability pensioners, etc. rose only by another 2–3 million. The fact that the increase in the number of disabled has fallen by 50 per cent in the last twenty years suggests that much greater attention has been paid to industrial safety in the USSR since 1960.

Table 6.3 also brings out one aspect of the human cost of the Second World War. In 1956 there were some 9.6 million Soviet citizens in receipt of war-disablement pensions of various kinds, and the numbers would surely have been higher in 1950 or 1946. Even in 1975, there were still more than 3.5 million war pensioners. The burden of support on this scale in the post-war period must have delayed the introduction of improved benefits for the rest of the population by several years.

Finally, as mentioned above, state pensions (both old age and disability) were provided for the collective-farm population only in 1965. As can be seen from Table 6.3, before 1965 some 8–10 million elderly or disabled peasants had been left to depend upon the support of their relatives or the charity of their fellow-villagers; or they were expected to support themselves from what they could produce on their private plots.

Thus one can suggest that the growth in the number of pensioners in the USSR reflects policy responses to the emergence of a sequence of social problems. Before 1940, or possibly 1960, the major social group for whom the state accepted responsibility was comprised of those disabled in the process of industrialisation. After 1945 one should add to this group the war-disabled. Before 1956, the elderly, both urban and rural, were left to the support of their relatives (or possibly private charity) or were expected to work on until they died. After 1956 and even more after 1965 substantial progress was made in catering for the elderly. Notice that between 1950 and 1960 the number of old age pensioners increases by five-and-a-half-fold; this is a far more rapid growth than was to be observed in the number of persons of pension-able age. It therefore implies that Khrushchev's 1956 Pension Law enfranchised substantial numbers of the urban elderly who had previously been without support.

It is tempting to ascribe the extensions in coverage provided for in the 1956 Pension Law and still more in the 1965 Pension Law to changes in social attitudes. After all, the doctrine of 'the state of all the people' was adopted at the XXII Party Congress (1961) and a policy of pensions for peasants might seem no more than a logical implication of such a doctrine. But the position is more complicated. As the figures in Table 6.3 show, between 1960 and 1970 the number of persons of pensionable age increased by 11 million. This is more than the gross increase that occurred in the preceding twenty years – and also three times the increase that occurred in the decade 1970–79. Many of these elderly people were collective farmers. In any circumstances, such an increase would have put a strain on the slender resources that Soviet collective farms have available for social purposes. Coming at a time when efforts were being made to raise the living standards of working farmers, the burden was excessive and state subsidisation was essential. That is, the decision to provide pensions (and other social security benefits) for the collective-farm peasantry was the result of an interaction between a demographic imperative and the new more humane social attitudes of the Khrushchev period. A similar argument could be developed to account for the Pension Law of 1956. It is these two laws that have been responsible for the enormous increase in the number of pensioners in the post-war period.

Changes in the number of pensioners are only one of the factors responsible for the growth in importance of pension payments re-corded in Table 6.2. It is also necessary to trace the evolution of the average value of pensions paid under various schemes. Unfortunately, the Soviet authorities have published very little information on this question. But some inferences can be drawn from the figures given in Table 6.4, which record an attempt to calculate the average value of pensions paid under the different legal frameworks.

According to Table 6.4, the average value of all pensions provided in 1940 was 6.9 roubles per month (in terms, that is, of post-1961

Table 6.4 Average Value of Pensions Paid under Different Schemes: USSR, 1940–80

	Expenditure on pensions from all sources	*Expenditure from state insurance funds*	*Average monthly pension all sources*	*Average pension from state insurance*	*Average pension from other sources*
	(million roubles)			*(roubles)*	
1940	300	—	6.9	—	—
1950	2,405	814	10.1	—	—
1960	7,098	4,946	28.7	28.7	28.6
1970	16,200	11,653	33.6	41.1	23.0
1971	18,200	12,795	36.3	42.8	26.5
1972	19,800	13,893	39.2	44.6	30.6
1973	20,800	14,732	40.5	45.9	31.4
1974	22,100	15,815	42.3	47.7	32.9
1975	24,441	17,761	45.9	51.7	35.3
1976	25,748	18,897	47.4	53.3	36.4
1977	27,080	20,133	49.2	55.2	37.3
1978	28,885	21,575	51.5	57.1	40.1
1979	30,601	23,202	52.3	58.9	41.7
1980	33,000	24,855	55.6	60.1	45.4

Source: Col (1) *Vestnik statistiki,* No. 2, 1981; *Narkhoz 1979,* p. 409.
Col (2) *Narkhoz 1979,* p. 557 and other years.
Col (3), Col (1) divided by the total number of pensioners as given in *Vestnik statistiki,* No. 2, 1979 and in Table 6.3.
Col (4), Col (2) divided by the sum of old age and disability pensioners receiving their pensions under the state scheme, *Vestnik statistiki,* No. 7, 1976, p. 85. (For 1977–80 it was assumed that the number of disability pensioners increased by 100,000 per year.)
Col (5) the difference between Cols (1) and (2) divided by the sum of war pensioners and collective farmers; *Vestnik statistiki,* No. 7, 1976, p. 85 and in Table 6.3. (For 1977–80 the number of war veterans is a residual.)

roubles). As the average monthly wage in the state sector in the same year was 33 roubles, it can be seen that state support for the disabled was far from munificent. In the next ten years the average value of a pension increased by 46 per cent. But since over the same period the retail price index increased by 86 per cent, this implies that the real value of pensions must have fallen by some 20 per cent. At that stage, pensioners were very badly off, which was still the case in 1960. In 1956/7 academic calculations set the poverty line at some 25–30 roubles per person per month – and this was the value of the *average* pension in 1960; this means that at least half of all pensioners were receiving a pension that was below the poverty line. Further, provided that one assumes that the value of pensions paid to the war-disabled does not fall between 1960 and 1965, the figures underlying Tables 6.3 and 6.4 imply that the average value of a collective farm pension in 1965 was approximately 13 roubles a month; this implies that the vast majority of collective farmers must have received the minimum pension of 12 roubles! Although pensioners remain relatively poor, their position has improved since the 1960s. In 1965/7 academic calculations put the poverty level at 50–56 roubles per person per month (using rather more liberal standards than ten years previously). In 1974, this standard was tacitly adopted by the Soviet authorities. As can be seen from Table 6.4, in 1975 the average value of state pensions met this standard and by 1979 the average value of all pensions did so. By the end of the 1970s it is probable that a half of all state pensioners were in receipt of pensions that put them above the poverty level, and since the average state-sector wage in 1979 was 163 roubles a month, the gap between state pension and wage has narrowed since 1940 (although the change since 1960 has been slight). The average value of collective-farm pensions must have increased also – and, given the relative numbers of farm members and war-veterans, is probably above the figures shown in Table 6.4 for non-state pensions for years after 1975. The gap between the average values of pensions paid under the different schemes has narrowed progressively during the 1970s but it is still substantial: in 1979 it was still some 40 per cent of the average collective farmer's pension. But in 1978 the promise was made to eliminate the difference by 1985.[6]

Analyses of the figures in Tables 6.3 and 6.4 permit the following conclusions: not only were there very few pensioners in 1940, but the payments they received were insufficient to permit them to approach the modest standard of living attained by other urban inhabitants. The position of pensioners in the early post-war years was probably worse. At this time, the state made little attempt to cater for the needs of the elderly; resources were concentrated on those who had been disabled during the Second World War – or were victims of industrial accidents; there was almost no social security coverage in rural areas.

In 1956 an expansion in the number of urban pensioners (the state began to assume greater responsibility for the elderly in urban areas) was accompanied by increases in the value of pensions paid; these increases succeeded in raising the average value of pensions to correspond with the contemporary conception of the poverty level.

In the 1960s, ideas about the state's responsibility were extended to include the bulk of the rural population. For the first time, almost fifty years after the so-called socialist revolution of 1917, some form of social security cover was provided for the peasantry. At the same time, conceptions of poverty were raised; subsequently attempts have been made to raise pensioner living standards above this new poverty level. For state pensioners, this was achieved (on average) by the middle 1970s but collective farmers still have some way to go before this standard is achieved. The authorities have undertaken to eliminate differences between the schemes by 1985. Thus it has been the decision to provide all persons of pensionable age with a standard of living that does not fall far short of the accepted poverty level, together with the demographic evolution of the Soviet population, that has resulted in the hundredfold increase in nominal expenditure on pensions in the past forty years.

The figures in Table 6.2 show that expenditures on other cash transfers have increased at roughly the same rate as total social consumption since 1940. This must conceal variations in the growth of expenditure on individual transfers since a number of new pro-

Table 6.5 Expenditure on Allowances: USSR, 1975, 1979
(millions of roubles)

	1975			1979		
	Total	Social insurance funds	Other sources	Total	Social insurance funds	Other sources
Sickness benefits	5,240	5,082	158	6,262	6,087	175
Maternity pay, etc.	1,369	1,257	112	1,567	1,467	100
Child allowances	389	—	389	325	—	325
Family income supplement	1,219	866	353	1,143	811	332
Other	1,011	9	1,002	1,136	10	1,126
Total expenditure	9,228	7,214	2,014	10,433	8,375	2,058

Source: Cols (1) and (4) *Vestnik statistiki,* No. 2, 1981; Cols (2) and (5) *Narkhoz 1979,* p. 557; Cols (3) and (6) residual.

grammes have been introduced in this period, but available data are not sufficient to allow such variations to be identified. For the most recent quinquennium, however, some interesting statistics have been published and these are given in Table 6.5. The figures in columns (2) and (5) of the table refer to expenditure or various transfers from

Social Insurance Funds (that is *po byudzhetu gosudarstvennogo sotsial'nogo strakhovaniya*); they thus refer to transfers received by civilian state employees. The figures in columns (1) and (4) refer to expenditures from all sources; thus the difference between the two sets must refer to receipts by collective farmers – and by dependents of military personnel. For most categories of expenditure, the relative magnitudes of entries in columns (2) and (3) or (5) and (6) make this interpretation plausible. But there is a large unexplained residual. Soviet statistical sources identify the residual as consisting of 'burial grants, public assistance, *edinovremennaya pomoshch'*, and other'. Burial grants are a small item available only to those earning the minimum wage or less. Similarly, all other indications suggest that public assistance in the USSR is niggardly.[7] Finally, the only benefit known to have been omitted from the table is the system of family allowances for the wives and children of married conscripts. But if military personnel are like their coævals in propensity to marry and to have children, such a programme could not cost the state much more than 25–35 million roubles a year in the 1970s. Thus we are left with the problem of accounting for the remaining 900–1000 million roubles shown as a residual in Table 6.5.

Let us turn to the remaining figures in the table. First, they show that about three-fifths of the total is absorbed by sick pay and only one-sixth by various family allowance programmes. These proportions are rather different from those to be observed in the rest of Eastern Europe. (Also, analysis of the data given in the table and of other figures suggests that there may have been an increase in morbidity or a relaxation in certification policy in the late 1960s or early 1970s.)

Second, the entry in the third row refers to the allowance for single mothers and for the mothers of many children introduced by Stalin in the 1940s. It should therefore be divided between the two social groups. Having done so, most plausible assumptions suggest that collective farmers receive some 5–7 per cent of total benefits (although they account for 12–15 per cent of the population and are among the poorest). This latter conclusion can be derived from the figures in row (4) of the table. These refer to the benefit introduced in 1974 and payable (at a rate of 12 roubles per month per child under the age of eight) to families with a per capita income of less than 50 roubles per month. If one assumes that the distribution of children between social classes corresponds to the distribution of the population as a whole and also that the total sum recorded in Table 6.5 was paid out in the form of benefits then one can calculate the incidence of poverty:

| | 1975 | | 1979 | |
	State fund	Other	State fund	Other
Expenditure on family income supplement (million roubles)	866	353	811	332
No. recipients (thousands)	6,014	2,451	5,632	3,306
Estimate of children in relevant cohort (thousands)[a]	24,666	4,839	26,635	4,737
Percentage in poverty	24.4	50.6	21.1	48.7

[a]Derived from Baldwin, op. cit.

Thus, on the assumptions made above, it appears that in the latter part of the 1970s, approximately a quarter of all children under the age of eight lived in families whose per capita income before allowing for family income supplement was less than the poverty level. Approximately a half of all collective-farm children live in such families. It seems only plausible to assume that similar proportions of children over the age of eight also live in poverty. Finally, unless one assumes that poverty in the state sector is concentrated almost exclusively on state farm workers, the figures above suggest that in absolute terms there are more poor children in urban areas than in the countryside – although a far higher proportion of rural children are in need.

Implicit in the figures that have been quoted in this section are the following conclusions: Soviet society in the 1970s was characterised by considerable inequality and continued to suffer from a range of social problems. To a considerable extent, the various transfers provided by the Soviet authorities have been conceived as responses to specific problems; they are not intended (nor do they in fact) operate conjointly to reduce or eliminate major social inequalities. The persistence of relatively high morbidity rates, of urban and rural poverty and so on will continue to pre-empt substantial sums of money. Proposals to extend the family allowance programme (described below) will add to this burden. The scope for radical innovations in policy is limited – unless the authorities can tap a new source of funds.

SOCIAL CONSUMPTION IN THE 1980s

Previous sections of this chapter have attempted to show how changing

Soviet attitudes towards the role of social consumption in the economy have led to the acceptance by the authorities of a range of commitments towards particular social groups, and have resulted in the adoption of specific programmes as a means of alleviating or eliminating individual social problems. At the same time, the evolution of the Soviet population has resulted in continued growth in the cost of these programmes. As Michael Kaser shows elsewhere in this volume, the evolution of the economy in the past decade or so (and its likely future growth in the 1980s) means that the potential resources available for innovations in social policy are almost non-existent. It is the purpose of this final section to spell out this conclusion in more detail.

The problems facing the formulation of social policy over the next five-year period can be posed more precisely than those dealing with 1985–90 and they will therefore be discussed first. The Eleventh Five-year Plan proposes that in 1985 social consumption expenditures (on Soviet definitions) will amount to some 139,000 million roubles and it is unlikely that even a new leadership would modify this total dramatically. On the other hand, if one attempts to project the cost of those programmes already in force in January 1981 forward to the end of the quinquennium one obtains a total cost for transfers of 73–75 thousand million roubles (see Table 6.6, column (1)). That is, pre-existing commitments imply that cash transfers will continue to account for some 52–54 per cent of total social consumption expenditure.

But such a calculation is slightly unreal. As pointed out above, in 1978 the authorities undertook to equalise pension regimes for collective farmers and state employees. Also, the plan itself proposed the introduction of partial payment for mothers between the expiry of their paid maternity leave and their child's first birthday. The terms on which this new allowance will be made available have now been spelled out more precisely.[8] From 1981 the new allowance is being introduced by region in stages; mothers in the Far East, in Siberia and in the north will receive 50 roubles per month for each month between the fifty-sixth day after birth and the 365th day after birth that they elect to remain at home to look after their baby. Mothers in the rest of the country will receive 35 roubles per month. To be entitled to this allowance, a woman must be employed at the time of the birth and must have been in state employment for at least a year beforehand. The decree which specifies the terms on which the new allowance will be made available also announces the introduction of cash payments for the first and second child; previously such family allowances had

Table 6.6 Projections of Social Consumption Expenditure:
Cash Transfers, 1985
(millions of roubles)

	If programmes are unchanged	*If commitments are honoured*
Pensions	40,002–40,978	42,935–44,064
Allowances	12,012–12,259	12,864–13,162
Sick pay	7,454–7,650	7,454–7,650(+)
Maternity benefits	1,917–1,968	2,579–2,656
Child allowances	250	478–503(+)
Family income supplement	1,038	1,000
Other	1,353	1,353
Stipends	2,541	2,541
Holiday pay	18,294–18,775	18,500–19,000
Total transfers	72,894–74,553	76,844–78,767
Total social consumption	139,080	139,080

Source: In column (1) I attempt to project existing programmes to 1985 on plausible assumptions, in column (2) I attempt to cost the measures announced in the decree of March 1981. Specifically:

Pensions (1): (persons of pensionable age)×(proportion in receipt of pension in 1979)+(estimated veterans and disabled)×(pension in 1979)×(wage index 1985/1979). Calculation was carried out separately for state employees and others.

Pensions (2): as above except only the state employee pension series was used. This perhaps exceeds the cost of measures announced in 1981 but was intended to reflect the 1978 commitment mentioned in the text.

Sick pay (1): (employment in 1985)×(sick pay per worker, 1979)×(wage index 1985/1979).

Sick pay (2): impossible to cost the provision of extra leave for mothers to care for their children; but should not be large.

Maternity benefits (1): (birth rate, 1979)×(estimated population, 1985)× (payment per child, 1979)×(wage index 1985/1979).

Maternity benefits (2): (maternity benefits (1))+(0.8 × births in 1985)×170 roubles. Births were estimated on the basis of the 1985 population and the alternative birth rates of 18.2 and 17.5 per mille. It was assumed that 80 per cent of births were to women who qualified for the additional benefit. The average cost of the benefit was based on the assumption that 10 per cent of recipients would come from regions such as Siberia and that on average women would stay at home with their babies for 5 months after expiry of maternity leave. This last figure derived from I. Katkova, 'Materinskii ukhod za novorozhdennym', *Narodonaselenie*, No. 21, 1978, pp. 38–46, p. 39.

Child allowances (1): arbitrary decline following trend of 1970s.

Child allowances (2): (child allowances (1))+(birth rate 1979)×(estimated population 1985) × 0.6 × 50 roubles)+(0.2 × (estimated births 1985)×100

Table 6.6 – continued

roubles). *Narkhoz 1979,* p. 37 reports that only 23 per cent of births in 1979 were of third or subsequent children; it was assumed that this would fall to 20 per cent by 1985; it was assumed arbitrarily that 60 per cent of births were of first children. No attempt was made to estimate the cost of improved allowances for single mothers.

Family income supplement (1): as per 1975–79 trend. *(2):* it was assumed that the above allowances might have a marginal impact on the incidence of poverty.

Other (1) & (2): as for Family income supplement (1).

Stipends (1) & (2): (stipend 1979)×(1985 population (20–24)/(1980 population aged (20–24)).

Holiday pay (1): (employment 1985)×(holiday pay per employee, 1979)× (wage index 1985/1979).

Holiday pay (2): (holiday pay (1))+((0.33 × female employment 1985)× (0.75 × holiday pay per worker 1979)×(wage index 1985/1979)).

Total social consumption: calculated from *Pravda,* 2 December 1980 and *Narkhoz, 1979,* p. 409.

not started until the third child. The new allowance will be 50 roubles for the first child and 100 roubles for the second. Allowances for single mothers have also been raised. Finally, it proposes to increase the number of days for which mothers can receive sick pay while caring for sick children aged 7 to 14.

The issue of *Pravda* containing the decree described above also contained a new decree on pensions. This proposed to raise the minimum pension for state employees from 45 roubles to 50 roubles a month some time in 1981; it also proposed that the minimum collective farm pension should be raised from 28 roubles to 40 roubles per month.

These two decrees also promised the introduction of improved benefits within the currency of the 1981–85 plan. For example, women with children under the age of 12 are to be granted additional holidays (an instance where holiday pay might legitimately be classified as part of social consumption expenditure) and those who retired on pensions at least ten years ago are promised some increase in the value of their pensions.

It is impossible to cost all these proposed improvements at all precisely, but on plausible assumptions they are likely to raise the cost of cash transfers to some 77–79 thousand million roubles in 1985. Since it is unlikely that total social consumption expenditures will be increased, the share of cash transfers is thus likely to rise to 56 per cent.[9] Thus, in the 1981–85 plan period, piecemeal additions to existing social programmes are likely to continue existing trends towards a growing role for cash transfers in Soviet social policy without any attempt to create a just and equitable society.

Predictions for the second half of the decade are inevitably more difficult but the following conclusions seem warranted. Over the past forty years there has been at least a loose relationship between rates of growth in output and rates of growth in social consumption expenditures. At least, as the rate of growth of output has declined in the post-Stalin period, so has the rate of growth of social consumption. Present Soviet forecasts suggest that growth in output will be modest for the rest of the decade. It is to be expected that consumption expenditures will grow only slowly over the same period – at 2.5–3.5 per cent seems the most plausible. At this rate of growth in total expenditure, given existing commitments, there will be no scope for radical innovations in policy for the rest of the decade.

Thus, extensive new policies will require new sources of funds. These are unlikely to become available under Brezhnev – and not much more probable under his successors whoever they might be. The two most likely sources, elimination of food subsidies and the introduction of progressive taxation, would not appeal in Moscow on political grounds. It is my impression that both would be intensely unpopular with the Soviet élite, with middle management and in skilled worker circles as well. All three of these groups have largely lost their social conscience if not their socialist consciousness. In the absence of civil unrest I regard any dramatic move towards greater social equality in the USSR as inherently unlikely in 1981–90.

NOTES

1. A. McAuley, 'Social Welfare under Socialism: a study of Soviet attitudes to redistribution', in D. Collard *et al.* (eds), *Income Distribution: the Limits to Redistribution* (Bristol, 1980), pp. 238–58. See also A. McAuley, *Economic Welfare in the Soviet Union* (Madison, Wisconsin and London, 1979).
2. *Programma Kommunisticheskoy Partii Sovetskogo Soyuza* (Moscow, 1964), Chapter 2.
3. V. S. Kulikov, *Rol' finansov v povyshenii blagosostoyaniya sovetskogo naroda* (Moscow, 1972), p. 58.
4. B. V. Rakitsky, *Obshchestvennye fondy potrebleniya kak ekonomicheskaya kategoriya* (Moscow, 1967).
5. M. Elizabeth Denton, 'Soviet Consumer Policy: Trends and Prospects', in Joint Economic Committee *Soviet Economy in a Time of Change* (Washington DC, 1979), pp. 760–89, especially p. 767.

6. V. N. Semenov, 'Programma dalneyshego ukrepleniya ekonomiki i finansov kolkhozov i sovkhozov', *Finansy SSSR*, No. 10, 1978, pp. 3–13, especially p. 11.
7. Bernice Q. Madison, *Social Welfare in the Soviet Union* (Stanford, Calfornia, 1968), Chapter 11.
8. *Pravda*, 31 March 1981.
9. In January 1982 S. S. Shatalin reported that total social consumption expenditure in 1985 would be 144 thousand million roubles, an increase of 3.5 per cent over the figure given in the XI Plan Report (S. S. Shatalin, 'Narodnoe blago-sostoyanie i sovershenstvovanie raspredelitelnykh otnosheniy', *EKO*, 1982, no. 1, 3–22 and especially table inside front cover).

7 Agriculture

Alec Nove

No one doubts that farming is a weak sector of the Soviet economy. There are serious shortages of food, especially livestock products and the leadership is conscious of the urgency of the need for higher production and greater efficiency. Brezhnev, in November 1980, described the food supply situation as even more serious than the energy, metal and transport bottlenecks (which were serious enough), and repeated his strictures exactly a year later.

The statistics (see Table 7.1) nevertheless show some progress, which over a long period appears to be quite impressive. Indeed, gross agricultural production in 1980 exceeded that of 1960 by over 50 per cent, which can hardly be described as a disaster. What, then, is the

Table 7.1 Soviet Agricultural Plans and Performance
(annual output in millions of tonnes)

	1966–70	1971–75	1976–80 Plan	1976–80 Actual	1980	1981	1981–85 Plan
Gross agricultural output[a]	100.4	113.7	131.8	123.7	121.2	—	139.8[b]
Grain	167.6	181.6	215	205	189.1	—	239
Cotton	6.89	7.67	9	8.93	9.96	9.6	9.25[c]
Sunflower seed	6.39	5.97	. .	5.32	4.65	4.6	6.8[c]
Sugar-beet	81.1	76.0	96.5	88.4	79.6	60.6	101.5[c]
Potatoes	94.8	89.8	. .	82.6	67.0	72	
Meat	11.6	14.0	15.3	14.8	15.1	15.2	17.25[c,d]
Milk	80.6	87.4	95	92.7	90.9	88.5	98[c,e]

[a] Thousand million roubles.
[b] 1985 goal 147.1.
[c] Draft goal of XXVI Party Congress (mid-point of range).
[d] 1985 goal 18.2.
[e] 1985 goal 102.
Source: Narkhoz 1980, pp. 201–2; *Izvestiya*, 20 November 1981; *Pravda*, 5 March and 24 January 1982.

nature of the trouble, what are the causes of the malaise, what remedies are proposed, and what are the prospects? It is to these questions that this chapter will be devoted.

The fact that agriculture is failing to provide the products demanded by the consumer is, naturally, a function not only of output but also of price. Retail prices of staple foodstuffs have remained unchanged since 1962; average money wages have risen since then by about 70 per cent. Allowing for the enlarged labour force and the (larger) growth of incomes of collectivised peasants, one can see that total money incomes must have approximately doubled. Agricultural production, especially of livestock products, while considerably higher, could not and cannot keep pace with increased demand due to the higher money incomes. The prices paid to the farms have been greatly raised. The gap between these and the low retail price is covered by an immense subsidy, which in 1981 amounted for livestock products to 25,000 million roubles, or some $33,000 million at the official exchange rate, the highest food-and-agriculture subsidy known in human history.[1] The attempt to build up livestock herds to try to meet this demand, and the resultant rise in requirements of fodder grain, explains why the USSR has a grain deficit despite the fact that grain harvests are considerably higher than they were twenty years ago (when virtually no grain was imported).

Soviet harvest yields, and the productivity of livestock and of labour, while certainly well above the levels of 1960, are still very low by international standards, even in comparison with other Communist countries. One should, of course, whenever possible compare like with like. Thus Soviet soil and climate conditions are much less favourable than those of the United States, or of Hungary, say. But when all allowance is made, performance is poor, and the fact that it is now much better than it was in 1960 merely proves how bad it was in 1960 (when it was well above the abysmal levels which prevailed in the last years of Stalin's rule).

Agriculture under Stalin suffered from acute neglect: underinvestment and low incomes could readily explain poor performance. Under Khrushchev there was a basic change of policy. Prices were raised, investment and incomes increased, the priority of agriculture enhanced. After an initial spurt in output (it rose by almost half between 1953 and 1958), Khrushchev's erratic policies and 'campaigning' methods brought the upward movement to a temporary halt. This and bad weather in 1963 contributed to his fall. Brezhnev criticised his predecessor's methods at the March plenum of 1965, but continued his policies, minus the excesses. Prices paid to farms were raised several times, without a corresponding increase in retail prices, investments in agriculture rose relatively and absolutely, incomes of peasants continued to increase faster than urban incomes (though from very low levels), the fertiliser programme was pressed forward, efforts were made to expand the supply of tractors and other machinery. Investments in land improvements, cowsheds, infrastructure, all rose, but as a consequence agriculture now absorbs vast resources. No longer can it be said that it is 'exploited' for the benefit of industry. On the contrary, agriculture has become a kind of ball-and-chain, a burden for the rest of the economy. There is not only the huge subsidy already referred to, itself in part the consequence of high costs of production. Investments in agriculture, the larger part of which are budget-financed, absorb about 27 per cent of total investments, an unusually high percentage for an industrialised country. To this must be added the investments in those industries which serve agriculture (tractors, fertiliser, etc.). Labour is much better paid, both in state and in collective farms, the increase in incomes far exceeding the gains in productivity, which naturally means that costs are rising.

Why has agriculture not done better? What prevents it from achieving its goals? Apart, of course, from the problems created by climate, which is indeed an important handicap.

All the causes which are listed below are discussed in various ways in Soviet published sources, or figure in speeches by Brezhnev and other leaders. Of course, there could be disagreements about the relative importance of these various factors, and also about remedies. But it is hard to imagine that any serious Soviet scholar would disagree strongly with the analysis that follows.

First on the list are problems connected with labour. These are of various kinds. There is the migration out of agriculture of skilled men and women, in search of a better life in towns, a tendency which exists in East and West alike, but seems to be particularly serious in the USSR, because of the very wide disparities in rural and urban lifestyles. This in turn is due to the remoteness and primitiveness of many villages, with their unpaved tracks which turn to deep mud, and the still inadequate educational opportunities – it is hard to recruit teachers for the 'uncultured' backwoods. The effect of all this is to create acute shortages of skilled labour, necessary for the operation and (especially) repairs and maintenance of machinery. The authorities are well aware of the importance of these facts, and plan a substantial improvement in village amenities, shops and housing.

At least equally important is the problem of labour incentives in the excessively large farms, which often have around 500 members or employees, scattered in several villages and engaged in a multitude of activities, cultivating numerous crops and keeping every kind of farm animal. A sort of diseconomy of scale (or alienation, if one prefers the word) then develops. The peasants do not feel responsible for the final outcome, and indeed there is often little visible connection between the quality of their work and the harvest. A frequently cited example relates to tractor-drivers engaged in ploughing. They are paid on piece-rates, measured in terms of hectares ploughed, and receive bonuses for economising on fuel and avoiding breakages. All these indicators 'benefit' from ploughing as shallowly as possible. The resultant losses in the harvest cannot be ascribed to the individuals concerned. So the fact that the tractor-drivers are well paid in no way ensures that they perform their work efficiently.

This lack of responsibility also contributes to labour shortages at peak times. Farmers the world over work very long hours to cope with the harvest rush. In the USSR, however, many do not bother. 'We will sow, God will send rain, then people will come from towns to gather in the harvest': this is how the attitude was described by a Soviet economist in private conversation. This, as well as gaps in mechanisation, causes the mobilisation every year of millions of townspeople and part of the army for work on the harvest. A particularly vivid letter to his fellow-villagers by Fyodor Abramov, reproaching them for their indifference, and the neglect of essential tasks, was printed in *Pravda*, 17 November 1979:

When was it known that able-bodied *muzhiki* go away at the time of the harvest? . . . The old pride in a well-ploughed field, in a well-sown crop, in well-looked-after livestock, is vanishing. Love for the land, for work, even self-respect, is disappearing. Is this not a cause of absenteeism, lateness, drunkenness. . . . We have indifference, passivity, fear of upsetting one's fellow-villagers. And with all this the hope for the strict and fair boss, who will arrive from somewhere and impose order. Almost like the Nekrasov poem: 'the master will come and will judge' (*vot priedet barin, barin nas rassudit*).

His cry from the heart produced a lively correspondence. This is no trivial matter. In agriculture more than anywhere, the attitude of those who work to what they do is decisive.

In an article devoted to labour shortage in other sectors of the economy, Manevich notes that, owing to lack of comprehensive mechanisation, the agricultural labour force has declined much more slowly in the USSR than in other major industrial countries, even if one omits the annual mobilisation of non-agricultural labour to help with the harvest. The scale of this mobilisation (*privlecheniye*) has rapidly increased: in 1970 numbers were 40 per cent above those of 1960, in 1978 they were 2.4 times above the level of 1970. His rough estimate is that 15.6 million people were involved in 1979, a phenomenally high figure, representing a major burden to the rest of the economy, especially as (according to Manevich) 7.8 million are 'workers from productive sectors'.[2] Evidently the labour situation at peak periods has been deteriorating fast.

Then there is the damage done by the excess numbers of orders from above, of imposed plans and detailed instructions. Compulsory delivery quotas can stand in the way of specialisation, and lead to loss when certain crops and livestock which the plans require are unsuitable to the circumstances of the particular farm. But this is only a small part of the story. Ample evidence exists of systematic petty interference. Orders are given about what should be sown, in what quantity and when. Sowing campaigns, machinery repair campaigns, harvest campaigns, are supervised by Party and state officials, who countermand decisions by farm managers and local agricultural advisers. Criticisms of these practices appear frequently. Thus: 'Too many compulsory indicators are imposed from above . . . Particularly frequent is the prescription of areas to be sown. The agronomist . . . in practice cannot decide himself what to sow, exact figures are imposed on him, and he is ordered strictly to carry out these orders . . . Thus our farm was forbidden to reduce the area under potatoes'.[3] 'Although the Party has long ago condemned the practice of giving detailed orders (*administvirovaniye*), this "style" has not disappeared. From the *rayon* and *oblast'* come orders: extend the area of this crop, cut the area of another. Thus the *oblast'* agricultural department calls in our specialist and orders him to double the area sown to maize this spring. But where can we find the hectares, without ruining our crop rotation?'[4] 'Why regulate our everyday activities? What field to sow on Friday and which on Saturday, where to have clean fallow and where not, surely this is a matter for the collective-farm specialists. . . . Yet up till now the Party secretary is apt to tell the farm chairman where and what to plough'.[5] In the same issue, permission by the management committee of a collective farm for the chairman to go on sick leave was reversed by the local authority and the Party secretary; not even such a decision as this is left to the farm management. Another source states that, in his area, one cannot slaughter a head of cattle without the written approval of Party and state officials.[6]

The absurdity of such practices is evident, the irresponsibility they cause is obvious. In the days when state purchase prices were extremely low, it was clearly in the interests of farm managements and of the peasants to avoid fulfilling state plans, and so it was 'rational' for Party and state organs to supervise closely every task, including routine tasks, of a sort which any industrial manager would be entrusted to carry out.(To fulfil industrial plans was and is in the material interests of their executants.) However, prices paid to farms are now much higher. Why, then, cannot the management of collective and state farms be trusted to do their job? Old habits? Instinctive distrust of peasants?

It must be added that the way in which farm management's performance is evaluated can produce perverse results, as is graphically shown in yet another critical article in *Pravda*, entitled 'Reward for being backward'. Not only are those farms rewarded for plan over-fulfilment who succeed in persuading the planners to give them an 'easy' plan, but there is a serious fault in the price system, for a 50 per cent bonus is paid for deliveries over the compulsory quota, or in excess of the amount delivered to the state in previous years. But suppose there is a drought, then the harvest is lower: 'In some countries this is taken into account, and prices are higher in a drought year. With us it is the other way round. A centner of grain in a favourable year, when its cost is lower, is paid the higher bonus price, while the (average) price is lower in a drought year'.[7]

Among the reasons often given in the press for high costs in agriculture are not only those connected with labour, but also of machinery. New machines often cost disproportionately more than old ones. Machines are allocated by the authorities and ones actually needed to cope with local conditions are often unavailable. A vast literature deals with what is called *nekompleksnost'*, that is the absence of complementary equipment, which reduces the effectiveness of the available machines and contributes to labour bottlenecks. Many complaints relate to lack of what is called *malaya mekhanizatsiya*, for example equipment for loading, unloading, materials handling, mowing. Plans for simple one-man-operated grasscutters, urgently needed for hay-making in farms and for individual peasant use, remain unavailable despite decisions to produce them. The quality of many kinds of equipment is poor. One reason given why women are little used as tractor-drivers is that the design of the tractors makes the work heavy, dirty and unpleasant,[8] and the lack of mechanised work for women is a source of discontent, especially as most village girls now receive a ten-year education. Shortage of spare parts is notorious; equipment requiring electric power (especially milking machines) cannot be used effectively because of frequent power cuts.[9] Specific items of equipment which farms seek to order, through the inter-mediary supply organisation Sel'khoztekhnika, often cannot be or are not provided. What is eventually provided is apt to arrive in separate parts, somehow to be assembled in farms' own workshops.

All this reflects the inadequacies of industrial planning, the lack of effective co-ordination and balance, the lack of influence of the customer over what is produced and allocated. One further example among many is fertiliser. Its output has greatly increased, which is, of course, highly desirable. But there is a shortage of bags, storage space, means of transport and machines to spread it on the fields. In consequence much of it piles up at railheads and on farms, and is wasted. Many cartoons relate to this theme: seeing a pile of fertiliser left out by the farm in the open, a visitor remarks; 'If an inspector sees this, out in the rain, there will be trouble'. To which a local man replies: 'What inspector would reach us on *these* roads!'.[10] But more about roads in a moment. Why so few grass-cutters? Are they not simple to make, and cheap? Answer: because they are simple to make and cheap, and are thus not a significant part of the value of output for plan-fulfilment purposes.[11]

Thus, despite very large investments, the return is low, and some processes remain undermechanised. The shortage of spare parts has been the subject of speeches, articles and cartoons, for fifty years, and seems incurable. One reason is the large number of breakages, due to poor maintenance and the appalling roads.

Which brings one to problems of roads and transport. Hard-surface roads are few. Although there is a sizable programme for highway construction, there are hardly any byways. Unpaved tracks between the farms and the outside world, and between units of the same farm, turn to deep mud in autumn and spring, and mud turns into deep ruts when it dries. Industrial supplies and consumers' goods can be held up for weeks on end, and farms face grave problems in getting their produce out. The state of the roads wears out tractors and lorries prematurely. Several Soviet economists, for instance Tigran Khachaturov, the *doyen* of the discipline, have been pointing out for years that 'roadlessness' (*bezdorozhye*) causes very heavy ecomomic loss. But there is the difficulty caused by lack of stones and quarries on the great Russian plain, which inhibits local efforts to make hard-surface roads and adds to the cost of building. (Invading German armies were known to improvise a hard surface by tying logs together and laying them over the mud.)

Matters are not helped by lack of specialised forms of transport, especially lorries adapted to their tasks. Thus grain is all too often carried to elevators on open lorries, and some of it blows away. Critics also point to many other related shortfalls: storage space is lacking, for grain, for vegetables and fruit, or there are not enough elevators or insufficient storage in wholesale and retail trade. There is a long-notorious shortage of packaging materials of all kinds. The effect is and can only be losses, so that part of the produce of the peasantry never reaches its users. This is well known and much commented on by Soviet critics. *Pravda* in 1980 ran a long series of articles about the reasons for lack of vegetables and fruit in urban shops (apart from the reasons mentioned above, there is also lack of incentives for the trading network to handle perishables). The Tenth Five-year Plan (1976–80) contained a decision to build grain elevators to a capacity of a further 30 million tonnes, but the plan was greatly underfulfilled, and a subsequent article observed that money for elevators had been diverted to other purposes, even though 'in the central areas of Russia alone, for lack of shelter, about 18 million tonnes of wheat remain in the open in autumn, unprotected from rain and snow'; losses under such conditions are supposed to be 1 per cent 'but, so to speak, this is only so theoretically'.[12] It is to cope with this complex of inadequacies that it has been decided to plan the entire agro-industrial complex as one interrelated whole, paying particular attention to infrastructure, packaging, distribution, etc. No one doubts that a great deal remains to be done.

Another and quite different bottleneck item is fodder for livestock. The shortage of fodder grain, and the resultant level of imports, has already been noted. But it must be stressed that one cause for the high demand for grain and grain concentrates is lack of other kinds of fodder: yields of hay are low and there are not enough root crops. The net effect is that Soviet livestock eat much more grain, per unit of livestock or of meat, than their American or West European equivalents, and the diet is unbalanced. There are plans to increase greatly various chemical additives, and recent decrees have sought to encourage hay-making by allowing the peasants who do the work to keep a big proportion for their own livestock. One handicap, already mentioned, is lack of small hay-making equipment, capable of being used in small meadows or on grass verges. It is quite clear that shortage of fodder is causing serious problems for the livestock industry. The United States embargo had only modest effects: as shown in Chapter 3, Soviet imports from Argentina, Canada and Australia in 1980 partly substituted for the frustrated purchases. None the less meat and milk production is stagnating (as Table 7.1 shows), and the key to progress is rightly seen as a substantial rise in production of all kinds of fodder in the Soviet Union itself.

Last on the list of problems (and high on the list of remedies) is the private plot. Official policies towards the little household allotment of land and to privately owned livestock have altered frequently since collectivisation, alternating between encouragement and obstruction. Thus Khrushchev in 1953 strongly criticised the policies of Stalin's last years, greatly reduced taxes, eliminated compulsory deliveries of private produce, sought to provide incentives for higher production. Yet in his own last years there were again restrictions, criticised in turn by Brezhnev at a Central Committee session of March 1965 held after Khrushchev's fall. Now again many critics point to obstruction of many kinds and the need to overcome them. Thus some markets refuse to allow the sale of produce brought from other oblasts,[13] some farm managements refuse to provide pasture for private cows (ibid). Why, asks another critic, is hardly any equipment, or tools, provided for individual cultivators: 'Over many years there developed a negative attitude to the requirements of private auxiliary enterprises'.[14] As we shall see, the present attitude is positive, and measures are being taken to stimulate private production, especially livestock. However, one other problem must be mentioned. Peasants are now much better paid for work for the state or collective farm, while it is troublesome to look after cows and pigs and to take produce to urban markets is costly in time and effort. As a result, sales in urban markets have shown little increase in volume, despite much higher prices, and one cause of shortage in urban areas has been the higher consumption of meat and other products in the villages. Young people prefer leisure to milking cows.

These, then, are the basic problems of Soviet agriculture. The authorities realise that they are interconnected, that what is termed a 'complex' approach is essential: thus there is clearly no point in expanding fertiliser production if it outruns the means of storing, transporting and spreading it, and investments in modern livestock farms make no sense unless there is more with which to feed the animals. The large investments currently being made in land improve-ments in central and north-West Russia will yield a poor return unless the mechanisation, labour incentives and infrastructure are radically improved. What, then, can be done? What is being done? What, finally, *should* be done?

Official policy lays stress on the need for still higher investments, on reorganisation based on agro-industrial complexes, that is essentially on better and more comprehensive planning. Missing from policy statements and the speeches at the XXVI Party Congress was any emphasis on the need to devolve authority and responsibility to the farms themselves, though, as already noted, occasional articles do criticise excessive interference from above. In fact such interference cannot diminish so long as Party decrees repeatedly urge the Party and state authorities to ensure that various tasks are carried out, that machines are repaired, seeds made ready, the harvest completed, etc., etc., and such decrees continue to appear. The ideas underlying the concept of the agro-industrial complex are sound. However, their imposition as a campaign of reorganisation can surely result in still further bureaucratisation, a diminution of the autonomy of farm management. These developments should be carefully watched.

A potentially positive reform would be the widespread introduction of the autonomous work-team (*beznaryadnoe zveno*). The idea was already the subject of experiment and discussion fifteen years ago. Its essence is simple: an area of land is handed over for the cultivation of a given crop or crops, together with the necessary equipment to a small group (say 5 or 6 people), who are allowed to organise their own work, without having work-schedules imposed on them (hence *beznaryad-noe*), and are paid by results. The scheme saves supervisory labour, and also ensures that it will not seem advantageous to gain on piece-rates by ploughing too shallow: everyone is interested in the size of the harvest. Experiments were described as successful, but they were halted for a number of years, partly (one imagines) because such a tendency seems contrary to the established practice of planning large units and exercising tight control, partly because of genuine organisa-tional and social difficulties: not all the work, and not all the workers, are suitable for such work-teams, and payment by results is apt to give rise to very large income disparities within the same collective or state farm, which causes friction.

Despite these complications, the idea has re-emerged in the official press. Newspaper articles have extolled this form of organisation of labour since late 1979 (some referring to a small *beznaryadnaya brigada*, but the principle is the same).[15] There has been no decree, nor yet a speech at the Party congress which explicitly advocates the introduction of this method, but it is very long since it has been condemned. It appears that it is being quietly adopted in some areas, but is still regarded as controversial and experimental. Its advantages are being publicly extolled, and it certainly does overcome the psychological diseconomies of scale, by identifying a small team with a specific area of land or a number of livestock. Unequal payment between *zvenya* (or between those in these teams and those not) can be, and in some reported cases is, accompanied by equal pay for all within the given *zveno*, justified by the fact that they share the work among themselves by their own decisions with the minimum of individual specialisation.

> We try to interest our personnel morally and materially in their work, to stimulate the achievement of good final results. We give preference to the autonomous (*beznaryadnoy*) system of organising and paying labour. We allocate fields and equipment to *zvenya*. Now it is no longer necessary to remind people what they have to do and when. The peasants appreciate this. Labour turnover has dropped.[16]

The likelihood is strong that this method will be adopted because, despite its disadvantages and its contradiction to the established habits of issuing orders to and through large-scale units, it works well. The authorities are by now very deeply concerned with the inadequacies of agriculture, and committed to putting them right as fast as possible. As long ago as 25 December 1979 *Pravda* published an article in which the author asked the Ministry of Agriculture to express its view on this kind of *zveno*. As far as I am aware, there is still no official 'line' on the subject.

The urgent need for more food undoubtedly underlies the much more positive policy towards private plots and livestock which even a *Pravda* editorial does not hesitate to call the individual sector (*individual'nyy sektor*).[17] In speeches, such as that of Brezhnev to the XXVI Party Congress, in numerous articles, in editorials, such as the one cited above, restrictions and obstruction are criticised, the need to encourage private production and marketing emphasised.[18] The point is made that to expand meat or vegetable production on private plots improves feeding of peasants and of townspeople, and is much less costly than a similar increase on state and collective farms. Published criticism refers to such obstacles as difficulty in acquiring piglets, calves, chicks, the unwillingness of some state and collective farms to provide pasture, the problem of fodder supply, the lack of interest on the part of co-operative trade to purchase private produce, which causes unnecessary journeys to markets by those willing to sell. Incredibly, one source reports that the co-operatives are forbidden, by a decree adopted in 1975, to pay cash directly to peasants selling private produce; sellers have to travel specially to the *rayon* centre and stand in a queue for payment.[19] It is also noted that some households are unwilling to bother with private livestock, and prefer to travel to the nearest town to buy such produce as eggs or ham. Land which could grow crops is too often denied to individuals even though it is not in use. All this, it is insisted, must now change: there is to be encouragement for peasants to produce more, and also a drive to provide allotments in the suburbs for townspeople; industrial enterprises are urged to set up more auxiliary farms, which already provide produce for canteens and for sale to employees.

Measures to expand private production which receive favourable press comment include using farm machinery to plough and cultivate household allotments,[20] and of course to ensure regular supplies of fodder and access to pasture.[21] Publicity has been given to the idea, adopted long ago in Hungary, under which a peasant household can undertake to fatten pigs or other animals, being provided with fodder at an agreed low price, and then sell them to either the farm or the state procurement agencies. It then makes little difference who actually owns the animals. In some quoted instances they are fattened by the households on behalf of collective, in others the piglets (say) are sold to the peasant. A *Pravda* editorial points out that peasant-owned livestock sold for meat to the collective farm can be delivered to the state as a collective-farm product and so benefit from the bonus price for above-quota deliveries.[22] The need is seen to make such deals attractive to peasants, some of whom may prefer not to bother to expand their private activities, now that they are much better paid for state and collective work (and there is not much to buy with the extra money, in village shops). Provision has also been made for the retention for private animals of part of the hay cut on collective and state meadows, as part of providing incentives for expanding hay-making. Articles have appeared urging the provision of small mechanised equipment suitable for the small allotments, ranging from motor-mowers to scooters with sidecars or trailers.[23]

Is this a genuinely new policy, or is it a repeat of a temporary pro-private-plot cycle, to be followed by obstruction and restrictions? We cannot yet tell, but my feeling is that it is something qualitatively different, that the authorities have learnt a lesson from the serious shortages that now exist. Private livestock raising may well tend gradually to decline as and when sufficient supplies are available from collective and state farms. Until then, it is important to stimulate it, to make it genuinely profitable, so as to cope with shortages at maximum speed and at minimum cost. The basic snag is the overall shortage of fodder. If there is not enough even for state and collective livestock, will the local authorities in fact carry out the obligation to supply private cows, pigs, etc.? We shall see. Meanwhile let us note that the correct policy is being followed, at least in this instance, at least for the time being.

However, the other measures being taken are much less promising. Agro-industrial complexes, schemes for linking state and collective farms and perhaps gradually merging the two kinds of farms, all add to bureaucratic complexities. It remains as difficult as ever to get the desired equipment and spares through Sel'khoztekhnika, which has been overcharging for the use of its own workshops and tends to hoard necessary spare parts and means of transportation. There are complaints too about yet another body. Sel'khozkhimiya, one of the functions of which is to spread fertiliser and herbicides on the fields, but whose rewards and plans are not linked with the size of the harvest.[24] As already mentioned, the habits of giving orders from above persist, and an examination of any recent agricultural decree shows that the local Party officials are repeatedly instructed to ensure that various measures are carried out, thus ensuring the continuance of interference, and of its negative effects. Better plans imposed from above, more discipline and tighter norms seem to be the traditional and persistent methods by which greater efficiency is to be realised. Surely such methods are unlikely to succeed. (I once saw among a list of norms imposed from above a utilisation norm for wire to be used for tying bales of hay together!)

What, then, is needed? Surely, more than anything else, greater freedom of decision by those on the spot, on the farms. I recall once being told by a Soviet farm official, shortly after the abolition of the Machine Tractor Stations (MTS), that this measure was a mistake. I was surprised, and asked why he thought that this apparently sensible decision was erroneous. He replied: 'Before 1958 collective farms were forbidden to buy tractors. After 1958 collective farms were forbidden *not* to buy tractors. The correct decision was to allow those who wish to buy to do so, and those who lacked workshops and maintenance personnel to hire them, that is to let them choose. After all, some American farmers hire combine-harvesters, for instance, others own them.' There is much wisdom in this. The enemy of agriculture is what the Russians call *shablon*, the imposition of some standardised decision or pattern on a vast variety of local conditions. The late Naum Jasny used to say that what was most needed was *samotek*; the word suggests uncontrolled spontaneity, and in the eyes of Soviet officialdom has a pejorative meaning.

In my view the basic principles of effective reform in Soviet-type agriculture are those which underlie the relative success of Hungarian farming. Its essentials are the following. Firstly, much greater freedom to choose what to produce, whether to specialise, what livestock to raise; there are neither compulsory delivery quotas nor any imposed plan indicators. This means that state purchase prices must be so fixed as to persuade the producers to choose the desired pattern of production. Secondly, in the place of administered allocation of inputs there is (more or less) free trade: farms can buy equipment, tractors, chemicals, from wholesalers or producers. This makes a great difference. Thirdly, the farm's management can make flexible work arrangements within the farm, to interest the peasants in their work; these include the Hungarian version of the autonomous work-team. Fourthly, farms undertake a variety of non-agricultural sidelines, ranging from building and decorating to small-scale manufacture and various services (for example motor vehicle repairs), which adds to revenues and provides off-peak employment. Fifthly, the private sector has been encouraged, to good effect, and with great flexibility. Thus there is no limit to the number of private animals, the owners can make contracts with their farm, or with the state food industry, or take meat to market, and can purchase fodder as required. Finally, the Hungarian authorities have dared to increase retail prices of food, to a level at which supply and demand is in approximate balance.

There is clear evidence in Soviet publications that the Hungarian experience has been carefully studied. Indeed, some of the recent proposals to encourage peasant households to fatten livestock may have been directly derived from such study. However, at present the chances of the Soviet leaders adopting the whole Hungarian package are very remote. It runs quite counter to their attitudes and policies. Equally strong arguments for major microeconomic decentralisation, and the greater use of the market mechanism, in other spheres of the economy have been put forward and rejected. In Hungary they have been accepted in principle and at least partially put into practice. It is for this reason that Hungarian farms can freely purchase their inputs: the reform has eliminated administered allocation of inputs in industry too. There is no sign either that the Soviet authorities are contemplating a change in the principles of price-fixing, or that they will face the necessity to increase retail prices of food (for political reasons that one understands).

So what will happen, in the absence of a major reform of the system? Large-scale investments in agriculture will surely have some limited effect, but a succession of three bad harvests (1979, 1980 and 1981) has continued to defer the gain. The grain crop of 1981 was so poor that a tonnage figure was – quite contrary to past practice – omitted from the annual plan results, which otherwise showed (as set out in Table 7.1) that drought had severely reduced the production of sunflower seed and sugar-beet and that the grain shortage was having its effect on livestock products. Table 7.1 also indicates the lack of ambition – as shown in earlier five-year plans – of the targets for 1985, but they rest on an assumption about an expansion of grain output which has been belied in the plan's first year. In the light of the planned rise in personal incomes, the smaller increment that must be anticipated for farm produce means that the present shortages of foodstuffs will persist. The outlook is neither catastrophic nor hopeful and the place between those extremes will depend, as usual, on luck with the weather.

NOTES

1. R. Lokshin, *Voprosy ekonomiki*, No. 10, 1981, p. 85.
2. E. Manevich, *Voprosy ekonomiki*, No. 9, 1981, p. 60.
3. *Pravda*, 30 March 1981.
4. Ibid., 26 March 1981.
5. Ibid., 11 May 1981.
6. Ibid., 16 January 1980.
7. Ibid., 9 March 1980.
8. M. Fedorova, *Voprosy ekonomiki*, No. 12, 1975, p. 5.
9. *Pravda*, 23 January 1981 provided vivid examples of the effects of the lack of spare parts on dairy farming in Western Siberia.
10. *Krokodil*, No. 14 (May) 1981.
11. *Pravda*, 4 May 1981.
12. Ibid., 16 May 1981.
13. Ibid., 16 May 1980.
14. Ibid., 4 May 1981.
15. Ibid., 25 November 1979, 14 July 1980, 26 March and 25 May 1981.
16. P. Kravchenko, chairman of a collective farm in Kharkov *oblast'*, *Pravda*, 25 March 1981.
17. *Pravda*, 10 June 1981.

18. An important and informative article appeared in *Voprosy ekonomiki*, No. 5, 1981, by G. Shmelev, and it is hardly accidental that he works in the Institute which studies other socialist countries, and shows himself particularly well-informed on the flexible ways in which private and co-operative activities are encouraged, and interrelated, in Hungary. He cites many figures not previously published. Thus, the average size of the private plot is 0.31 hectares in *kolkhozy*, 0.17 hectares for workers and employees in rural areas (0.21 hectares in *sovkhozy*), and the author notes that collective farmers' plots and livestock are substantially below the permitted maxima. In 1979, private plots accounted for 26.5 per cent of total agricultural production. (This is higher than the amount I had calculated and published in *The Soviet Economic System*, but the reason is plainly that I had used figures in 1965 prices, while Shmelev's are in 1973 prices; as livestock products account for two-thirds of the value of private output, and prices for livestock products have been substantially raised, this has the effect of increasing the share of private produce in the total.)

19. Ibid., 16 May 1980.
20. Ibid., 31 July 1980.
21. Ibid., 16 May 1980, 29 April and editorial of 10 June 1981.
22. Ibid., 10 June 1981.
23. *Inter alia*, ibid., 4 May 1981.
24. Ibid., 30 March 1981.

POSTSCRIPT

After this book was sent to the press, the Central Committee (in May 1982) adopted a much-publicised 'Food Programme'. Its key features are:

(1) Further development of the agro-industrial complex concept, with new co-ordinating organs at the centre, in the republics and in the localities. How much effective power they will have over organisations owing allegiance to different ministries is not yet clear.

(2) Substantial additional expenditures on infrastructure, rural amenities, transport and storage.

(3) Sizeable increases in procurement prices, apparently without any increase in retail prices of basic foodstuffs. The already huge subsidy bill will thus grow still huger.

(4) Some new ideas on incentives for peasants include what is called *brigadnyy podryad*, with (small) brigades responsible for a range of tasks, but no mention is made, positively or negatively, of the *beznaryadnoe zveno*. Payments in kind, especially in fodder, are being revived.

It is much too early to comment on the effectiveness of these measures, but they certainly show the very high priority which the leadership attaches to overcoming food shortages.

8 Economic Policy
Michael Kaser

PLANNING CONTROL

Every other chapter in this book is relevant to Soviet economic policy because a centrally-planned economy is of its nature directed by the state. It is a form of the 'command economy', which is one of the three procedures used by communities to order their economic activities; the two others (in the taxonomy formulated by Hicks as an alternative to that of Marx[1]) are 'custom' and the market, but there are many differently-weighted combinations of the three. A 'command economy' need not be planned: Hicks points to regimes in which a military ruler or a religious hierarchy may determine the use of resources without any thought necessarily having been given to the forward assessment of cause and effect which is the essence of planning. A 'command economy' may be mixed with a 'customary' mechanism – as in Calvin's theocratic economy of the Geneva republic – but is more usually associated with some elements of a market, for plans may be disaggregated and decentralised to allow the agents of economic activity to act within constraints and parameters chosen by the planning authority. Where the parameters are expressed by market relationships, typical systems are the mixed economy of 'late capitalism' (a marxist phrase I favour, while eschewing the implication of a terminal phase), the variant types of 'market socialism' employed in Hungary and in Yugoslavia, and the 'second economy' coexisting, with increasing weight, alongside the state-run part of the Soviet system.

What all economies employing the 'command' must share is the use of a priority ranking from above which need not coincide with priority rankings which are (or would in other circumstances be) expressed from below. This dichotomy is part of Hicks' spectrum running from absolutist 'aboveness' to anarchic 'belowness' and, although neither extreme could ever be fully adopted, the forced-labour sector of the

186

Soviet economy under Stalin was a modern example near the upper limit.[2]

The dichotomous characteristic more relevant to the present is that the rankings of those who participate in the economy are not harmonised by the 'command' economy as in theory they could be by perfect competition in a market or through perfect computation in a planned economy.[3] In the 'classic Soviet model' – Stalin's system formalised – the priorities of those above overrode those desired below with respect to a broad range of economic decisions. On Drewnowski's map of such decisions[4] much the greater area was subject to 'state planners' preferences' but that area has been encroached upon by 'household preferences' since Stalin's death. The preponderance of the former was publicly argued in terms of social priorities and ideological principles – that they rather than market prices or consumers' purses determine the allocation of resources – but the ultimate objective was political, not economic. Stalin's principal aim was to remove all foci of decision-making which were not subject to his will. In so doing, he also removed much of the information on which decentralised decisions had previously been based and consequently his decisions were less informed (and probably therefore less rational) than they could have been. The loss of potential welfare was exacerbated by the implicit assumption that central choice should be exercised exclusively among options generated centrally, as if the relevant state or Party officials had a 'monopoly of brains'. If agents below did not generate information, or were only sparingly allowed to use that information, their thinking function atrophied and it is one of the problems of the inherited 'bureaucratisation' of the Soviet economy today that managers have been chosen for their ability to comply rather than to deny, to replicate rather than to refute.

There was a second objective whereby economic interests were brought in touch with political ones: a planned economy is capable of mobilising resources to meet major goals – such as raising the rate of saving or of defence expenditure – and of ensuring that specific projects accorded priority be met to the exclusion of other, lower-ranked projects. The attainment of some goal – a rapidly developing structure of capital assets or the exploitation of natural resources – is easier with such mobilisation – Stalin's 'heavy industry' or Khrushchev's 'virgin lands campaign' are instances. They can be used to justify the non-attainment of other desirable objectives – adequate housing was not in Stalin's 'bill of goods', nor were private motorcars in Khrushchev's; an analogy can be found in the most ancient of command microeconomies, a ship – 'All hands on deck' – and Lange's famous characterisation as *'sui generis* a war economy' is well known.

But if the economy fails to meet those objectives, the advantage of mobilisation under a command, legitimating the monopoly of decision-making by the Party, is called into question. The economic problems of the 1980s hence have an important political dimension. One such problem, the slowing down of industrial growth, and the intractability of agriculture evoked Brezhnev's affirmation to his Central Committee in November 1981 that 'the food problem is on the political as well as the economic plane the crucial question of the Five-year Plan'.[5] Another has been the failure of Brezhnev's combination of augmented military expenditure (in absolute, though not in relative, terms) and quest for East–West detente to yield the stable international equilibrium that the Soviet people have been led to expect from their leadership.

What may be perceived as a struggle between competing objectives and their supporters has been rendered more acute by a prospective reduction in the resources available in the next one or two decades: although the transfer from what is called by Soviet economists 'extensive' to 'intensive' exploitation has been urged since the 1960s, the certain decline in manpower numbers and the likely diminution of foreign technology provision has rendered immediate the need to raise both labour and capital productivity. The keen future competition for scarce resources should be assessed in the light of past and present repositories of economic power in the Soviet planned economy, the five to which such power could be attributed being workers' agencies, the peasantry (and others who seek the permissiveness of the market), the 'military-industrial complex', the managerial technocracy and, of course, the Party.

The seizure of power by Lenin and Trotsky in 1917 was in the name of the workers, but their slogan and banner, 'All power to the Soviets', meant (soon, if not immediately) the abstraction of power from the factory committees (*fabzavkomy*). From the dissolution of such committees (culminating in the Party's struggle to control the railwayman's executive, *Vikzhel*) through the suppression of the 'Workers' Opposition' to the expulsion of Tomsky from the leadership of the trade-union movement, which thenceforward remained wholly under Party management, the history of the first dozen Soviet years was of the emasculation of workers' agencies. Attempts to form 'free trade unions' in late 1977 and early 1978 were soon repressed and these and the Soviet government's concern at the Polish free trade union,

Solidarity, until its quashing by martial law in December 1981 have been the only recent signs that some stirrings might be found of dissent focused upon any organisation of workers as such.[6]

It is the other four channels of group interest – they are too broad to be termed 'interest groups' – which are relevant to control of the Soviet economy in the 1980s, but one of them, the Party (as constituted by its officials) must participate in any ruling alliance – and, as this chapter seeks to prove – is continuing to control all three. The fifth, the workers' interest, is involved in the outcome because, although that part of the townsfolk who (or whose parents) migrated from the countryside over the past half-century are the beneficiaries of 'heavy' (military-oriented) industrialisation, they must be supplied with sufficient food and consumers' goods from agriculture, 'light industry' and imports if they are to be prevented from threatening whatever ascendancy is achieved.

Brezhnev has, as already stated, made 'the food problem' the prime economic and political issue of the day, and it is clear from the various concessions in late 1980 and early 1981 to the private household plot that the peasantry is to be allowed to react more to market incentives. In Chapter 7 Nove shows the deficiencies of incentives to the individual collective farmer and to the profitable operation of state and collective farms, and notes the accumulation of permitted public criticism during 1980 and 1981 of restrictions on private farming. Both he and Hazard in Chapter 4 draw attention to a series of measures in 1977–81 which require collective farms to allow their members the use of machinery, access to pasture and the provision of supplies to raise crops and livestock more productively (within the still severe area and number constraints).[7] Hazard goes so far as to conclude from the government's concessions that 'in a sense there has emerged a neo-NEP, although it does not return farming to private farmers as was the case in the 1920s' page 105). A further decree, of 17 January 1981,[8] not only made explicit the right of collective farmers to raise their (few) livestock for profit by private sales but required state farms to lend funds for (or in the case of young families to donate) livestock for private rearing and to help in the improvement of household plots.

Decrees of 10 March 1975 and of 3 May 1976 codified the rights of Soviet citizens to engage respectively in private prospecting and in private handicrafts – though each specified branches in which such activity remained forbidden. Some minor concessions were made to private operations, but the codification was in itself a liberalisation since it made public precisely what was allowed.

Openly-acknowledged pressure to extend such codification to consumer services has more recently emerged. A section chief in the Institute of Economics of the World Socialist System (IEMSS), where privatisation, for example in Hungary, can be cited as a successful case, has observed that 'it would be useful not to limit individual work activity to handicrafts but to extend it to other parts of the service sector, which would be directly in keeping with Article 17 of the Constitution'.[9]

Because private gainful activity has grown in response to the widening gap between aggregate household incomes and the state's provision of goods and services on open access,[10] and because prosecutions under Khrushchev's laws against speculation and 'parasitism' were relaxed by Brezhnev, bribery and peculation seem to have become more widespread. In 1981 the Party revived a practice virtually abandoned under Brezhnev of the confidential circularisation of Party primary organisations. Such a 'closed letter' was despatched in September to warn Party members of food shortages in the wake of the country's third bad harvest in succession and another was sent in November to call on them to stiffen measures against corruption and the theft of food from state stocks.[11] It noted extensive bribery in retail trade, the manipulation of supplies to create shortages from which private profit could be derived and payments to medical staff to obtain treatment.[12]

The extension of the second economy in the 1970s[13] has been wholly due to the government's failure to respect relationships posed by the volume and process of supply and the volume and direction of demand, by the exacerbation in other words of the 'shortage economy'.[14] Four types may be distinguished outside the officially-sanctioned areas of transaction (which with respect to sales for private gain include household plots, commission shops and licensed handicrafts). The first is theft. Stealing state property seems scarcely to be regarded as morally blameworthy in the USSR and may often be the only means whereby a private citizen may receive a product he would be perfectly prepared to pay for: allocations of producers' goods with a household use are mostly to state enterprises, leaving trivial quotas for retail sales; if an unplanned shortage occurs it is usually the household quota that is cut, to leave the available supplies for state enterprises; consumers' goods in short supply at the official price are diverted to 'closed access' outlets and the non-privileged buyer has no licit source. Many of such thefts are for personal consumption, but where theft is for sale to others a second type is to be distinguished, which combines with the resale of private property. As Hazard in Chapter 4 considers in more detail, buying for resale is characterised in Soviet law as 'speculation' for which there have been some increases in prosecutions, though not to the prevalence of Khrushchev's days. A number of second-hand markets (notably that in Odessa) have been closed or greatly restricted and transactions driven 'underground'. The third type is illicit production – some of which the proponents noted above wish to legalise – which may take place in state enterprises or privately. Such activity 'on the side' (*na levo*) extends to many services, among which the use of state-owned cars for private hire is so prevalent that severe restrictions were imposed by a decree of 31 May 1973 and are still enforced.[15] The fourth type is corrupt purchase, private payment being made to gain preference in the supply of a 'deficit' good or service. The series of agricultural failures in 1979–81, when set against higher urban money incomes, brought food shortages which were the worst for two decades. As Table 8.1 shows, the five-year plan targets for the consumption of key foodstuffs were seriously underfulfilled (though overfulfilled for consumer durables). In each plan, however, real incomes per head (money incomes deflated by consumer-price changes plus social consumption) were closer to that planned.[16] Such side-payments would almost disappear if market-clearing prices

Table 8.1 Consumption per head of Important Consumers' Goods

| | Eighth Plan | | Ninth Plan | | Tenth Plan | |
	Plan	Actual	Plan	Actual	Plan	Actual
Kilogrammes per head:						
meat and meat products	50[a]	48	59	57	63	57
fish and fish products	20[a]	15	22	17	21	17
fruit	42[a]	35	89	39	53	34
vegetables	99[a]	82	109	89	113	93
Consumer durables per 100 households:						
radio sets and record players	—	72	86	79	83	86
television sets	48	51	72	74	84	85
refrigerators	35	32	64	61	85	84

Source: Compiled from five-year plan texts and *Narkhoz* for relevant years in M. A. Crosnier and G. Mink, *Le courrier des pays de l'Est* (November 1981), p. 15; for earlier years, a caveat and slightly variant statistic see G. E. Schroeder and B. S. Severin, in US Congress JEC, *Soviet Economy in a New Perspective* (Washington DC, 1976), pp. 623, 625, 642.

obtained or if the government adjusted aggregate household incomes (net of tax and savings) to aggregate consumer supplies at the set prices.

Both alternatives are being pursued in a very hesitant fashion. Commission shops for foodstuffs have reportedly been opened in some provincial cities – Rostov-on-Don, Lvov, Odessa and Vladimir have been noted – in which state supplies of foodstuffs (mainly meat and dairy products, where shortages are most acute) are sold at prices close to those ruling on the free collective-farm markets: meat is reported at double, and sausage nearly three times, the state-shop price.[17] Limited price increments for state shops have become an annual event since 1977 but by 1981 the official retail price index was only 4 per cent above 1976.[18] At the other option of adjusting quantities instead of prices, scope is limited for increasing the provision of the products which are most out of alignment with demand at the official retail price. Although increasing, and considerable, quantities of meat and dairy products have been imported (aggregating 1.83m roubles or $2.8m in 1980 against 0.73m roubles or $1.1m in 1979, that is a two-and-a-half-fold rise in the single year[19]), inadequate fodder, due to the poor harvests of 1979–81, has held back domestic output. Instead, the quantities have begun to be rationed – only locally, according to supply conditions, and only since the spring of 1980: reports suggest a range of from one-third to one kilogram a month for meat and sausage and the same amounts for butter.[20]

Resort has been made to food rationing in three previous periods of Soviet history and the technique for lifting it has differed on each occasion. In 1921 Lenin effected the dramatic conversion from 'War Communism' to the 'New Economic Policy' (NEP) by reinstituting the market; in late 1935 and early 1936 the rationing which had begun with the first Five-year Plan was lifted simultaneously with a big increase of state-shop prices to market-clearing levels; and wartime rationing was terminated in 1947 by a currency reform which wiped out nearly all of the inflationary overhang.[21]

There are few indications which technique the Soviet government will employ when it decides on normalisation (for it must regard the present rationing, queues and irregular supplies as abnormal). In Chapter 4 Hazard discerns the introduction of another NEP as a distinct possibility, but only on the supply side, that is by authorising more private production in the consumer sector. There was no sign in the passing references made in the Soviet press that the sixtieth anniversary of the X Party Congress, which on 8 March 1921 approved

Lenin's proposal for NEP (accepted the previous day by his Central Committee), has such relevance today; more attention was, for example, paid (Soviet anniversaries being usually commemorated for their present-day significance) to the sixtieth anniversary of the Soviet-Afghan Treaty.[22] The 1936 solution of a very sharp rise in retail prices was implemented in Poland in February 1982 in conditions of con-sumer-good disequilibrium more serious than those of the con-temporary USSR. But just as Polish popular protest had been stilled by the imposition of martial law two months previously, so the start of the Great Purges in the USSR of 1936 was an effective concomitant to so sudden an inflation. There is nothing, however, to suggest that the Soviet authorities are today heading for an abrupt change – in either the level of prices or the degree of repression.

The choice of technique, if experience is to be followed, is con-fiscation as in 1947 of the inflationary overhang (money involuntarily saved because there were no desired goods which possessors could purchase). There has been a subsequent currency reform, that of January 1961, but it was only an exchange of currency (one new rouble for ten old), without any cancellation. Nevertheless, Soviet citizens feared worse and engaged on a spending spree to convert cash into any good that could be got.[23] So vast is today's unspent purchasing power ('postponed demand' in Soviet usage) that the possibility of con-fiscation is real. Its advocacy could be found among proponents of a continuingly command economy, such as might be found in the groups considered in the next two sections – the 'managerial technocracy' or the 'military-industrial complex' respectively, but, because the overhang mutes wage incentives and distorts effective demand, proponents of more decentralised, market-oriented practices might take it as necessary medicine.

MANAGEMENT AND MANAGERS

A 'seller's market' (though 'market' is not quite the appropriate term) operates in the USSR as much for producers' goods as for consumers' goods, and has the same effect of blunting the buyer's discrimination. Where retail sales or household services are concerned, readiness to take a 'second-best' when a first-choice good or service proves un-available merely reduces the welfare that a consumer could derive from spending the equivalent sum. If the shoppers do not protest,[24] there is no overt manifestation of the demerit arising. But where wholesale (interenterprise) transactions are similarly conditioned, the effect is much more deleterious to the economy, because clients for materials and machinery are inhibited from selection on grounds of utility, performance or quality for the production process they employ: they accept products or services which perpetuate inefficiency or avert innovation. Part of the rise in the capital-to-output ratio in the 1970s must be due to a preclusion of capital efficiency by lack of incentive on the part of purchasing enterprises to seek the cheaper machinery or the equipment which generates cheaper outputs. As the Chairman of the Council of Ministers, N. A. Tikhonov, put it to the XXVI Party Congress in March 1981: 'Speaking of engineering, I want to dwell on yet another problem. This branch is called upon not only to produce modern technique but actively to contribute to its effective operation in the hands of the user.'[25] Addressing the Central Committee as it reviewed the final draft of the Eleventh Five-year Plan (1981–85) the General Secretary, Brezhnev, ended his report: 'It is necessary to draw up plans better and to carry them out better. It is necessary to organise better production and to produce better. In short, to work more efficiently. This, in the final count, is the main, decisive thing.'[26] In that same speech he had criticised the implementation of the decree of July 1979 on economic management as being 'put into effect slowly, in half measures' and called for a Central Committee meeting exclusively devoted to economic reform, stressing that 'while working to fulfil the five-year plan we should at the same time improve the economic mechanism'.[27]

The decree of 12 July 1979[28] fell into three parts. The first section was principally addressed to the industrial ministries and to Gosplan itself and, on the face of it, was no more than a requirement that those central bodies should plan in greater detail, in better time and for further ahead, though with the important proviso that the projected product-mix should be established, once the drafting had reached a phase concerned with such specifics, on the basis of contracts negotiated between the enterprises of production and distribution.[29] The section also comprised another significant change, in the substitution for enterprises and the associations grouping them[30] of 'normed value-added' as the 'indicator' for calculating labour productivity and the wage bill. A market or a profit-oriented incentive system would require that actual value-added be used, but the objective of the 1979 reform was to reward conformity to a planned relationship of inputs other than labour to final output. It spelt the end of reliance on a measure of final output alone, which (whether as the traditional 'global output' or as the 'realised output' of the 1965 reform) was subject to deviations from plan of the mix and quantity of inputs; only the 'increase in the volume of sales' remained among 'plan indicators' as a measure dependent on inputs as well as on the efficiency of their transformation into outputs. The second section of the 1979 decree complemented the first in the sphere of capital formation – specifying a number of sensible measures to reduce construction time and enhance investment efficiency. The third took up two themes of the 1965 reform in instructing enterprises and associations to adopt 'direct economic relations' among themselves on the base of stable plans and long-term contracts and rearranged and increased the incentive funds at the disposition of enterprises.

The 1979 reform went contrary to that of 1965, however, in enhancing the priority for physical indicators of output (that is, measures in natural units which by their nature cannot reflect the quality or performance requirements of users – as production values at market-clearing prices would). Finally, the 1979 decree required less haste and more stability in the process of planning: draft long-term plans (to 1990 in the present instance) were to be submitted eighteen months in advance of the start of the quinquennium (1981–85 in this instance), a final detailed plan at least five months before the start of the quin-quennium and physical balances established for the entirety of the five-year period.[31]

The proposed time-table went by the board. In the first place Gosplan's instructions on plan procedure were promulgated much later for the 1981–85 Plan than had been the corresponding instructions for 1976–80.[32] In the second place the publication schedule for the 1981–5 Plan proved to be no better than that of its predecessor. The Central Committee's draft guidelines appeared on 2 December 1980, only one month before the starting date, were ratified as 'Basic Guidelines' by the XXVI Party Congress (published on 5 March 1981), were revised by the Central Committee on 16 November and were approved as the final text of the Plan by the Supreme Soviet, with publication as a law on 20 November 1981. Finally, Gosplan's instructions on stable contractual relations were not published until that same November.[33]

Nor could the price relativities in which the material balances (and thence the long-term contracts) were planned have been those to be paid during the execution of the contracts, because the wholesale price list of 1 July 1967 was (apart from a limited adjustment on 1 January 1973) only replaced on 1 January 1982.[34] This does not exclude the use of the 1982 price list for planning purposes in advance of their actual application (indeed the new list has a special column for the coefficients to be applied to calculate 'normed value-added').

The price obstacle to effective management is twofold. First, prices, even in the 1982 revision, are not those at which customers would buy as much as producers supply (the 'market-clearing' criterion); even the relative costs of production they are intended to reflect do not indicate the production forgone by applying resources to that use (the 'opportunity cost'), because no price of an alternative product has embodied a utility value. Although taken out of context – which was that of investment – a Soviet newspaper comment encapsulates the problem: 'utterly hopeless plans are based on equally utterly hopeless measures'.[35] The second problem is rigidity. Not only are prices not (as in a market) subject to negotiation between customer and supplier, but those fixed by the USSR State Committee on Prices (Goskomtsen) remain unchanged for long periods and changes when introduced are small. Until the price series was reconcealed (it did not appear in the 1980 edition of the official statistical yearbook), a certain amount of branch detail was available on wholesale-price movements (Table 8.2).

Table 8.2 Industrial Wholesale-price Index, 1949=100

	Producers' goods		Consumers' goods		Total industry	
	Before tax	After tax	Before tax	After tax	Before tax	After tax
1948	—	64	—	95	—	86
1950	80	80	90	83	83	80
1955	61	61	85	64	68	61
1965	55	58	104	65	70	60
1967	65	66	105	64	77	64
1970	64	66	106	65	77	64
1975	59	62	111	67	75	63
1978	57	62	111	67	74	63
1979	57	61	111	67	73	62

Source: Narkhoz 1978, pp. 138–9; *1979*, pp. 164–5.

The elimination of most subsidies under Voznesensky's price reform of 1 January 1949 raised prices of producers' goods (designated 'heavy industry' or 'Group A') inclusive of turnover tax by 56 per cent; no series has been published before tax, which from 1949 was almost exclusively levied on consumers' goods. Voznesensky's dismissal almost as soon as his reform was implemented (and before other steps he might have taken to rationalise the economic mechanism) and his execution in 1950 left Stalin free to retrogress. Wholesale-price reductions, effected by the reintroduction of widespread subsidies, were effected in 1950 and 1952 but as industrial productivity rose reductions genuinely based on cost declines became possible. Price lists were revised in 1955 and 1967. By the latter date, prices of producers' goods and consumer durables were just two-thirds of the level prevailing in 1949. Wholesale prices for consumers' goods, as represented by the food-processing and footwear and textiles industries (designated 'light industry', or 'Group B'), were likewise reduced in 1950 and 1955 – but those for the food sector were raised in 1958 as state agricultural procurement prices were increased. The relevant increases were only passed on to the consumer to a modest extent – due to the provision of heavy subsidies, to which reference is made in Chapter 7.

The economic reform decided upon in September 1965 required new wholesale prices to be implemented (chiefly to absorb the charge on capital assets which was one of the principal features of the reform). These were introduced in the 'light industrial' sector between October 1966 and March 1967, and in the 'heavy industrial' sector on 1 July 1967. The net impact was to bring about a 9 per cent increase, exclusive of turnover tax charges (modified for the tax-inclusive price to 7 per cent by reductions in turnover tax).

A further revision took place on 1 January 1973. This involved an increase of 8 per cent (tax-exclusive; but of 5 per cent, tax-inclusive), in respect of 'light industry', which was offset by reductions of 8 per cent in respect of engineering goods (tax-exclusive; 6 per cent, tax-inclusive). The increase in the price of motor spirit applied in 1978 was too small to affect the aggregate index; but the index (1949 = 100) for fuel prices as a group rose from 113 to 127 during 1978 – that is, by 24 per cent, but remained stable during 1979 while energy prices world-wide rushed upwards under the effect of the 'second oil-shock'. The 1982 revision has only admitted part of that 'shock', as it did of the first in 1973: the average of energy prices has been put up about one and half times.

Such protection of the world's lowest relative price for energy draws attention to the continuing absence from interenterprise prices of any of the relationships which foreign-trade corporations face when they sell Soviet exports or buy imports: price isolationism lives on when it has been killed off in the more trade-dependent members of Comecon.[36] Without 'market clearing' prices confronting them either on home or foreign transactions, therefore, it may seem questionable why the Soviet government in the 1970s shifted so many ministries, administrations and foreign-trade corporations from its payroll as 'budget institutions' on to autonomous (*khozraschetnye*) finance. An explanation – elaborated below – may be that prices are only a monitoring device: although the price relativities and the various incentive schemes attached to profit or value-added were not instruments to an optimal allocation of resources, the requirement to cover corporate outlay by corporate revenue kept managers on their toes. Such 'reforms' could render managers less willing to take delivery of 'second-best' goods and more anxious to create greater value from the capital assets, material inputs and manpower at their disposition. Specialised management training and the harnessing of better knowledge and fast analysis by computers, programming and sophisticated data-processing were measures in the same direction.[37]

The extent of the transfer to autonomous finance is impressive. One All-Union Ministry, that of Instrument-making, Automation Equipment and Control Systems, was converted as early as 1970, and for most of the decade was regarded as the crucial experiment. By 1980 four other all-Union ministries were classed with it (Tractors and Farm Machinery, Heavy and Transport Engineering, Energy Engineering and Electrotechnical Industry), as were some republican ministries. Following promulgation on 2 March 1973 of a decree on (and a General Statue for) All-Union and Republican Associations, enacted in conformity with Brezhnev's call at the XXIV Party Congress (1971) that associations and combines 'must in future become the main elements of social production on a *khozraschet* basis',[38] the share of global industrial output within associations rose from 12 per cent (at end-1972; it had been 7 per cent at end-1970) to 48 per cent at end-1980; by the latter date just over half (50.1 per cent) of industrial workers were in the association network.[39]

Foreign-trade corporations were to shift to autonomous finance under decrees of 31 May 1977 and 31 May 1978. As Hewett surmises, the conversion of foreign-trade organisations to autonomous accounting (and their supervision by boards comprising equal representation by the Ministry of Foreign Trade and the relevant industrial ministry) was the outcome of an extensive investigation of the operation of the Ministry by a working party under V. P. Gruzinov of the All-Union Academy of Foreign Trade, whose report was published, probably with exisions, in 1975.[40] Pursuant to a decision of August 1976, but clearly in preparation for the joint management participation authorised in 1978, industrial ministries were instructed to establish their own 'Departments of External Deliveries' (*zagranpostavka*) for liaison with the corporations.

The linkage of industrial ministries with foreign trade corporations was a microcosm of what should be done elsewhere in the economic administration. Already in the early 1970s 'territorial-production complexes' – recommended in a resolution of the XXIV Party Congress in 1971 – were being created to co-ordinate the operations of many ministries in new development areas. Thus one of the first, in northern West Siberia, had oversight of the exploitation of oil, gas and timber, the Surgut gas-fired electric-generating station, construction agencies and pipelines; another, the Bratsk-Ust'-Ilimsk, was responsible for the Bratsk and Ust'-Ilimsk hydroelectric plants, an aluminium works, forestry, cellulose and woodworking enterprises and construction agencies;[41] a zonal task which was beyond the national confines since various Comecon states were involved in the investments.

The territorial-production complexes are an attempt, like the transfer to autonomous finance, to inveigle the staff of industrial ministries from their administrative entrenchments behind 'departmental barriers'.[42] But above the ministries stands Gosplan, which hitherto has to a significant degree reinforced those barriers by its own organisation into 'branch departments'. In such departments there is a *kurator* whose function is to liaise (*kyr'erovat'*) with the corresponding departments of a ministry: a liaison can become an alliance! Gosplan has always had its 'functional departments' and, more powerful, a composite (*svodny*) department to make decisions and advise across ministerial boundaries, but at the start of the 1981–85 Plan, the Council of Ministers specifically instructed Gosplan to improve its arrangements to co-ordinate and direct across branches and regions, a task underlined by Tikhonov in his speech to the XXVI Party Congress.[43] The principal new co-ordination instrument is the 'target programme' (*tsel'ovaya programma*), to the fulfilment of which all appropriate resources can be directed. Such programmes were introduced into planning practice in the mid-1970s,[44] but have not altered Gosplan's branch departments. Their implementation is supervised at two levels: major projects by interbranch commissions chaired by a Deputy Chairman of the Council of Ministers (fourteen persons held that rank in July 1981) and other projects by complexes within Gosplan and chaired by an official of that agency. The target programmes are also a means of concentrating resources to greater effect – to counter for example, the dispersion of investment projects and the small scale of consumers' good production – and a vehicle for Comecon integration – 'long range target programmes' have been adopted by that organisation since its Session of 1976.[45] Domestic and Comecon-linked programmes in such broad fields as food and energy will include evaluations of the domestic use of imports and the comparative cost of exports and the former will be developed on a new interbranch concept, the agro-industrial complex (*agropromyshlenny kompleks*).[46]

The changes in economic management effected for the elaboration and implementation of the 1981–85 Plan (which also comprises goals for 1990) are directed towards improving the process of central decision-making and of assuring their implementation. In short, they are instruments of a 'command economy' which enlarge freedom neither for a market nor for a manager outside the central agencies. But the key to the new commands is the 'norm' which the manager or technician should be in a position to shape more accurately to his requirements.

The ambit of the traditional 'norm' has been greatly extended under the July 1979 decree, and together with that decree's 'enterprise passport'[47] furnishes the central agencies with much more detailed constraints to impose on the units they supervise. But because the instructions through the norms will have to be much more precise, recipients will have more influence over them. Moreover, because the norms are more diversified at the microeconomic level and now constitute aggregates at the macroeconomic level, they should be much less arbitrary and more rational, both as to technical efficacy or economic efficiency.

The use of norms in the value-added plan indicator is discussed above; the new norm system as a whole was set out in a Gosplan decree of 11 January 1980. In addition to those long in being to establish material balances and the enterprise *tekhpromfinplan* (manpower, materials, energy productive assets and investment), there are six new groups: 'social product generated' (that is the aggregate from which external inputs are deducted to yield normed value-added), financial resources, money expenditure on equipment, outlay on transmission installations, environmental protection and socio-economic norms.[48] The agencies elaborating the norms – Gosplan, Gosstroy, Gossnab, GKNT, the State Committee on Labour (Goskomtrud) and the Ministry of Finance – have worked with the relevant technical research institutes, and part of the objective of the new system is to accelerate the operational commissioning of technical change.[49]

The emphasis in the 1981–85 plan documents and commentaries on the introduction of new technology needs no reiteration here. It has long been the *leitmotiv* of the 'intensification' of resource use but has been strengthened, as Hanson shows in Chapter 3, as his 'explanation (7)' by the Soviet government's turn from imported towards domestic technology. The augmenting of the number of material balances and fuller use of computerised information and control systems[50] are further instruments in the penetration (albeit more enlightened by managerial-technical expertise) of the operational units by commands of the central bodies.

Taken as a whole, the reforms pursuant to the 1979 decree illuminate more than ever the systemic differences between market capitalism and Soviet socialism, which 'can be thought of as being bifurcated: allocation in physical terms, control via the price system'.[51] Moore's new insight allows us to see the reforms as compatible with effective control of a command economy: prices have not and will not be used for allocative decisions but to facilitate monitoring of such decisions taken in physical terms. Thus interenterprise transfer prices should be constant for long periods because 'what does matter is that the valuation procedures be consistent and easily understood – that they be relatively low-cost information devices'.[52] It makes little difference if price relativities are out of date (even as limited supply-side constructs), as they must be because each Soviet price reform takes three years and some relativities are obsolete by the time it comes into force. The more extended use of 'commands' in physical units in the reforms is evident – the augmentation of *ex ante* material balances; the penetration of norms and of programmed data-reporting (4383 'ASU' were installed in 1971–80) further into measures of management; the continued isolation of flexible foreign price ratios from the domestic set of prices – as is their combination into the macroeconomic plan not by budget appropriation (as in capitalist practice) but by 'target programmes'.

Many of the elements in Moore's interpretation have for long figured in western analyses of Soviet practice – Grossman called constant prices 'crypto-physical units', Ames perceived the need to monitor 'agency costs' (the cost of devolving operational decisions) in a Soviet enterprise, I took the planners' need for stability,[53] to name three. Although Moore's interpretation of a bifurcated system is not so formulated by Soviet economists, they have when describing the 1979 reform to western economists seen merit in its improvement of central instruments of control while continuing to regret the inability of those instruments adequately to identify demand relationships.

Mention was made above of the weak penetration of customer discretion in a 'buyer's market' and of the new attempts to write utilisation characteristics into plans for producers' goods. One final point may be made with respect to consumers' goods from a study by Gorlin of recently-introduced instruments for improving the quality of soft goods – textiles, clothing, knitwear and footwear – notably centrally-set quality certification (*znak kachestva*).[54] She concludes that the measures 'far from representing a movement towards de-centralization and price flexibility, actually increase the administrative burden on the ministries and the agencies responsible for the main-tenance of standards. The "reforms" described lead the economy further away from decentralizing change'.[55]

THE 'MILITARY-INDUSTRIAL COMPLEX'

The one large production zone in which the customer's requirements are paramount is armaments and other provision for the armed services. It is sometimes remarked ironically that the only 'buyers' market' in the USSR is within the 'military-industrial' complex, but the traffic in resource allocation is by no means in the obvious direction – from the military to the industrial. This section examines the manner in which economic constraints and rigidities affect the scale and pattern of military equipment and installations. The editors of a recent col-lection of studies on Soviet strategy have observed that 'While it is not true that the US has a military-industrial complex, nevertheless the role of these groups is clearly important in determining the Soviet force posture'.[56]

There is in the first place something of a cost-effectiveness constraint on specific weapon systems. 'For example, in the ABM treaty in SALT I, while the armed forces probably opposed limitation of what it considered an important component of its damage limitation policy, it recognised that the costs and inefficiency of the system were too great.'[57] The relevant assessments are many fewer than are manifest in a pluralistic society because 'in the area of devising strategic needs, force sizing, force employment or overall strategic theory-doctrine, there is no effective counter to the Soviet military. Indeed, in this regard, there may be only a smattering of civilians that even have knowledge of the character and composition of Soviet military capabilities'.[58] Secondly, the institutions of the production sector, at least on occasion, impose rigidities on the military establishment's selection of weapon system. Examples include a tendency to favour the improvement of old designs over completely new ones, to select weapon systems on the basis of the 'institutional interests' of a design and production group, and the allegedly decisive influence of the 'Soviet missile design and manufacturing establishment' on the negotiators' unwillingness in SALT II to accept United States measures of nuclear-weapon symmetry.[59] The need for such domestic calibration during negotiations on SALT reportedly led to the establishment early in 1969 of a co-ordinating committee between the Ministries of Defence and of Foreign Affairs and representatives of research institutions and production ministries.[60] Previously, and continuingly, a Military Industrial Commission (VPK)[61] has been the nexus of the nine industrial ministries administering military production, the Academy of Science, running the research units, and the Ministry of Defence. The VPK is subordinate to the Council of Ministers, which also, at least since 1970, has had a specifically military body, the Defence Council, as during the Second World War.

The Defence Council – chaired by Brezhnev and believed to include the leading defence chiefs and all members of the Politburo – must be the forum in which the third constraint is exercised by economic institutions, namely the aggregate expenditure on defence and the opportunity cost of specific resources as revealed, notably but not solely, by planning the material balances. In Chapter 2, Holloway is careful to cite estimates, all from United States government sources, without commitment (pp. 43 and 54), and advances two developments indicating caution on aggregate military spending. Holloway takes as evidence of Soviet use of a cost-effectiveness formula the decision not to seek nuclear superiority over the United States,[62] a position re-inforced at the XXVI Party Congress (see p. 44). On the cost side at least three recent statements draw attention to the opportunity cost of military spending. One of Brezhnev's closest foreign-policy advisers, himself a Central Committee member, N. N. Inozemtsev, wrote in 1981 (again as Holloway notes) that competition among the objectives of growth, welfare and security will 'complicate economic development' in the 1980s (page 54).[63] Brezhnev himself at a Central Committee meeting of 21 October 1980 required the industrial ministries serving defence needs to increase their contribution to the civilian sector both in research results and in output: their growth of production of consumer durables 'must not be allowed to slow down in the next five-year period'.[64] Finally, a Soviet economist warned in 1981 that 'an excessive increase in military-economic might cannot be allowed because in the final analysis this could slow the development of the very foundation of military power – the economy – and do irreparable harm to defence capability'.[65]

Becker has so cogently reviewed the difficulties of estimating Soviet defence expenditure[66] that there is no need to take space in this chapter, but, put very briefly, he shows the difficulty of uncovering the various groups of military expenditure from Soviet sources and the problems of valuing, either at rouble or at dollar prices, the physical items (as revealed by intelligence sources) which go to the military: 'the complexity, costliness and intelligence-dependence of the "building block" system effectively prevents its use outside of the U.S. Government'.[67] The CIA has in the past (publication policy under the Reagan Administration has become more secretive) made available those rouble- and dollar-priced estimates,[68] which have therefore been subjected to outside criticism, particularly on the pricing procedures. Some claim as a consequence that the CIA figures are an underestimate,[69] others that they are an overestimate[70] and Becker that they are probably just right.[71]

I use here a new variant of uncovering Soviet magnitudes, restricting the compilation to the supply of goods and excluding services. This permits comparison with national income in the Soviet definition (net material product, NMP) and consequently avoids having to estimate either armed services pay (which does not generate NMP, being classed with such as education, science and health-care as a 'nonproductive service') or GNP. The results cannot be used for comparison with countries where military expenditure can only be compared to GNP but they do show the 'defence burden' as perceived by the Soviet leadership, which does use NMP as its standard macroeconomic aggregate. As I also show, the opportunity cost of a largely conscript force is probably perceived as low by that leadership; indeed, they may be seen as having a value outweighing earnings forgone. Examples can readily be drawn from problems raised earlier in this book. They constitute a rapidly deployable bloc of labourers, not only for emergencies – for which all governments use their armies – but regularly in harvesting (among the sixteen million temporary workers – the staggering figure which Nove notes on p. 174). They are a resettlement channel, for many do not return to their native village on demobilisation and thus assist the relocation policy noted by Helgeson in Chapter 5. Because regiments are not designated with regional associations, they can foster an ethnic mingling which Miller in Chapter 1 shows to be a political need.

The government could have before it figures which demonstrate its maintaining strategic-weapon parity (on its measures; those used by the US government give the USSR superiority) while reducing the share of NMP devoted to the military, if the comparison between 1970 and 1979[72] set out below is tenable.

From the very beginning of the Five-year Plans military requirements have been intimately integrated with civilian[73] but have been concealed from public (and potential enemy) scrutiny by restriction to a single entry in the Soviet budget; the absence of parliamentary enquiry into appropriations has protected such hypersensitivity. The single entry has a history coterminous with the five-year plans[74] and is not a novelty of post-war secrecy. Textbooks on Soviet budgetary practice specify that in the classification of expenditure entries (groups, divisions, chapters, paragraphs and articles), Group 3, expenditure on defence has only a single division: '208 USSR Ministry of Defence',[75] but it is defined as 'expenditure on defence within the structure of the state budget', as distinct from 'funds of the union budget appropriated against the estimate of the USSR Ministry of Defence'.[76] The question is which of these three constitutes 'Group 3', the published outlay.[77] Certainly it is not investment which must be included as 'capital investment' under Group 1 'finance of the national economy', within Division 100, Chapter for the USSR Ministry of Defence.[78] Of the 112 weapon types in production in 1980, 44 are clearly classifiable as 'investment' by the Ministry of Defence.[79].

If it is accepted, against the opinion of many, that Group 3 is meaningful (that is, represents actual outlays) its very constancy excludes 'pay and subsistence', because wages have risen too fast (government salaries by 27 per cent between 1970 and 1980[80]); it must be non-capital 'procurement', prices for which are close to those of engineering goods (which in 1979 were 77 per cent of those ruling in 1970[81]). One reason for believing that expenditure on current supplies is Group 3 is that these are the flows of funds that need closest control under material-balance planning. The cost of conscript military forces can be virtually neglected: military personnel are simply omitted from the gainfully occupied.[82] The approach in terms of opportunity cost is defensible: resources used in the economy for investment and current goods are scarce and subject to allocative planning, while conscription mostly draws on low-productivity farm labour and is outside the plan.[83] The heading under which 'labour costs' are funded is unknown but it is of little import: there are 15,200 million roubles of undistributed expenditure in the 1980 budget which is remarkably close to my tentative estimate of 'pay and subsistence'.[84]

The computations detailed in Table 8.3 show it to be possible to demonstrate that Soviet allocations of physical goods to military uses fell as a percentage of NMP from 9.6 per cent in 1970 to 8.6 per cent in 1979, even though in constant (1969) prices they rose 53 per cent. Commentators observing the paradox of unchanged (even declining)

Table 8.3 Estimates of Appropriations for Military Goods
(thousand million roubles)

	1970 1969 = current prices	1969 prices	1979 current prices
1 Procurement	19.7	22.4	17.2
2 Investment	5.0	11.3	13.9
3 Research and development	4.4	8.2	6.3
4 Total goods	27.3	41.9	37.4
5 Net material product utilised	285.5	—	432.9
6 (4) as per percentage of (5)	9.6	—	8.6

Source: Because conclusions contrary to many western assessments may be drawn from these estimates, their calculation is set out in detail at the end of the Notes.

current-priced outlays and the evidence of an increase in the absolute quantity of armaments[85] and the like have dismissed the evidence of a price decline in both engineering goods and investment costs over the 1970s. Once this price decline is allowed for (by suitably inflating current-priced estimates), the volume (constant-price) rise agrees precisely with the US agencies' estimate of a 4 to 5 per cent annual rise in the 1970s:[86] a 53 per cent rise over those nine years is, of course, 4.8 per cent.

Because the US agencies also employ 1970 prices (which are virtually the same as the 1969 prices I use in Table 8.3), a comparison can be made with the 'material component' here estimated as 37,400 million roubles and their 58,000 to 63,000 millions on 'the narrow definition of defense'.[87] The 'labour cost' of defence, shown by the difference between the two estimates, of some 23,000 million roubles would be distributed between some 4.6 million men at 5000 roubles per man for pay and subsistence.[88] It is thus possible that on its own measure, the Soviet government considers that there has been a relative reduction in material resources allocated to defence during the 1970s. Whether that measure is realistic, or whether the government believes it to be so, depends on whether the price cuts have reflected genuine cost reductions or have been manipulations to yield level spending on the defence budget. This would have required subsidies which could have been raised by taxation or other levies but could also have been provided by borrowing from the State Bank – the equivalent of 'printing money'.[89] A second caveat relates to the identity of actual defence spending, as reported, with that planned since 1967. This does add to the suspicion of manipulation, but could indicate stricter control over defence outlays than over the other two major budget groups ('national economy' and 'social and cultural measures'), at least while the Defence Council has been in being to act as allocator and monitor.

For the 1980s the indications are that if the 'parity policy' is implemented, the burden of defence as a call on material resources would only be enlarged in response to a real increase in the armed might of potential enemies (NATO and China). If the USSR has during the past decade had to devote only some 9 per cent of NMP to military uses, continuance should not impose difficulty in meeting other objectives. Finally, the renewed concern that there should be spin-off from the defence industry – in technology for industry generally and as consumer durables in particular – suggests that if anything defence might ease the two crucial shortages of the Eleventh Five-year Plan – the diminution of the flow of foreign technology and the shortage of consumers' goods with respect to household purchasing power and its inflationary overhang.

PRODUCTION TARGETS FOR THE 1980s

By contrast, the 'labour input' into military uses is likely to exacerbate a severe problem of the 1980s. As Helgeson has shown in Chapter 5, four Union-Republics will experience a decline in the active labour force in the second half of the 1980s; those republics (the Russian Federation, Ukraine, Latvia and Estonia) employed four-fifths of wage earners and 85 per cent of the industrial workforce and generated 82 per cent of the electricity.[90] The increments in numbers of active working age will accrue in the least industrially developed republics. The contrast is particularly stark between the Russian Federation, where the labour supply will diminish, and Central Asia and the

Transcaucasus where the labour supply will continue to rise. Using the standard Soviet division by five-year plan period, the Russian Federation had increases in working-age population of 6.0 million in the first half and of 3.9 million in the second half of the 1970s. But in each of the next three quinquennia there will be decreases (of 0.8 million in 1981–85, 0.9 million in 1986–90 and 0.4 million in 1991–95); the rise in the number of pensioners, described by McAuley in Chapter 6, is a corollary. Not until the last five years of the century will a positive increment emerge (of 2.0 million). It is, of course, in the Russian Federation that most of the nation's capital assets and deposits of natural resources are located. In Central Asia there will be an increment of 3.0 million in each of the three next quinquennia and even of 4.0 million in 1990–2000 and in the Caucasus 0.7 million more in every quinquennium to the end of the century.[91] These regions have a lower capital-stock per head, fewer energy and natural resources and, as Helgeson shows (p. 143), an excess of labour in agriculture.

Migration from the Caucasus and Central Asia to the principal labour-deficit area of the Russian Federation, Siberia, would solve some of the problem and the measures Helgeson describes (strengthening the organised recruitment service and increasing family allowances in areas of low demographic growth) are in this direction. Furthermore, the Plan for 1981–85 envisages pay supplements such as are already paid in the Far East and East Siberia (there are still higher supplements for the Far North) to the Urals and North Kazakhstan.[92] The inhibitions to migration are nevertheless considerable, for community in Central Asia and the Caucasus exercises a much stronger tie than is to be found in Russia or the Ukraine, and the conditions of life, including the climate, are more attractive.

Some demobilisation of the armed forces by diminishing the annual intake of conscripts could contribute to a solution, but the main channel must be the substution of capital for labour in the regions of insufficient manpower. The need for 'intensification' has long been recognised, dictated particularly by a rising ratio of capital assets to output, partly due to the exhaustion of natural resources near to the zones of established industry and the need for heavier investment per unit of product in the remoter regions. The demand for natural resources has been reinforced by a wasteful use of materials which has been fostered by poor technology and a lack of incentives for managers and technicians to economise on inputs. The norms (and the attachment of incentives thereto) which constitute so marked a feature of the 1979 reform are part of the redressment on this score.

Gains in labour productivity must also be expected in the 1980s from technical progress, but Hanson has shown in Chapter 3 that the deterioration in Soviet relations with the United States in the late 1970s and especially in 1980 (Afghanistan) and 1981 (Poland) was a setback for proponents of the purchase of technology from the West. A reaction against reliance on the West for technology is indeed apparent from 1979; its obverse, greater integration with other Comecon members, is evident from 1976 (but especially from 1981).

The allocation problem for the 1980s is thus one of severe, but not unmanageable constraints. The diminution of the labour supply in the regions where capital and resources are principally located makes growth of collective-farm investment within agro-industrial com-technology from the West to enhance that productivity will, on present indications decelerate and be inadequately replaced from within Comecon. Capital formation is nevertheless being held unusually steady – by 1985 state investment will only be 5.4 per cent larger than in 1980 (that from all sources may be a little higher because of the growth of collective-farm investment within agroindustrial complexes). Restraint on accumulation, which will fall from 24.7 per cent of NMP in 1980 to 22 per cent in 1985, frees some of the incremental product (NMP for distribution is to rise 18 per cent over the same period) for personal consumption. Evidence of the latter is the target for real income per head: since this is 16.5 per cent over the five years and population growth will be of the order of 4.0 per cent, consumption will rise 2.5 per cent faster than material product. The projected rise in 'social consumption', which counts towards 'real income per head', is still larger, 23 per cent over the five years, but as McAuley points out in Chapter 6, much of such spending is to keep pace with demographic change and there is little room for innovation in social policy. The 'social consumption fund' also provides for military requirements, but the 'accumulation fund' is proportionately to decline. Because it covers the outlay on such capital items as warships, military aircraft and defence construction works, and because demographic factors urge reduction rather than expansion of military manpower, there is no evidence within the Plan of the increase in the weight of military expenditure foreseen in US government estimates.[93]

Two resources 'outside' the economy remain to be noted. The likely gain from trade is reviewed by Hanson in Chapter 3 and is small. If account is taken of the cost of Comecon to the USSR, the balance is certain to be negative: in the first year of the Plan, above all because of the need to satisfy minimal Polish import demand, the USSR ran an export surplus of some $7300 million with Comecon ($2500 million of which went to Poland) and had to incur an import deficit of some $1300 million with the developed West.

The other 'outside' source is the country's natural resources: the exploitation of richer ore deposits (such as Udokan copper) or the discovery of a 'supergiant' oilfield (such as Samotlor) boosts output per unit of capital and labour input. The same sort of gain can arise from the more efficient use of natural resources. This chapter, therefore, concludes with some considerations on natural-resource availablity in the 1980s and, because the survey must be brief, concentrates on energy (the principal targets for which are in the summary data on the Five-year Plan in Table 8.4).

Table 8.4 Output in the 1970s and Plans for 1985

	Unit	1970	1975	1980	1981	1985 Plan
Oil[a]	Mn tonnes	353	491	603	609	630
Natural gas	Th. mn cu. m.	198	289	435	465	630
Coal	Mn. tonnes	624	701	716	704	775
Electricity	Th. mn kWh	741	1039	1295	1325	1555
Rolled steel	Mn tonnes	81	99	103	103	118
Chemicals	Index 1970=100	100	165	218	229	288
Engineering[b]	Index 1970=100	100	173	256	271	358
Consumer durables	Th. mn rbls[c]	—	22.2	27.5	27.5	38.5
Agricultural output	Th. mn rbls[d]	108	113	121	—	147
Grain	Mn tonnes	187	140	189	155[e]	239[f]
Freight transport	Th. mn t/km	3829	5201	6165	6300	6865
Passenger transport	Th. mn p/km	553	747	891	926	1029
NMP utilised	Th. mn rbls[c]	286	363	451	474	530

[a] Includes gas concentrate.
[b] Includes metal-working.
[c] At current prices (but constant prices for 1985).
[d] At 1973 prices.
[e] Estimate (no official data).
[f] Average for 1981–85.
Source: 1970, 1975, 1980 from *Narkhoz 1980, passim;* 1981 from *Ekonomicheskaya gazeta,* No. 5 (1982), 5–6; 1985 Plan from Baybakov's report to Supreme Soviet, *Pravda,* 18 November 1981.

As already mentioned (p.200) by a decree of 1980 environmental protection is the subject of a new 'norm'; 'the protection of nature' figured for the first time as a separate chapter in the Directives on the

Five-year Plan; and shadow pricing has been used to assess policies for the conservation and exploitation of minerals (particularly for energy sources) and for the ecological balance.[94] Depletion charges on producers seem, however, no nearer imposition than they were when the book to which this is a sequel was written.[95] Conservation by users has been only modestly attempted through changes in relative prices. The doubling of the retail price for motor-gasoline in 1978 (after constancy since 1947) was only a gesture – partly because it was so minimal when set against the world-market rise and partly because other domestic oil products were unaffected (the retail price of kerosine, still widely used in town and country, was in 1980 still the same as in the 1950s, as were apartment heating charges – a few kopecks a month per resident); Soviet car owners, unused to price shocks, seem nevertheless to have reduced their motoring mileage.

Whereas throughout the world big price increments pushed up the weight of energy costs, in the USSR the share of energy in enterprise and household budgets alike has actually fallen, as Table 8.5 shows. Given the known stability of prices, the comparison is testimony to

Table 8.5 Percentage Share of Energy in Outlay

	1970	1980
Industrial production	6.4	5.9
Catering	0.79	0.69
Households — industrial workers	0.3	0.1
— collective farmers	1.8	1.5

Source: Narkhoz 1970, p. 175; *1980,* pp. 153, 384–5, 436.

either conservation or quotas (or to combinations of them) but it is also evidence that the State Committee on Prices has not tried rationing by the purse. The Chairman of Goskomtsen, N. N. Glushkov, observed in 1978 that among retail prices 99 per cent of foodstuffs and 90 per cent of non-foods had not been altered for ten years or more,[96] and in 1980 that energy was the most difficult issue in the preparing of the 1982 wholesale-price reform.[97] In fact charges to enterprises for electricity and for heat were increased in advance of the reform, being effective from 1 April 1981.[98] As Table 8.6 indicates, consumption of energy per rouble of net product in 1980 was 7.4 per cent below that of 1970, a saving achieved more from reducing storage and shipment loss and use as raw material than from reducing burning for fuel.[99] The Plan Directives for 1981–85 noted this differential and made a specific point of reducing the consumption of oil as a fuel.

On the production side it is oil which, having increased by 70 per cent in the 1970s is, as Table 8.4 shows, to rise by only 4.5 per cent under the 1981–85 Plan, due partly to the difficulty of maintaining output from existing Siberian wells and partly to slowness in opening up new deposits. Natural gas, by contrast, continues its dynamism (a 2.2-fold rise in 1971–80) with a planned 45 per cent rise in 1981–85. The most prominent use in which gas is to replace oil in the 1980s is exports: the planned construction in the five years of 48,000 km of gas pipeline

Table 8.6 Aggregate Energy Consumption

	1970	*1980*
Net material product produced[a]	281.5	456.0
Consumption of energy[b]	1117.3	1676.7
Kg energy per rouble of NMP	3.97	3.68

[a] Thousand million roubles at 1973 prices.
[b] Million tonnes of coal equivalent.
Source: NMP was valued in 1970 at 1965 prices and in 1980 at 1973 prices (*Narkhoz 1978,* p. 574); to the 1973 NMP at current prices (*1978,* p. 385) an index to 1970 (ibid., p. 578) was applied to obtain 1970 at 1973 prices; index 1970 to 1980 from *1980,* p. 379. Energy consumption in coal equivalent (1 tonne = 7 mn kcal) from ibid., p. 53.
Note: My Table 11.6 in Brown and Kaser (eds), op. cit., 2nd edn, p. 285 is not precisely comparable, being in current prices, but whereas the 1976=80 Plan anticipated a rise in kg of energy per rouble of NMP, the actual experience was a decline.

includes a major undertaking from Urengoy to the western frontier which, despite strong West European opposition, is threatened by a United States technology embargo. Table 8.7 indicates how rapidly Soviet exports of energy to other Comecon members have grown: from 6.3 per cent of USSR production in 1971–75, they will become 9.4 per cent in 1981–85. Of the 980 million tonnes of coal equivalent to be supplied, oil represents 58 per cent (572 million), but this assumes fulfilment of undertakings given by the late Aleksey Kosygin to the Comecon Council in 1979 and 1980 that a 20 per cent increase in energy deliveries and a total of 400 million tonnes of oil would be delivered (that is about the same rate for 1981–85 as was sold in 1980).[100] But a pressing need for convertible currency led to some reduction of the oil supply to Comecon in 1982, as Hanson reports in Chapter 3 (p. 76).

That need to earn convertible currency underscores the earning value of oil: sales in 1979 accounted for just over 56 per cent of total Soviet export earnings to the developed West and for 34 per cent of its export earnings from all partners; gas exports in that year were a mere 5 per cent. A close investigation of the prospects for hydrocarbon exports is to be found in Hanson's Chapter 3.

In the first year of the Eleventh Plan, the hydrocarbons were on course for fulfilment of the 1985 goals – as already noted, modest for oil but large for gas – but coal output continued to regress from its record of 723 million tonnes in 1978. The problem of coal, according to Campbell, is 'getting the equipment that it needs to meet its goals of modernization and productivity growth',[101] and of opening up large

Table 8.7 Soviet Energy Production and Exports to Comecon
(million tonnes of coal equivalent)

	Output	Exports to Comecon	Percentage of output
1961–65	4150	145	3.5
1966–70	5647	260	4.6
1971–75	7128	446	6.3
1976–80	8945	815[a]	9.1
1981–85 Plan	10460	980	9.4

[a] Exports 1516.3 (imports 146.0) to all partners.
Source: References cited in my Table 11.5 in Brown and Kaser (eds), op. cit., p. 285; outputs in coal equivalent from *Narkhoz 1980*, pp. 53, 156 (and corresponding tables in previous issues); 1981–85 Plan Law; Soviet declarations to Comecon.

opencast operations in Siberia. In 1980 there were 12m kW of nuclear power capacity installed, which generated 10 per cent of electricity supply; it is on this source in the longer term that Gosplan places its reliance for the solution of its energy problem. Because of the high cost of extracting further large quantities of hydrocarbons from remote areas, and their eventual exhaustion, such a nuclear programme must be cost-effective. But in that cost no account need to be taken of the delay familiar to corresponding projects in the West, for an 'anti-nuclear lobby' is as potentially destabilising as any form of dissidence and would be repressed. That the political monopoly supports the economic is the return coupling of the articulation which, at the start of this chapter, was taken as fundamental to the Soviet system.

NOTES

1. J. R. Hicks, *A Theory of Economic History* (Oxford, 1969).
2. Very high estimates of the contribution of forced labour to the Stalinist economy have been recently made by S. Rosefielde ('The First "Great Leap Forward" Reconsidered', *Slavic Review*, 39, No. 4 (December 1980), 560–87; 'An Assessment of the Sources and Uses of Gulag Forced Labour 1929–1956', *Soviet Studies*, XXXIII, No. 1 (January 1981), 51–87). Most of his critics (ibid., 528–611, his 'Reply' is 612–15) concentrate on assessing the rate of economic growth under Stalin, but two (R. W. Davies and S. G. Wheatcroft, ibid., 593–602 and S. G. Wheatcroft, 'On Assessing the Size of Forced Concentration Camp Labour in the Soviet Union', *Soviet Studies*, XXXIII, No. 2 (April 1981), 265–95) are *inter alia* concerned with his estimate of the share of forced labour in industry and construction, which he puts at 26.7 per cent in 1940, p. 614. Wheatcroft accepts for 1939 a forced-labour total of 4 to 5 million (p. 286) and shows non-forced employment in industry, construction and transport at 23.7 million (p. 281); thus the percentage in forced labour would range from 14.4 (if 4 million) to 17.4 (if 5 million). R. Conquest, 'Some Comments', ibid., XXXIV (July 1982), 434–9, argues for the higher end of the range.
3. P. D. L. Wiles, *Economic Institutions Compared* (Oxford, 1977), pp. 273–4.
4. J. Drewnowski, *Journal of Political Economy*, 69 (August 1961), pp. 341–54.
5. L. I. Brezhnev, as reported in *Pravda*, 17 November 1981.
6. Speeches at the XXVI Party Congress to activate the official unions towards members' interests, may have been a prophylactic against the Polish movement rather than a concern at domestic dissent.
7. See also references to private farming in note 33 of Chapter 4 and note 20 of Chapter 7. The entire sphere of non-state economic bodies is being reviewed. A decree of the Presidium of the Supreme Soviet of 22 March 1978 requires codification of laws on 'voluntary societies and unions and of legislative measures on the rights of worker collectives'. In noting this, however, *Svod zakonov, SSSR*, 1 (Moscow, 1980), 345–70, reproduces only laws on trade unions (of 27 September 1971) and the collective farm (of 28 November 1969), omitting all other decrees on non-state economic bodies, for example that on prospecting teams (though promulgated openly in *Sobranie postanovlenii pravitel'stva SSSR* No. 9 (1975), 163–4).
8. *Sel'skaya zhizn'*, 18 January 1981.
9. E. Ambartsumov, *Sovetskaya rossiya*, 3 January 1982; a similar argument had just previously been published by G. Lisichkin, *Literaturnaya gazeta*, No. 52, 1981.
10. This 'inflationary gap' has prompted the diversion of consumers' goods to 'closed-access' outlets on what seems to be an increasing scale. The incomes of those without such access must figure prominently in the demand for privately furnished supplies.
11. Reported in the *Financial Times*, 17 November 1981.
12. Judging from private comments – since details are not published – informal payments for health care are now running at more than double

those for the late 1960s, as noted in M. Kaser, *Health Care in the Soviet Union and Eastern Europe* (London, 1976), p. 66.

13. This growth has been reflected in increasing awareness in the West. Among economists, the most attention has been paid by G. Grossman: see his 'The "Second Economy" of the USSR', *Problems of Communism*, XXVI, No. 5, (September–October 1977), 25–40; 'Notes on the Illegal Private Economy and Corruption', in US Congress Joint Economic Committee (JEC), *Soviet Economy in a Time of Change*, Washington DC, 1979, vol. 1, pp. 834–55. See also A. I. Katsenelinboigen, 'Coloured Markets in the Soviet Union', *Soviet Studies*, XXXIX, No. 1 (January 1977), 62–85 (who gives details *inter alia* on the paucity of commission shops and closure of second-hand markets); D. O'Hearn, 'The Consumer Second Economy: Size and Effects', ibid., XXXII, No. 2 (April 1980), 218–343; and H. W. Morton, 'Who Gets What, When and How? Housing in the Soviet Union', ibid., 235–59.

14. For the term and a seminal analysis see J. Kornai, *Economics of Shortage*, 2 vols (Amsterdam and New York, 1981).

15. V. S. Pavlov (ed.), *Gosudarstvennyy byudzhet* (Moscow, 1980), p. 279.

16. The growth of real income was planned in the original Directives for 1976–8 at 20 to 22 per cent and confirmed in the Plan Law of 29 October 1976 at 21 per cent. Using the former set of data (from *Pravda*, 7 March 1976) the SRI-WEFA Soviet Econometric Model ('SOVMOD II') showed that the other targets of the Directives would yield only an 18.3 per cent rise over the five years, D. W. Green *et al.*, 'An Evaluation of the 10th Five-year Plan Using the SRI-WEFA Econometric Model of the Soviet Union', US Congress JEC, *Soviet Economy in a New Perspective*, Washington DC, 1976, p. 308: in fulfilment, the increment was 18 per cent (*Pravda*, 5 March 1981).

17. M.A. Crosnier and G. Mink, 'Le face à face pouvoir – consommateur en URSS et en Pologne', *Le Courrier des pays de l'Est* (November 1981), 3–32.

18. *Narkhoz 1980*, p. 437 and implicit price index in *Ekonomicheskaya gazeta*, No. 5 (1982), p. 7.

19. *Vneshnyaya torgovlya SSSR v 1980g.* (Moscow, 1981), pp. 41–2: quantities imported in 1980 included 820,948 tonnes of meat and meat products, 70,088 tonnes of dried milk and 249,000 tonnes of dairy butter.

20. Tabulated by town in Crosnier and Mink, op. cit., p. 19.

21. On 1936 and 1947 see J. Chapman, *Real Wages in Soviet Russia since 1928* (Cambridge, Mass., 1963), pp. 19 and 24; and on all three A. Nove, *An Economic History of the USSR* (London, 1969), pp. 219, 305 and 308–9; prices in state shops and on collective-farm markets were brought into line in 1936–7 and again in 1948 (a parity between them which has existed at no other time in the USSR since 1928).

22. The occasion could have been taken to quote Lenin on the virtues of decreasing central economic controls, which is not of course current policy. The commemoration of an anniversary usually serves to draw a moral – see at-the-time note of the 60th anniversaries of the Soviet Afghan Treaty (*Pravda*, 19 February 1981), and of the founding of the Italian Communist Party (ibid., 17 March 1981), but there was no

mention at the time of the Anglo-Soviet Treaty of 16 March 1921. On the other hand, O. Latsis (ibid., 18 December 1980) saw merit in joint-stock companies of local authorities and state industries as under NEP; it is thought that this was to have been the first of a series, but no sequel was published.

23. G. E. Schroeder and B. S. Severin, 'Soviet Consumption and Income Policies in Perspective', in US Congress JEC, *Soviet Economy in a New Perspective* (Washington DC, 1976), pp. 627–8.

24. Crosnier and Mink, op. cit., p. 21, have gathered from the foreign press or *samizdat* a list of seven strikes in Soviet plants or towns during the twelve months from the summer of 1980 due to shortage of retail supplies.

25. *Pravda*, 28 February 1981.

26. Ibid., 17 November 1981.

27. Ibid. Delays were still being reported in applying the 1979 practices in *Pravda*, 15 February 1982, but the tone of an interview with a Deputy Chairman of Gosplan, A. V. Bachurin, in *Ekonomicheskaya gazeta*, No. 1 (1982), 2, was brighter.

28. Dated the 12th, a summary appeared in *Pravda*, 29 July 1979, and an almost full text in *Ekonomicheskaya gazeta*, No. 32 (1979), 9–16. The complete text is in *Sobranie postanovlenii pravitel'stva SSSR*, No. 18 (1979), 118ff.

29. The decree is examined by Nove in 'USSR: Economic Policy and Methods after 1970', in A. Nove, H. H. Höhmann and G. Seidenstecher (eds), *The East European Economies in the 1970s* (London, 1972), pp. 17–44, and 'The Soviet Industrial Enterprise' in Ian Jeffries (ed.), *The Industrial Enterprise in Eastern Europe* (Eastbourne and New York, 1981), pp. 29–38.

30. On the 'association' structure as established by the decree of 4 April 1973 see the present writer's Chapters 9 and 11 in A. Brown and M. Kaser (eds), *The Soviet Union since the Fall of Khrushchev*, 2nd edn (London, 1978), pp. 199–200 and 296–7, and A. C. Gorlin, 'Industrial Reorganization – The Associations', in US Congress JEC, *Soviet Economy in a New Perspective*, op. cit., pp. 162–88.

31. As *Pravda*, 5 December 1979 observed: 'The list of materials and manufactures centrally planned has been lengthened and will be stable for five years'. Bachurin, op. cit., writing just after the Plan Law had been enacted, states that in the 1981–85 Plan there are 409 types or groups of production in material balances against 234 in the 1976–80 Plan; in total, the USSR Gosplan and the USSR Gossnab have elaborated 624 balances with annual breakdowns for 1981–85. That these are, however, intended to be not just administrative manipulations of supply but reflections also of demand, is evident from his statement that the 55 balances for engineering goods 'fully reflect the attributes required by customers'.

32. *Metodicheskie ukazaniya k razrabotke gosudarstvennykh planov razvitiya narodnogo khozyaystva SSSR*, Moscow, 1974, was confirmed by a Gosplan decree of 22 April 1974 and promptly published, but its successor for the 1981–85 Plan was confirmed as late as 31 March 1980 and published only at the end of that year, when the Plan was ostensibly due to start. A commentary by M. Chistyakov, the sub-departmental chief

responsible in Gosplan, explains in *Planovoe khozyaystvo*, No. 7 (1980), 73, that this was due to the revisions required by the decree of 12 July 1979.

33. Instruction on the Procedure for Recording the Fulfilment of Tasks and Obligations for the Delivery of Products and Goods in Conformity with Agreed Contracts', *Planovoe khozyaystvo*, No. 11 (1981), 123–7.

34. Only selective quotations from the 1982 price-lists were published in advance of their introduction. The estimate here for energy prices is based on percentage increments for electric power (12), coal (42), firewood (40), and purchased heat (70) and the statement that oil and gas prices were raised by more than that for coal (p. 35); the same editorial notes that energy and raw material prices had remained almost constant since 1967 and that the 1973 review affected only engineering and consumer non-food manufactures (p. 29), 'Price Formation – an Important Component of Businesslike Management', ibid., No. 5 (1980), 29–43. An index of farm procurement prices 1965–78 is in A. Stolbov, 'Prices for Farm Produce and Incentives for Production', ibid., No. 6 (1980), pp. 92–6, and the last meeting of the Price Committee before the reform is reported in 'In the USSR Goskomtsen', ibid., No. 7 (1981), 123–5.

35. *Pravda*, 26 February 1980.

36. See Jeffries, op. cit., p. 3 and country chapters, *passim.*; J. M. van Brabant, *Socialist Economic Integration* (Cambridge, 1980), Chapter 3.

37. The rapid assimilation in the earlier Kosygin–Brezhnev period of specialised training and data-processing for management was discussed by the present writer in Brown and Kaser, op. cit., Chapters 9 and 11; a much fuller analysis has since appeared in M. Cave, *Computers and Economic Planning: The Soviet Experience* (Cambridge, 1980); and In V. V. Tolstosheev, *Avtomatizatsiya upravleniya narodnym khozyaystvom* (Moscow, 1978). The ASPR network described in each is according to the Plan Directives for 1981–85, to be 'introduced and effectively utilized' (*Pravda*, 5 March 1981). The first non-Soviet citizen to attend a graduate course in management (started in 1966) at the Plekhanov Institute observes that Soviet managers found much of the course irrelevant to their experience (S. M. Puffer, 'Inside a Soviet Management Institute', *California Management Review*, XXIV, No. 6 (Fall 1981), 90–6; I owe the reference to John Hutton of The Management College, Henley).

38. *Pravda.*, 31 March 1971.

39. *Narkhoz, 1980*, p. 121.

40. V. P. Gruzinov, *Upravlenie vneshney torgovley: tseli, funktsii, metody* (Moscow, 1975), translated by M. Vale as *The USSR's Management of Foreign Trade* (London and White Plains, NY, 1979); the conclusions of E. A. Hewett are from his 'Foreword' to that translation, p. x.

41. *Bol'shaya sovetskaya entsiklopediya*, 3rd edn, Vol. 25, p. 508. On the concept of territorial production complexes see J. Pallot and D. J. B. Shaw, *Planning in the Soviet Union* (London, 1981), pp. 72, 77–81.

42. Reference is made in Chapter 4 (and its note 23) to the endowment of many central agencies with new statutes. The legislation has conveniently been gathered in *Svod zakonov SSSR*, op. cit., and shows that, at the time

of publication, the current statutes of the Council of Ministers date from July 1978, those of ministries from July 1967, those of the main State Committees with economic functions from the second half of the 1960s (Gosplan September 1968; Gosstroi January 1968; Gossnab May 1969 and GKNT October 1966) and of local authorities from July 1981. At the lower level an innovation in the July 1979 decree was the establishment of a 'passport' linking the capacity and resources of the enterprise; the decree of 4 October 1979 is commented by Chistyakov, op. cit., p. 80.

43. Tikhonov, op. cit.

44. The emergence of the target programme is described in Cave, op. cit; for their content as defined in the 'methodology' for the 1981–85 Plan see Chistyakov, op. cit. p. 75 (who notes that they subsume 'territorial-production complexes').

45. At its Berlin Session, 7–9 July 1976, Comecon established five 'long-range target programmes' (DTsP): on energy and raw materials, on engineering, on agriculture, on consumers' goods and on transport and communications. It may be assumed that the Soviet elements in each are target programmes also for Gosplan. See also G. Schiavone, *The Institutions of Comecon* (London, 1981).

46. Pallot and Shaw, op. cit., pp. 178-80, find three forms of agro-industrial complex: state farm-factories (*sovkhoz-zavody*), agro-industrial associations (*agrarno-promyshlennye obedineniya*) and intercollective-farm enterprises (*mezhkolkhoznye predpriyatiya*): the first have a long history but their number has recently increased, the second are new, and the third emerged in the 1950s. N. Smetanin, 'The Development of the Country's Agro-Industrial Complexes', *Planovoe khozyaystvo*, No. 6 (1980), 77, states that at the beginning of 1978 there were 661 enterprises and associations of 'an agro-industrial type'; if chicken farms with a cycle complete to retail-ready stage were added the total would be 'nearly 1400'; in addition there were 124 production agro-industrial associations.

47. See note 42.

48. G. Pokaraev, 'On the introduction into Planning of a Unified System of Progressive Norms and Normatives', *Planovoe khozyastvo*, No. 5 (1980), 53–4.

49. The new system is examined from this aspect in G. Plekhov, 'On Plan Normatives and the Finance of Science and Technology', ibid., No. 1 (1982), 47–57; he points out that in 1979 56 per cent of new machine types got from documentation to experimental production in less than two years, against 52 per cent in 1970.

50. See notes 31 and 37.

51. J. H. Moore, 'Agency Costs, Technological Change and Soviet Central Planning', *Journal of Law and Economics*, XXIV (October 1981), 207.

52. Ibid., 206.

53. G. Grossman, 'Gold and the Sword' in H. Rosovsky (ed.), *Industrialization in Two Systems* (New York and London, 1966); E. Ames, *Soviet Economic Processes* (Homewood, Ill., 1965); M. Kaser, *Soviet Economics* (London and New York, 1970).

54. The share of industrial products receiving top certification is rising, but not yet very large: 7.5 per cent at the beginning of 1977 (*Pravda*, 3 May

1977) to 15.5 per cent at the beginning of 1982 (*Ekonomicheskaya gazeta*, No. 5 (1982), 5).

55. A. C. Gorlin, 'Observations on Soviet Administrative Solutions: The Quality Problem in Soft Goods', *Soviet Studies*, XXXII, No. 2 (April 1981), 163–81 (citation from pp. 177–8).

56. G. Segal and J. Baylis, 'Soviet Strategy: An Introduction', in G. Segal and J. Baylis (eds), *Soviet Strategy* (London and Montclair, New Jersey, 1981), p. 29.

57. Ibid., p. 27. Puffer, op. cit., p. 91 notes that staff from 'the military industry' attended the management course she was on.

58. D. Ross, 'Rethinking Soviet Strategic Policy: Inputs and Implications', in Segal and Baylis, op. cit., p. 135.

59. Sources cited by Ross, ibid., pp. 139–41.

60. R. L. Garthoff, 'The Soviet Military and SALT', in Segal and Baylis, op. cit., p. 166.

61. Ibid., p. 167; C. Donnelly, 'The Soviet Armed Forces since 1945 ' in *Cambridge Encyclopedia of Russia and the Soviet Union* (Cambridge, 1982), p. 441; VPK is given only as a 'pre-revolutionary' abbreviation in *Slovar' sokrashchenii russkogo yazyka* (Moscow, 1963), p. 87.

62. *Pravda*, 19 January 1977.

63. *Mirovaya ekonomika i mezhdunarodnye otnosheniya*, No. 3 (1981), 7.

64. For context, details and commentary see *L'Aggravation du dilemme défense-croissance en U.R.S.S.*, Centre d'Etudes Prospectives et d'Informations Internationales (Paris, April 1981), p. 6, and statement of Major-General R. X. Larkin and E. M. Collins, US Defense Intelligence Agency, to US Congress JEC, Subcommittee on International Trade, Finance and Security Economics, 8 July 1981, p. 93 (to be published in *Allocation of Resources in the Soviet Union and China 1981*).

65. Book by A. I. Pozharov (1981), cited by Larkin and Collins, op. cit., pp. 91–2.

66. A. Becker, 'The Meaning and Measure of Soviet Military Expenditure', in US Congress JEC, *Soviet Economy in a Time of Change*, Vol. 1 (Washington DC, 1979), pp. 352–66.

67. Ibid., p. 361. Other NATO governments do nevertheless use this technique.

68. Notably in the periodic Congressional *Hearings* published as *Allocation of Resources in the Soviet Union and China* (with year added) and special papers of its National Foreign Assessment Center (NFAC).

69. S. Rosefielde, *False Science: Underestimating the Soviet Arms Building, 1960–1980* (Transaction Press, Rutgers University, forthcoming); he ingeniously integrates much higher defence appropriations into CIA's own national product accounts.

70. F. D. Holzman, 'Are the Soviets Really Outspending the U.S. on Defense?' *International Security* (Spring 1980), 91–2.

71. A. Becker, *CIA Estimates of Soviet Military Expenditure*, Rand Corporation Report, Santa Monica, California, August 1980; and especially *The Burden of Soviet Defense. A Political-Economic Essay*, Rand Corporation Report, Santa Monica, California, October 1981, pp. 12–21, 60–1. For the CIA figures see sources in notes 15 and 44, chapter 2.

72. Nothing can be said of 1980 because in pursuance of a policy of reducing statistical information published, the wholesale price series, an essential element of Table 8.3, was suppressed from *Narkhoz 1980*.
73. D. Holloway fully demonstrates this, starting with a 1927 citation of Voroshilov, in R. Amann and J. Cooper (eds), *Industrial Innovation in the Soviet Union* (Yale University Press, forthcoming).
74. See *Narkhoz 1932*, p. 577, reporting 1927/28 to 1929/30.
75. Pavlov, op. cit., p. 39.
76. M. K. Shermenev (ed.), *Finansy SSSR* (Moscow, 1977), pp. 255–6. Both this and Pavlov, op. cit., are designated textbooks for use in finance courses.
77. I conclude this from the separation of each use into individual sentences (ibid., p. 256). It is to be noted that *Narkhoz* (e.g. *1970*, p. 536) deliberately obfuscates by terming 'expenditure on defence' in its tabulation of distributed NMP (a series since suppressed): the figures given are merely the budget entry.
78. Pavlov, loc. cit.; he does not list the Ministry of Defence or the military industrial ministries (using such innocuous examples as the Ministry of the Motor Vehicle Industry and the Ministry of Agriculture). Nevertheless, *Metodicheskie ukazanie*, op. cit. (1974), pp. 724–5, 778, lists the military industries, including investment expenditure, for 'enterprises and organizations on a special list' (*no osobomu spisku*).
79. Aircraft and vessels as listed in Table 43, 'Weapon Types Produced in 1980', in Larkin and Collins, op. cit.
80. *Narkhoz 1980*, p. 365.
81. *Narkhoz 1979*, p. 164.
82. This omission was admitted in the 1960s but not since. The tabulation of the gainfully occupied in *Narkhoz 1967*, p. 645, and *Narkhoz 1970*, p. 507, show the same figures but in the former are said to 'exclude armed service personnel and students' and in the latter merely to 'exclude students'.
83. Collective-farm members are not included in 'employment in the national economy', which is the principal manpower balance (*Metodicheskie ukazaniya*, op. cit. (1974), pp. 370–3).
84. See note 88. An expert on the Soviet budget rejects the view that non-overt defence outlay is outside the budget (R. Hutchings, 'Soviet Defence Spending and Soviet External Relations', *International Affairs*, 47, No. 3 (July 1971), p. 518); this seems confirmed by Shermenev, loc. cit.
85. See, for a recent case, statement of Lt. General E. F. Tighe, Director of the Defence Intelligence Agency, US Congress JEC, *Allocation of Resources in the Soviet Union and China, 1980*, p. 42.
86. Ibid., p. 44; the CIA figure is the same: see statement of Admiral S. Turner, Director of the Central Intelligence Agency, ibid., *1979*, p. 13.
87. Ibid., *1980*, p. 43.
88. The 4.6 million men overstates the number implicit in the US estimates because they include MVD and KGB troops, which are only within the US estimate's 'broad definition'. On the data on Soviet forces and pay in Donelly, op. cit. pp. 439 and 453 and the 'labour content' of military research (see notes to Table 8.3), I can account for 17,000 million roubles. Officers' pay is, however, lavish and could account for more. A higher

estimate does not necessarily prejudice my theory that pay is financed out of undistributed outlay, because the labour cost of research (4,900 mn roubles in 1970) is under the 'science' appropriation.

89. That such inflationary borrowing takes place has been demonstrated in a paper by Professor P. J. D. Wiles (London School of Economics) for the 1982 Conference of NASEES.

90. Wage-earners in 1980 from *Narkhoz 1980*, p. 362, but the industrial component has been another casualty of the policy of withdrawing published statistics: that quoted is for 1974 from *Narkhoz 1974*, p. 188; electricity generation from *Narkhoz 1980* p. 154, in lieu of industrial output by republic.

91. G. Baldwin, *Population Projections by Age and Sex for the Republics of the USSR*, US Department of Commerce (Washington, DC, 1979).

92. Tikhonov, op. cit.

93. Evidence to the US Congress JEC, *Allocation of Resources in the Soviet Union and China 1980*, p. 44 spoke of a rise in defence outlay from 12–14 per cent in 1979–80 to over 15 per cent in the mid-1980s; the corresponding evidence in 1981 (Larkin and Collins, op. cit. pp. 1–2, spoke of the Five-year Plan as 'opting for further growth in military strength as the standard of living of the population stagnates or even declines in some areas') is a modified formulation.

94. Intervention of L. V. Kantorovich (the Soviet Nobel Laureate for Economics) to an International Economic Association Round Table, Athens, 31 August 1981 (the Proceedings, edited by B. Csikos-Nagy and G. Hall, are forthcoming, Macmillan).

95. Kaser, in Brown and Kaser, op. cit., pp. 201–2. So dead does the issue now seem that the two most recent (and substantial) books on Soviet energy by western economists pass it by in silence (R. W. Campbell, *Soviet Energy Technologies: Planning Policy, Research and Development* (Bloomington, Indiana, 1980), and M. I. Goldman, *The Enigma of Soviet Petroleum: Half-Empty or Half-full?* (London and Boston, 1980).

96. Moscow Radio in English, 15 March 1978.

97. *Ekonomicheskaya gazeta*, No. 17 (1980); Goskomtsen had elaborated sixteen variants of energy prices before reaching a decision for the 1982 relativities.

98. Ibid.; prices for the radio and electronics industry were also raised in advance, on 1 January 1981.

99. *Narkhoz 1980*, p. 53, shows the former to have risen by 58 per cent between 1970 and 1980, the latter by 45 per cent.

100. See Goldman, op. cit., Chapters 6 and 7, and chapters by P. Hanson and A. H. Smith, in K. Dawisha and P. Hanson (eds), *Soviet-East European Dilemmas* (London, 1981).

101. Campbell, op. cit., p. 133.

Sources and Methods for Table 8.3: Outlay in 1970 in the defence estimate was communicated by an informant to the CIA (see US Congress JEC, *Allocation of Resources in the Soviet Union and China, 1976*, p. 82) and is hence taken as the sole definitive statistics. Because 1969 prices are used for the official investment series, and did not change in 1970, information is maximised by use of that year. Row 1 is the 'defence' outlay stated in the budget (*Narkhoz 1980*, p. 523), inflated by the index of wholesale prices without turnover tax for engineering and metal-working (*Narkhoz 1970*, p. 175, shows 1970 to have been identical with 1969 and *Narkhoz 1979*, p. 164, shows 1979 to have been 76.9 per cent of 1970).

Row 2 is derived as follows (thousand millions of roubles at 1969 prices) from total investment in the relevant branches:

	1970 (*Narkhoz 1970*)		1979 (*Narkhoz 1979*)	
Engineering	6.12	(p. 484)	11.10	(p. 368)
Transport	7.81	(p.483)	16.25	(p.367)
Construction	3.01	(p. 483)	5.17	(p. 367)
Non-productive n.e.s.	9.55	(p. 483)	13.00	(p. 367)
Total	26.5		45.5	
of which 'defence'	5.0		11.3	(residual)
hence 'civilian'	21.5	(residual)	34.2	

'Defence' in 1970 is the CIA estimate of investment in defence (NFAC, *USSR: Towards a Reconciliation of Marxist and Western Measures of National Income*, October 1978, p. 16) and 'civilian' in 1979 is the 1970 figure multiplied by the index of growth of all investment (59.3 per cent, *Narkhoz 1970*, p. 483, and *1979*, p. 367). Since that index is in 1969 prices it can be applied to the growth of accumulation (*Narkhoz 1980*, p. 380) of 29.8 per cent in current prices to yield an index of investment prices (1969 = 100) of 81.5. This is applied to yield a current priced figure for 1979. A fall in unit costs for military procurement is contrary to western experience and there is evidence from Soviet sources that prices of civilian engineering goods have not declined as the index states. Even so, it could be argued that if the price index is realistic, more of the decline was consequently due to military goods.

Row 3 was constructed with the advice of Dr J. Cooper (University of Birmingham), whose help on planning topics I also acknowledge with thanks. Total expenditure on 'science' in 1970 was 11.7 thousand million roubles (from *Narkhoz 1970*, p. 732) of which supplies for science were 6.8 thousand million roubles (ibid., p. 535), or 58 per cent. The CIA estimate of total military research and development for 1970 is 7.5 thousand million roubles (NFAC, loc cit.) from which 42 per cent was deducted for labour costs. The 'material' share (4.35 million roubles) was multiplied by the current-priced outlay on 'science' (44.4 per cent increase, *Narkhoz 1980*, p. 525) and inflated by the price index used in (1) above to yield 1969 prices. NMP could not be deflated because the constant price series (*Narkhoz 1980*, p. 380) is aggregated over quinquennia and no annual series appear to be available.

9 Leadership Succession and Policy Innovation

Archie Brown

Though the possibility that Soviet policies in the remainder of the 1980s will turn out to be 'more of the same' is an option which can by no means be excluded, the present decade provides two of the main preconditions for significant shifts of policy. The first is the change which will certainly take place (and which has, indeed, already begun to take place) in the composition of the top political leadership and the second is the existence of very serious problems in a number of areas of policy.[1]

Before we turn to the question of leadership change and policy innovation, and the relationship between the two, it is necessary to look first at the structure and style of Soviet political leadership in the Brezhnev era and especially during recent years (the late 1970s and beginning of the 1980s).[2] The Soviet Union has never known such a prolonged period of collective leadership as it has had under Leonid Brezhnev. It is true that Brezhnev has gradually widened the gulf in terms of status between himself and his colleagues and gradually brought more of his known supporters of many years' standing into high political office, but he has not attained more power individually than the Politburo wields collectively.[3]

It was only in 1977 that Brezhnev was able to add one of the two highest state offices to his Party General Secretaryship when he became Chairman of the Presidium of the Supreme Soviet. Nikolay Podgorny (not surprisingly, since for him it meant the loss of a prestigious post he had held for almost twelve years) opposed the move to make Brezhnev the first Party leader in Soviet history also to be head of state, and this oposition led to his removal from the Politburo as well.[4] This left only three people within the Politburo, apart from Brezhnev himself, who had been full members of it in Khrushchev's time. The fact that two of them combined Secretaryships of the Central

223

Committee and the third, the Chairmanship of the Council of Ministers, with such membership made Suslov, Kirilenko and Kosygin authoritative and influential leaders whose acquiescence in decisions had to be won rather than merely taken for granted.

The resignation and death of Kosygin, and his replacement by Nikolay Tikhonov – a founder-member of Brezhnev's Dnepropet-rovsk group[5] – undoubtedly strengthened Brezhnev's position vis-à-vis the ministerial network and added impetus to a process already under way whereby a number of changes were made in the headships of ministries. Tikhonov had earlier taken K. T. Mazurov's place in the Politburo, first as a candidate member in November 1978 with full membership following just a year later. Mazurov was but one of a number of Politburo and Secretariat members in the middle and late 1970s (Katushev in 1977 is a particularly striking example) to be asked to step aside to make room for an older man.[6]

Kosygin, though no rash or radical reformer, had unquestionably shown a stronger disposition towards economic reform than Brezhnev, who responded to those forces within the Party who feared the consequences for their authority and, indeed, power of any move towards a socialist market economy. Kosygin, moreover, had been conspicuously less fulsome in his tributes to Brezhnev on public occasions than had most of his colleagues. The Brezhnev-Kosygin relationship would appear to have been 'businesslike', rather than warm, as was indicated by the manner in which the latter's departure both from office and from this world was announced.

On 23 October 1980 Brezhnev reported to the Supreme Soviet that a letter had been received in the Central Committee the previous day in which Kosygin had asked to be released, on the grounds of his ill-health, from Politburo membership and the Chairmanship of the Council of Ministers. In advising the Supreme Soviet to accede to the latter request and to ratify the nomination of Tikhonov in his place, Brezhnev offered no word of thanks to the man who had headed the government for sixteen years, though he did put on record Kosygin's thanks to him.[7] It would, of course, have been a break with normal practice to have thanked a retiring politician. The lack of a tradition of honourable retirement in Soviet politics is such that Polituburo members, Secretaries of the Central Committee and ministers cling to office partly because if they were to leave it, it would generally be believed that they had been sacked. Thus, eventually, in many cases, their fear becomes self-fulfilling; they stay on until they are indeed dismissed. To be certain of glowing tributes to their service to the Party and state, Politburo members must die in office, as the examples in recent years of Grechko,[8] Kulakov[9] and Suslov[10] bear witness. It is probable that this has been a factor influencing Brezhnev's own decision to defy declining health and those western commentators who have a hundred times prematurely pensioned him off.

Kosygin's illness was genuine, not political, and within two months he was dead. Though he died on 18 December, the *Pravda* obituary did not appear until 21 December. Most of *Pravda*'s front page on 19 December was instead devoted to Brezhnev's seventy-fourth birthday and the award to him, for a second time, of the Order of the October Revolution. Verbatim reports of Suslov's speech in Brezhnev's honour and of the latter's reply were published. It would appear that the decision to accord Kosygin full honours on his death (for after the delayed announcement, there was an official lying-in-state of his body[11] and a prominently-reported state funeral, at which Tikhonov was the main speaker[12]) may have been taken only following representations from some of his closer colleagues.

If the replacement of Kosygin by Tikhonov added further strength to Brezhnev's already strong position within the leadership, the consequences of the death of Suslov were bound to be more ambiguous. On the one hand, the departure of such an authoritative figure may have left Brezhnev freer to promote his own candidate for the succession to the General Secretaryship; on the other hand, so long as Suslov was there and lent his support to Brezhnev (as he had done since 1964) this, taken in conjunction with the support of Brezhnev's own placemen, rendered the latter's position virtually impregnable.

Even if it were to be argued that the loss from the Politburo of both of these men with independent power bases could not but be to Brezhnev's advantage, their departure came when he was of an age and in a state of health which made it unlikely that he would adopt a more assertive style of rule, even supposing he had the disposition to do so. Moreover, events in recent years have not made it easy for Brezhnev to exercise a more vigorous role in Soviet policy. Given that he had invested much personal prestige in improved East–West relations, he could not have welcomed the developments in Afghanistan in 1978–79 and the 'anarchy' (as Soviet spokesmen saw it) in Poland in 1980–81, and may well have been a relatively reluctant interventionist in Afghanistan in December 1979 and an important advocate of restraint so far as mooted direct Soviet military intervention in Poland was concerned. Given, too, that as long ago as March 1965, Brezhnev, in a speech usually recalled in years of good harvests, had put his full weight behind the effort to raise production and productivity in Soviet agriculture and accord that sector a higher priority, it can have been of little comfort and no support to him to observe its rather dismal performance in recent years.

For these many reasons, the Soviet leadership under Brezhnev has remained collective as well as cautious. Indeed, on the basis of two not insignificant indicators, its degree of collectivity may be said to have increased in the late 1970s and beginning of the 1980s as compared with the early and middle 1970s. During the period of 255 weeks between the XXIV Congress of the CPSU in 1971 and the XXV Congress in 1976, the Politburo met 215 times and the Secretariat of the Central Committee on 205 occasions.[13] In the 259 weeks between the XXV Congress and the XXVI Congress in 1981, the Polituburo met 236 times and the Secretariat held 250 meetings.[14] On the assumption that the Politburo still ceases to meet as a body during lengthy vacation periods, the increase in the proportion of meetings, as compared with the previous five-year period, may provide support for the view that during periods of political activity there have been more twice-weekly meetings.[15] A more dramatic rise in the incidence of meetings is, however, to be found in the case of the Secretariat which held 45 more meetings than in the previous inter-Congress period, so that there were very few weeks in which a meeting of that body was not convened. It would appear to have been been the Secretariat which has provided continuity of political control during the Politburo's summer recesses. It has the advantage of being a smaller body than the latter, since Politburo meetings are attended by candidate as well as full members and by the Secretaries themselves, though only full members have a vote. The Secretariat has the further advantage that its members (ten at the time of the XXVI Congress, nine since Suslov's death) are all based in Moscow, whereas the full and candidate members of the Politburo include First Secretaries of distant republics.

One feature of the Politburo's work mentioned by Brezhnev in the Central Committee report to the XXVI Congress may represent a significant innovation, and a broadening of the base of expertise brought to bear on particular questions, though the amount of information given in the Central Committee report is insufficient for this to be asserted categorically. It has been the practice for the Secretariat of the Central Committee to organise the preparation of the agenda and of background papers for the Politburo, in the writing of which leading officials in the Central Committee apparatus have played the main part. At the 1981 Congress, however, Brezhnev noted the increasing complexity of many of the problems facing the Party leadership and went on to observe that in some cases the Politburo had created special commissions for the detailed study of and the drawing of generalisations from the phenomena in question and to facilitate the taking of the necessary practical measures (presumably by making policy recommendations).[16] It must be assumed that these *ad hoc* committees reporting to the Politburo represent something more than the familiar preparatory work done within the Central Committee building. The fact that they were mentioned by Brezhnev at the XXVI Party Congress but not on previous such occasions makes it reasonable to infer that they are a relatively recent development and that they bring in as policy consultants experts from outside (as well as inside) the ranks of the Central Committee apparatus.

The extraordinary age structure of the top Party leadership has also been conducive to collective leadership and to resistance to radical innovation. With the most important Soviet leaders men in their seventies, a sharing of the burdens of office became a matter of physical as much as of political necessity. When these same leaders were people who had taken substantial steps up the political ladder in Stalin's time, who were beneficiaries of Stalin's rule but who knew it too well to wish to see a return to the extreme insecurity for Party cadres which it entailed, who reacted no more favourably to the less lethal (but nevertheless dangerous) unpredictability of Khrushchev, it is hardly surprising that order, stability and 'tranquillity'[17] have been their watchwords and their most immediate policy goals. The leaders are of an age when it as natural for them to be set in their ways as for a child to jump over the cracks in paving-stones. They can see the dangers of every radical reform and can be reasonably confident that the way in which the Soviet Union has been governed since 1964 will suffice for their time.

Historically, a change in the topmost leadership position in the Soviet Union has opened up the way to policy innovation. Indeed, the point about the significance for policy of new leaders can be (and has been) made more generally. On the basis of an interesting and stimulating comparative study of the impact of leadership succession on public policy in a variety of states both East and West, with particular attention paid to the Soviet Union and the United States, Valerie Bunce concludes that 'new leaders mean new policies and old leaders mean the continuation of old priorities – it is almost as simple as that'.[18] What may be more different than Bunce allows for, however, is the pattern of the individual leader's power over time when the Soviet

Union is compared with the United States or Britain. Whereas American Presidents and British Prime Ministers tend to enjoy greater power and authority in the earliest period of their incumbency than after they have been in office for some years, the policy innovation which takes place in the Soviet Union in the immediate post-succession period is not a reflection of the greater power then than later of the General Secretary vis-à-vis his Politburo and Secretariat colleagues, for the General Secretary inherits a top leadership team which cannot instantly be changed. Whereas the President begins by appointing new department heads and the British Prime Minister by appointing a new Cabinet, the General Secretary has to move more cautiously and gradually in engineering changes within the Politburo and Secretariat. If the General Secretary does have a 'honeymoon' period, it is a less personal one than that enjoyed by his western counterparts (and, in particular, the American President) and more in the nature of a group honeymoon.[19]

It is not because a General Secretary's individual power is at its strongest in the earliest years of his tenure of office that much policy change occurs then, but, on the contrary, because his power accumulates so much over time that it becomes increasingly difficult for his colleagues to push through innovatory policies or for institutional interests to effect really significant shifts in priorities. Thus, it is the death or removal of a powerful General Secretary which opens up the way to policy change. Even when that person has been a 'consensus leader' as Brezhnev has been – and Stalin and Khrushchev, in their different ways, were not – there is no question but that he was to become the most powerful individual within the Politburo or that the nature of the consensus changed as he brought in more and more people with similar views to his own and with long-standing personal loyalties to him. The changes in Politburo membership between 1971 and 1980 are of particular importance in this respect.[20]

When the General Secretary, as an individual, pushes through policy changes, this tends to be after he has more firmly established his power base within the leadership. Until 1928 Stalin appeared in the garb of a 'centrist' and maintained an alliance with Bukharin and his supporters on the 'right' of the Party. It was in the period of the First Five-year Plan and the compulsory collectivisation of agriculture at the end of the 1920s and in the early 1930s that Stalin began putting his own distinctive mark on Soviet policy. Though two of Khrushchev's boldest initiatives came within three and four years of his accession to the highest Party post – the attack on Stalin in his 'secret speech' to the XX

Congress of the CPSU in 1956 and the abolition of almost all the industrial ministries, together with the creation of regional economic councils (*sovnarkhozy*), in 1957 – some of his most important policy innovations, which (as was to become clear) were far from welcome to his colleagues, occurred in the early 1960s – less than three years from his removal. Among these were his attacks in open session on Stalin at the XXII Congress in 1961 and instigation at the same Congress of compulsory fixed percentage turnovers in Party committees from the Politburo downwards, his division of regional Party bodies and soviets into organs for industry and organs for agriculture, his creation of the Committee of Party-State Control and the placing of missiles in Cuba (all in 1962). In Brezhnev's case, though he has never struck out on his own to the extent of Khrushchev, the more active pursuit of detente began only at the end of the 1960s and beginning of the 1970s[21] whereas the early post-Khrushchev years represented a change in the style of conduct, rather than policy content, of Soviet foreign policy.[22]

That having been said, it is clear that in many areas of policy important changes took place within the first few years of Khrushchev succeeding Stalin and of Brezhnev succeeding Khrushchev. But, as already noted, it does not follow that one should interpret this in terms of the new General Secretary as an individual leader being allowed a 'honeymoon period' or 'grace period'.[23] Change in the top political leadership is one of the major ways of generating policy change within political systems generally, Communist systems more particularly and the Soviet system quite specifically.[24] On this central point,[25] Valerie Bunce rightly observes that the major contenders for the top position in the Soviet Union are forced to undertake (or extend support to) fresh thinking about the major problems of the day, if only to show that they have something useful to offer the various élites whose support they hope to gain. Thus, succession can be described as 'a time of criticizing the status quo, generating new ideas and proving one's worth'.[26]

The new policies which emerged, however, in the case of the post-Stalin and post-Khrushchev successions, were, in the first place, the product of collective revulsion against, or at a minimum dissatisfaction with, the style of rule and certain of the policies of the former leader. It is especially in the 'group honeymoon' period that very important inputs into the policy process may be made by leaders other than the General Secretary; it is at this time, for example, that the Chairman of the Council of Ministers tends to play a more distinctive policy-making role. Thus, the attention to the interests of the Soviet consumer and to light industry which Khrushchev, once he had achieved ascendancy within the Soviet leadership was to make one of his own policies, was first promoted by Malenkov and opposed by Khrushchev at a time when the latter still felt it necessary to curry favour with heavy industry and military institutional interests. Similarly, the 1965 economic reform owed much more to Kosygin than to Brezhnev.

There was no agreement among Stalin's successors as to the policies which should be pursued, and the 'collective leadership' up until Khrushchev's defeat of the 'anti-Party group' in 1957 came close to consensus only on the necessity to do things differently from Stalin and, in particular, on the need to put an end to the extremes of arbitrariness which had characterised Stalin's rule and to subordinate the security forces to strict Party control. In the case of Khrushchev's successors, the early reversals of such Khrushchevian policies mentioned above as the abolition of industrial ministries, the liberty to attack Stalin and 'the period of the cult of personality', the existence of a joint Party and state organ (the Committee of Party-State Control) to check up on Party as well as state bodies, the bifurcation of the Party, and the institutionalised insecurity of tenure for senior Party office-holders embodied in the compulsory percentage turnovers on Party committees cannot convincingly be interpreted as specifically 'Brezhnev' policies since there is every reason to believe that the entire leadership was in favour of the reversal of those decisions of Khrushchev.[27] It is, moreover, a measure of Khrushchev's ability to get his way in his last years of office, notwithstanding the constraints upon his power at that time which have been given due (and perhaps more than due) emphasis in the academic literature,[28] that it was virtually the same Politburo (Brezhnev included) which formally approved the major institutional innovations of 1962 as consigned them to oblivion in 1964–66.

As a generalisation, then, it will not do to say that it is particularly in the immediate post-succession, or 'honeymoon', period that 'the new leader has the power and desire to make a change'.[29] 'Desire' and 'power' do not necessarily go together; desire and energy may indeed be at their greatest then, but study of the Stalin, Khrushchev and Brezhnev leaderships does not lead one to the conclusion that the individual power of these leaders was greatest then. It is necessary to make a distinction, often overlooked, between, on the one hand, the power and capability of the executive as a whole to introduce policy changes and, on the other, the power of the top leader vis-à-vis the rest of the executive (that is, in relation, most notably, to the Politburo,

Secretariat and Presidium of the Council of Ministers). Succession provides the top leader with the opportunity to express views and policy preferences which he had to keep to himself or, at best, express in restricted circles when serving in the Politburo of his well-entrenched predecessor, but it is in the early years especially of a new General Secretaryship that this change at the top provides somewhat similar opportunities to senior colleagues whom the General Secretary has 'inherited' rather than appointed. Succession also opens the way to policy changes through the renewal of leading cadres more generally. Ultimately, this extends to members of the Politburo and Secretariat – at which point the General Secretary's *individual* power over policy tends to reach its peak – but it may much more quickly embrace heads of departments in the Central Committee, ministers and other leading officials who also have parts to play in the policy process.

To accept this account of the early post-succession years as a time of policy innovation, though not the period of the greatest personal power of the General Secretary, does not, however, mean that Brezhnev's successor will necessarily take as long to establish a personal dominance as did Stalin, Khrushchev or Brezhnev. The style of each one of these leaders differed from that of the others and there is no reason to suppose that the next Soviet leader will replicate the style of any one of them. What he will do is to inherit a Politburo with a radically different age structure from that which has confronted any incoming General Secretary in Soviet history (unless a totally unexpected degree of rejuvenation of the top leadership were actually to precede Brezhnev's departure).

Though Lenin was Chairman of the Council of People's Commissars and not General Secretary of the Central Committee of the party, so long as he was alive his authority was greater than that of Stalin, though latterly (because of Lenin's ill-health) his day-to-day power was not. In looking, therefore, at the leadership succession precedents, it is right to consider first the Politburo just after Lenin's death. The entire Politburo[30] was aged between 40 and 44 and the average age of the membership was 42. The two oldest members were Stalin and Trotsky, both of whom were 44 at that time.

The Politburo immediately after Stalin's death on 5 March 1953 had an average age of 57. Khrushchev was 58 when he became acting first Secretary of the Central Committee on 14 March and 59 by the time he was accorded the official title of First Secretary in September of that year. Malenkov, who was Chairman of the Council of Ministers, and whose power rivalled Khrushchev's until at least 1954, was 51 when

Stalin died. Only one member of the Politburo was over the age of 70 – Voroshilov who was 72 – the second oldest being Molotov at 63.

The average age of the Politburo immediately after the removal of Khrushchev was 59 if F. R. Kozlov (who died in January 1965 but was already at the time of the leadership succession very seriously ill and taking no part in political life) is excluded from the calculation (60 if Kozlov is included). Only one member was aged over 70 – the 76-year-old Shvernik – the second oldest being Mikoyan at 68. Brezhnev was 57 when he succeeded Khrushchev.

Thus, at the time of the three previous leadership successions, the General Secretary has in each case been under the age of 60 and also within three years of the average age of the Politburo. At least one of those precedents is not going to be followed in the next succession. At the end of February 1982 the average age of the Politburo was 69. Of the thirteen full members, eight were over the age of 70 and one, the 83-year-old Pel'she, who joined the Party before the revolution, was well into his ninth decade.

Though in much western academic and press speculation about the next General Secretary the most favoured names are Politburo members already in their seventies, the arguments for choosing a younger man do not come down merely to precedent. It is one thing for a leader to continue in office until he is in his middle seventies (Brezhnev is 75) and quite another for a leader to be first appointed at such an age. Apart from the fact that such a General Secretary would in all probability lack the energy and vigour needed to tackle pressing problems, his prospective tenure would be so short that the replacement of a leader sufficiently well-entrenched to keep manoeuvring for the succession within circumspect bounds by one who would have far fewer committed supporters in vital places might lead to a much less inhibited power struggle and one which, until it in turn was resolved, could scarcely contribute coherent answers to policy problems (even if it did, along the lines Bunce has suggested, stimulate useful policy proposals and counter-proposals[31]).

Other things being equal, precedent and prudence alike would suggest that the next Soviet leader should be someone under the age of 70 and preferably under the age of 60. But, of course, other things are not equal, and there are a number of other factors of great importance to be taken into account, among which special attention must be paid to the present position, relevant experience and nationality of the potential candidates.[32]

In terms of position, there is one requirement which has been regarded as an essential prerequisite in the past and which is an important one both in terms of gathering support in the most vital quarters and from the standpoint of relevant experience. It is usually overlooked by western observers[33] though its structural significance should be immediately apparent. That is the desideratum that the incoming General Secretary should already combine full membership of the Politburo with a Secretaryship of the Central Committee. Stalin in 1924, Khrushchev in 1953 and Brezhnev in 1964 were all members both of the Politburo and of the Secretariat when they succeeded to the leadership.[34] This is a logical requirement for the General Secretary who, as his title suggests, is head of the Secretariat as well as chairman of the Politburo.[35] Apart from the desirability of his having gained experience of the workings of both bodies, there is a sufficiently strong sense of hierarchy within the Soviet political establishment to make it difficult either for someone who has attended the Politburo in a non-voting capacity (as a candidate member or as a Secretary of the Central Committee) to leapfrog over the entire full membership into the chairman's seat or for someone who (albeit a full member of the Politburo) has never attended the weekly Wednesday meetings of the Secretariat to turn up for the first time in the capacity of General (that is leading) Secretary.

So far as experience more generally is concerned, the ideal candidate for the General Secretaryship will have served as a Party secretary at various levels and have a thorough knowledge of how Party organisations should be run. So far as policy is concerned, his future responsibilities make it highly desirable that he should have knowledge and experience of foreign and economic policy, including agriculture. If he has some experience of a state as well as a Party post, so long as his career has preponderantly been on the Party side of the hierarchy, that may be counted an advantage. Of the three General Secretaries who have been the supreme leaders in the Soviet Union over the past six decades, Brezhnev's career profile fits these desiderata most perfectly. Though he came up through the Party secretarial hierarchy and had experience in both industrial and agricultural areas, he also served as Chairman of the Presidium of the Supreme Soviet from May 1960 until July 1964 and so was taking back the formal headship of state he had once held when he added it to his General Secretaryship of the Party in 1977. The significance of Brezhnev holding that office in the period before he acceded to the Party leadership was that it brought him into contact with foreign statesmen and gave him a closer acquaintance with foreign policy than that attained by the average member of the Politburo.

Such direct responsibilities in the foreign policy area are far, however, from being a *sine qua non* for the aspiring General Secretary. The point is that every conceivable candidate for the General Secretaryship gains some inside knowledge and experience of foreign policy simply by reading the papers attached to his Politburo agenda and by attending Politburo meetings. There is no reason to doubt, and ample evidence to support, Brezhnev's statement to the XXV Congress of the Party in 1976 that 'a large place in the work of the Politburo' is occupied by questions of foreign and defence policy.[36] Politburo members also have personal assistants and, if they so desire, may get briefings on foreign policy issues from them. The most cautious observer of the Soviet political scene would be hard put to produce a short-list for the General Secretaryship longer than the combined membership of the Politburo (full and candidate members) and the Secretariat of the Central Committee – twenty-four people (excluding Brezhnev himself as the current incumbent) as of February 1982. Any one of these two dozen men, by his attendance over a period of years at Politburo meetings, acquires an inside knowledge of, and some collective responsibility for, foreign policy. That is more than can be said of the office of Governor of Georgia or even of governor of California. Cabinet systems and 'Politburo systems' have in common the feature that before a person reaches the office of Prime Minister or General (or First) Secretary, that person has almost invariably held Cabinet or Politburo rank under another Prime Minister or General Secretary and so been privy to the highest-level foreign policy discussions. It is in the United States, rather than in the Soviet Union, that a person can become chief executive without any such experience, so that there is something a little odd about American commentators on the Soviet leadership succession problem ruling out (as often happens) this or that member of the Politburo on the grounds that he lacks sufficient background in foreign affairs.

Nationality is the other main factor, in addition to age, present position and career profile, which has a bearing on the chances of possible contenders for the Party leadership. There has only been one non-Russian top leader in Soviet history even when one includes Lenin as well as Khrushchev and Brezhnev and, taking account of the ambiguous power relations of 1953–54, adds for good measure Malenkov. But the single example of Stalin (a Georgian) is hardly the happiest precedent to fall back on. It is the less likely to be followed at a time when Russian national feeling has been growing in strength, and however much the Soviet leadership must pay attention to the sensibilities of other nationalities within the Soviet Union, that already disproportionately Russian leadership[37] can hardly afford to risk a diminution of its authority in the eyes of the Russian people who still (albeit only marginally) comprise more of the Soviet population than all other nationalities put together.

If one looks at existing members of the Politburo in terms of position, career experience, age and nationality, several members can be ruled out as possible General Secretaries – Pel'she, Tikhonov and Kunaev on a number of grounds, including age (especially of the first two) and nationality, and Gromyko on grounds of age but, still more, because of his exclusive background in international diplomacy and lack of any Party organisational experience. Of the remaining nine members of the Politburo – a long 'short-list' which is, of course, liable to change the longer Brezhnev remains in office – V. V. Shcherbitsky, the First Secretary of the Ukraine, has in some respects the right kind of career profile and at 64 is below the Politburo average age but he has neither experience as a Secretary of the Central Committee nor is he a Russian and would be a most surprising choice. G. V. Romanov has both age and nationality on his side. At the age of 59 as of 1982, he is the only Politburo member in the same age band as Khrushchev and Brezhnev at the time they took over the leading Party post. It is unlikely, however, that he could move straight from his Leningrad regional party secretaryship to the General Secretaryship without first acquiring experience and support (which at the moment he appears to lack) in the Secretariat of the Central Committee in Moscow. Moreover, the precedents are not encouraging for a Leningrader to reach the top Party post, though it is true that Romanov, as a candidate member of the Politburo from 1973 and full member since 1976 (and member of the Presidium of the Supreme Soviet since 1971) has accumulated significant experience within the collective leadership in Moscow.

The three other Politburo full members who do not hold Secretaryships of the Central Committee cannot be ruled out as possible Brezhnev successors. One, Dmitriy Ustinov (born 1908) is conceivable, however, only as a stopgap General Secretary. He has age against him, but he has in the past served as a Secretary of the Central Committee, office he had to give up when he was given the no less important post of Minister of Defence in 1976. He has experience of both the Party and state side of the higher echelons of Soviet politics and throughout virtually his entire career has been concerned with defence industry and defence-related matters.

More plausible candidates, if only because they are six years younger, are Yuriy Andropov and Viktor Grishin (both born 1914). Andropov, regarded as one of the abler members of the Politburo, has extensive Party secretarial experience, including the period 1962–67 as a Secretary of the Central Committee. During the years 1953–57 he was Soviet Ambassador to Hungary which gave him a foretaste of large-scale East European crises. His position since 1967, as Chairman of the KGB, can virtually be regarded as both a Party and state post, since though the KGB has membership of the Council of Ministers and is thus formally part of the ministerial network, it is – to a higher degree than in the past – responsible essentially to the Party leadership. By definition, his institutional position gives Andropov exceptional knowledge both of foreign and domestic problems and policies. It is probable, however, that his long occupancy of this post will be seen as a potential complication for a General Secretary in his dealings with foreign statesmen and the view may well be taken that the image of Soviet policy projected by such an appointment would be a damaging one. Though it is wrong in this instance to infer from his KGB Chairmanship that Andropov is the hardest-line of Soviet leaders (even if that has often been true in the past of Soviet security police chiefs), his fifteen-year occupancy of his current post, while not ruling him out of contention, probably does more harm than good to his chances.

It is arguable that if a contender for the General Secretaryship cannot be both a full member of the Politburo and a Secretary of the Central Committee, then the next best thing is to combine Politburo membership with the First Secretaryship of the Moscow city Party organisation.[38] It is that combination of posts, together with the fact that he has extensive experience in the leadership (candidate member of the Politburo from 1966, full member from 1971, member of the Presidium of the Supreme Soviet from 1967) while being (at 67 in early 1982) below the Politburo average age, which puts Grishin in the running. He is, however, one of the less educated and more conservative Politburo members, and not close to Brezhnev.

One of the great imponderables is whether closeness to Brezhnev will turn out to be a strength or a weakness. Given the extent to which Brezhnev has over a period of years succeeded in placing known supporters in high places, and given the more recent deaths of Kosygin and Suslov, he should, in principle, be very well placed to influence, if not determine, the choice of his successor. But though Brezhnev himself was given the kind of career experience by Khrushchev which made him virtually the heir apparent, no Soviet leader thus far has been able to determine the choice of his successor when the moment for decision came. Moreover, when they succeeded to the Party leadership, Khrushchev and Brezhnev, in turn, found it desirable and expedient to dissociate themselves from the leadership style, and many of the policies, of their predecessors. If, however, Brezhnev were to be dismissed from the pages of Soviet history to the extent that his two predecessors were, this would, to say the least, call into question the collective wisdom of the highest echelons of the Party in permitting successive deficient leaders to occupy the top post for some sixty years.[39] An 'unpersoning' of Brezhnev might provoke dangerous questions about the legitimacy of the system. Without going so far, however, Brezhnev's successor may well feel the need to distance himself from him if only to respond to the feeling that the time has come for changes in leadership style and for new policies and to disclaim responsibility for policy failures under Brezhnev, such as the continued food (especially meat) shortages outside the major cities and the deterioration, rather than improvement, in international relations during recent years, even though the Soviet Union's pro-claimed goal has still been that of détente.

As was noted earlier, General Secretaries up until now have already been full Politburo members and Secretaries of the Central Committee at the time when they attained the top Party post. That is but one reason for paying special attention to the three members of the Politburo not discussed thus far in the context of the leadership succession, the only people apart from Brezhnev who combine Central Committee Secretaryship with voting membership of the Politburo. Of these three, the one who has most frequently been seen as the next General Secretary is Andrey Kirilenko; the second most canvassed name is that of Konstantin Chernenko; and the one whom no western observer thus far seems to have suggested as Brezhnev's immediate successor is Mikhail Gorbachev. Though conjecture in this area cannot but remain tentative at a time when it is probable that not all members of the Soviet selectorate have made up their own minds about the succession and when, indeed, they cannot count on still being in the Politburo and able to exercise their vote when the moment for decision comes, there are grounds for believing that this conventional ranking order of potential candidates should be reversed.

All three of these men are Russians, but Kirilenko and Chernenko can be assumed to have Ukrainian ancestry since they have Ukrainiansounding names. There are Soviet citizens who believe that this in itself somewhat damages their prospects since most Russians do not consult such reference books as *Deputaty Verkhovnogo Soveta SSSR*[40] and assume they are Ukrainians. To this it may be objected that the General Secretary of the Central Committee of the CPSU is not elected on the basis of universal adult suffrage. If only at the margin, however, anticipated popular reaction is one of the factors which Politburo members who make the choice are likely to bear in mind. So long as Tikhonov, a real Ukrainian (though with a Russian-sounding name), is Chairman of the Council of Ministers, the appointment of either of them would be unlikely, though it must be added that it is improbable that Tikhonov's occupancy of that position will outlast Brezhnev's tenure as General Secretary.

In other respects, Kirilenko and Chernenko have different political strengths and weaknesses. They are sometimes put in the same category as Brezhnev 'clients', but in fact Kirilenko, like Brezhnev, owes his rise into the Party leadership to Khrushchev. He became a candidate member of the Politburo[41] in 1957 (when Khrushchev brought in his own supporters to replace members of the 'anti-Party group') and has been a full member since 1962. This puts Kirilenko in a very different position from that of Chernenko who is a Brezhnev client *par excellence*. Having worked in the apparatus of the Central Committee of the Moldavian Communist Party as head of its department of propaganda and agitation from 1948–56, Chernenko (as his subsequent career was to demonstrate) established excellent relations with Brezhnev in the period when the latter was First Secretary of the Moldavian Central Committee (1950–52). When Brezhnev became a Secretary of the Central Committee (for a second time[42]) in 1956, Chernenko was made a sector head in the Agitprop department of the Central Committee at all-Union level, and when Brezhnev was translated to the Chairmanship of the Presidium of the Supreme Soviet in 1960, Chernenko moved there too as head of the Presidium's (and thus Brezhnev's) secretariat. On his accession to the General Secretaryship[43] in 1964, Brezhnev lost little time in availing himself of the services of Chernenko. In 1965 Chernenko became head of the General Department of the Central Committee (the nearest Soviet equivalent to the Cabinet Secretariat in Britain) and, accordingly, the Central Committee official who works most closely of all with the General Secretary. Promotion of Chernenko into the highest Party elected organs (which in reality, of course, are the subject of collective co-option) was a less straightforward process, since it required a higher level of support from a sufficient number of colleagues in the leader-ship. It was only in 1976 that Chernenko became a Secretary of the Central Committee, followed by candidate membership of the Politburo in 1977 and full membership in 1978.

Kirilenko, in addition to his much longer service in the Politburo and Secretariat, has been, and remains as of early 1982, the Secretary in day-to-day charge of the Party organisation, the very position Brezhnev held at the time he succeeded Khrushchev and, other things being equal, an important base from which to build support in a leadership contest. What is not equal in Kirilenko's case, however, is age. He was born in 1906, four months earlier than Brezhnev, and there would be something more than a trifle absurd about replacing the present General Secretary by an older man with little in the way of fresh thinking to offer. Even prior to his long experience at the top of the Party hierarchy (twenty-five years of attendance at Politburo meetings, sixteen years as a Secretary of the Central Committee), Kirilenko had the kind of career background appropriate to the top leadership post, having come up through the Party secretarial hier-archy. It is this long and relevant experience, together with the significance of his current post, which gives him still an outside chance of being an interim General Secretary while more time is allowed for the 'real' successor to Brezhnev to emerge.

Chernenko's career profile is less impressive from a leadership succession standpoint than Kirilenko's. It is doubtful whether many of his colleagues in the Politburo believe that what they most require in a leader is long experience as a propagandist and chief clerk. Cher-nenko's extremely close connection with Brezhnev is also a double-edged sword. On the one hand, it gives him his only chance of suc-ceeding to the top post. He has been pushed into prominence by Brezhnev in recent years, and has been increasingly seen at inter-national gatherings. If Brezhnev were to deploy all the authority at his disposal to make Chernenko General Secretary, it is possible that he might succeed. Chernenko is five years younger than Brezhnev and Kirilenko and from that point of view at least a more plausible interim leader than the latter. Yet given that he was born in 1911, age is hardly, in a more general sense, on his side, and he is very dependent on Brezhnev voluntarily handing over the reins of power at a time when the General Secretary is still physically and politically strong enough to have a large say in determining into whose hands they will be thrust. This could, indeed, happen but it would be rather surprising and certainly unprecedented. Even if Chernenko were to succeed

Brezhnev, the fact that he has faithfully echoed Brezhnev's policies for so long and has no Party standing independently of him would make it difficult for him not only to provide a different kind of leadership and new policy initiatives but to survive long in the leadership once his patron was no longer in a position to protect him.[44] Given that the next General Secretary may find it necessary to put some distance between himself and Brezhnev's style and policies, it must be said that Chernenko is in an especially weak position to do that.

This leaves Mikhail Gorbachev. Since Gorbachev is by a very wide margin the youngest member of the Politburo (he was born in 1931) and is twenty years younger than anyone else who combines Politburo membership with a Secretaryship of the Central Committee, and since, furthermore, he has been in the leadership for a shorter time than almost all of his colleagues – becoming a Secretary of the Central Committee in November 1978, a candidate member of the Politburo exactly a year later and a full member of the Politburo in October 1980 – he has attracted little or no attention as a potential successor to Brezhnev. Yet he is in a number of respects the most obvious choice. There is, of course, many a slip 'twixt cup and lip in Soviet politics, and over the past decade ambitious younger men within the leadership have proved to be even more vulnerable to sudden demotion than their elders, but Gorbachev's career and qualifications are impressive in Soviet terms and worth rather more detailed examination than that of the other contenders.

Gorbachev, on leaving school, became an agricultural worker attached to a Machine-Tractor Station. He was apparently an exemplary worker, for he stood out among fellow-students at Moscow University in the early 1950s by virtue of the fact that he wore the insignia of the Order of the Red Banner.[45] Few Soviet students have already gained such a distinction and, for that matter, not so very many early school-leavers from the Russian countryside enter the Law Faculty of the Soviet Union's most prestigious university. Yet when Gorbachev became a full-time student, at the beginning of the 1950s, he was scarcely any older than those who had had a complete pre-university schooling.[46] Gorbachev, who is remembered by some of his contemporaries at Moscow University as being both able and open-minded, joined the Party while a student (in 1952, a year before Stalin's death) and went into the apparatus of the Komsomol after graduating. He became First Secretary of the Stavropol' City Komsomol organisation and began a speedy rise through the Komsomol and Party organisations of Stavropol' city and region which saw him attain the position of First Secretary of the Stavropol' regional Party committee by the age of 39.

During his period in the Party apparatus, he acquired experience overseeing both industry and agriculture, but it was agriculture (the sector in which he had early experience as a manual worker) which he made his speciality, adding to his Moscow University law degree an agricultural degree from the Stavropol' Agricultural Institute. When he became First Secretary of the Stavropol' *kraykom*, he was following in the footsteps of both Suslov and Fedor Kulakov who had each held that regional Party secretaryship and for whom it represented a major regional base. Clearly, it was Kulakov, who vacated the Stavropol' regional First Secretaryship in 1964 to become head of the agriculture department of the Central Committee and from 1965 a Secretary of the Central Committee, who was Gorbachev's most immediate patron, but it is likely that he received support also from Suslov. The very fact that the sudden death of Kulakov in 1978[47] led not to a setback in Gorbachev's career but to his entry into the central Party leadership indicates that his record had come to the attention of, and had favourably impressed, other powerful members of the Politburo. That he was then accorded Kulakov's Secretaryship of the Central Committee (with responsibility for Agriculture) and that within two years he was a full member of the Politburo, while retaining his Secretaryship, indicates how quickly he made a very significant impact indeed.[48]

Gorbachev's position could, perhaps, be regarded as vulnerable on two counts. First, the fact that agriculture has proved to be such an intractable problem in the Soviet Union and has performed badly in the most recent past might well be held against him. Against this it may be argued that nothing short of the powers of the General Secretaryship enable a Soviet leader to do anything drastic about agriculture (and even then Khrushchev and Brezhnev did not find it easy to get their way on agricultural policy) and, furthermore, that there are straws in the wind to suggest that Gorbachev is thinking seriously about reform in this area (a point which will be touched upon when agriculture is discussed briefly below). The second possible source of vulnerability arises from the death of Suslov. How important Suslov's support was to Gorbachev only time will tell. It is worth recalling that Gorbachev's immediate patron, Kulakov, was close also to Brezhnev. It is evident, too, that Gorbachev has connections in more than one quarter. John Hazard has noted in Chapter 4 that his very presence in the Politburo is welcomed by jurists and taken by them to mean that 'they now have an advocate at the very top'. His presumed attachment to legality and his opposition to arbitrariness may seem incongruous when placed alongside the fact that he was one of four members of the Politburo who signed the *Pravda* obituary in January 1982 of S. K. Tsvigun, the First Deputy Chairman of the KGB, and (unlike its Chairman, Andropov) a member of the security police since 1939.[49] However reform-minded in certain areas a prospective General Secretary may be, he would, however, have little chance of reaching the top post if regarded as unsound by such important interests as the security police and the military. It should not, therefore, be assumed that the jurists' hopes are entirely misplaced; it is rather that any conceivable General Secretary at the present time is going to continue to see the KGB as a necessary instrument of the Party's goals and that a further strengthening of legal norms as compared with Stalin's time is likely to be accompanied by a continued commitment to the use of coercion against political opposition (broadly defined).

On leadership succession and policies there are two more general points to be made. The first is that it is impossible to predict in detail what a prospective Soviet Party leader's policies will be if and when he attains that office not only because that would presuppose knowledge of the balance of pressures and constraints upon him in the post-succession stage but also because on his way up the Party hierarchy and in his attempts to make a favourable impact on the most powerful individuals and institutional interests, he has to temper any innovative zeal with reassurance that he is sound on fundamentals. Once a person has the political resources of the General Secretaryship at his disposal, his political style and policy preferences become much more readily apparent. It would have been difficult, if not impossible, to predict before 1953 that the ardent Stalinist, Khrushchev, would take the lead in demythologising and criticising Stalin.

The second general point is that whoever succeeds Brezhnev – whether Gorbachev or anyone else – changes in Politburo and Secretariat membership cannot but follow much more quickly than they did when Brezhnev succeeded Khrushchev. The age structure of the top leadership is, as was noted earlier, totally different from that at the time of any previous succession and this provides opportunities for a new General Secretary more rapidly to promote like-minded people from among his associates. With such an almost total change in the composition of the top leadership in prospect during the present decade, it is likely that the posts of Chairman of the Presidium of the Supreme Soviet and General Secretary of the Central Committee of the CPSU will be separated again when Brezhnev goes, in spite of the plausible arguments adduced in favour of the Party leader being also head of state at the time when Brezhnev assumed the latter position.[50] It seems improbable that an incoming General Secretary will be handed two of the three most prestigious positions 'on a plate', and if the General Secretary of the CPSU, the Chairman of the Council of Ministers and the Chairman of the Presidium of the Supreme Soviet are indeed to be three different people again, this would mean – as is usual in the early stages of a General Secretaryship – that there would be significant counterweights to the General Secretary within the new leadership. At the same time, there is little reason to doubt that the person who attained the top Party post, assuming he was young and vigorous enough, would be able to establish a dominant position vis-à-vis the others and to achieve this more quickly than in the past.

The link between leadership change and policy change is likely to be especially clear in the Soviet Union in the 1980s because of the seriousness of the problems confronting the new leadership, the more so since many of the problems have been the object of only tinkering, piecemeal reforms on the part of the present elderly leaders. In concluding this chapter with a very brief survey of some of the problem areas in Soviet policy which have already been discussed in greater depth in the chapters of the other contributors to this volume, I should make clear that such an emphasis does not imply that western countries do not also face severe problems. In some cases they are the same. If international tension has increased, that is a problem for western states as much as for the Soviet Union. In other cases, they are quite different. The high unemployment of the early 1980s in the United States and Western Europe is not reproduced in the Soviet Union; it is, however, possible to buy meat in any part of the United States, Britain or France. In yet other cases, the problems are somewhat similar but may have different consequences. An important example is the slowdown in economic growth in the Soviet Union. By international standards even the declining Soviet growth rate is by no means as bad as the economic performance in this respect of a number of western countries. The effect on the Soviet political and economic systems of a growth performance as poor, say, as that of Britain in recent years might, however, be much more drastic than the impact on the British system.[51]

A combination of rising expectations and rising money incomes has put enormous pressure on the supply side of the Soviet economy, especially where foodstuffs are concerned. Complaints in private conversation about food shortages are an increasingly prominent feature of Soviet life and if this seems surprising in the light of the 50 per cent increase in agricultural production between 1960 and 1980 noted by Alec Nove in Chapter 7, it is less so in the light of Nove's observation that money wages have risen by about 70 per cent in the same period and that when the higher incomes of collective-farm peasants are taken into account, there has been an approximate doubling of total money incomes in the past twenty years. During that same period, moreover, the price of basic foodstuffs has remained unchanged. The nettle of pricing policy is one which the present Party leadership has scarcely begun to grasp, but given that agriculture is absorbing 27 per cent of total investments (Nove, Chapter 7) and that the enormous element of subsidy in the prices of meat, milk and dairy products alone accounts for more than 9 per cent of total budgetary expenditure (as Alastair McAuley observes in Chapter 6), it is difficult to see how a new Soviet leadership can continue to add to the agricultural subsidy year by year for the rest of the decade in a period of substantially reduced economic growth.

Agriculture is, however, one area of policy where (as Alec Nove, John Hazard and Michael Kaser have already indicated in this volume) there has been some movement in Soviet policy over the past few years. Not only has there been more support for private farming, but much stronger support in *Pravda* (though it is not yet by any means an adopted policy) for granting substantially greater autonomy and initiative in the organisation and schedules of their work to farmers – the *beznaryadnoe zveno* discussed by Nove in Chapter 7. It is, perhaps, pertinent to observe that this greater support for the private sector in farming and increasingly open-minded and sympathetic consideration of the *zveno* (or link) system in agriculture has occurred since Gorbachev joined the top Party leadership team as Secretary of the Central Committee responsible for agriculture. It is also worth adding that the Central Committee report delivered by Brezhnev to the XXVI Congress of the Party contained for the first time in such an authoritative Soviet source explicit praise for Hungarian agricultural arrangements.[52] Nove has drawn attention in this volume to some of the advantages of the Hungarian agricultural reform and has rightly pointed to the weight of resistance to such radical measures likely to be found within the Soviet bureaucratic establishment. Commendation for precisely this sector of the Hungarian economy in the Central Committee report to the Congress could hardly, however, have appeared without the approval of the Secretary responsible for agriculture and, given that the compilation of the General Secretary's report for these occasions is very much a collective effort, it is not unreasonable to conjecture that the passage was inserted on Gorbachev's initiative. In the same section of his speech, Brezhnev praised aspects of economic policy in several other East European states and concluded with an admonition to the delegates to 'study the experience of the fraternal countries more closely and utilise it more widely'.[53] It is far from clear, though, whether Brezhnev has any strong personal commitment to translating such sentiments into action or the physical or intellectual energy required to pursue a major reform at this stage in his career. It is a matter which is likely still to be on the agenda when the next General Secretary takes office.

Many other economic problems and dilemmas will take their place alongside it. 'The unreformed economic system', in the judgement of Philip Hanson (Chapter 3) 'performed relatively poorly in commercially acquiring, assimilating and diffusing Western technology.' How large a place trade with the West should be accorded in Soviet policy remains an open question, for, as Hanson points out, it has an important political as well as economic dimension. On this reading, trade with Western Europe or with Japan is not an adequate substitute for trade with the United States, even if desired as a complement to it. It is, as he observes, possible that 'Kissingeresque arguments' are not without appeal in Moscow and that when the idea of trade creating 'a vested interest in mutual restraint' is aired there, it is trade with the United States which is accorded the highest degree of political importance.

Both John Hazard and Michael Kaser point to another problem which has serious political and social as well as economic implications – the rise in economic crime. It is not only that the 'second economy' becomes ever more important in the Soviet Union, but that serious economic crime, including bribery and corruption, is apparently on the increase. A new leadership might well adopt an even more vigorous 'law and order' line than that proclaimed, and in some measure acted on, by the present leaders in recent years. Whether they will tackle some of the more systemic deficiencies of the Soviet economy which provide fertile soil for economic crime is more doubtful. As Kaser notes, some of the theft of state property is of goods which the individuals involved would buy if only they were available for sale. While there would appear to be considerable support among the intelligentsia for moves towards a socialist market economy, there are powerful vested interests who do well out of the present system of administrative allocation and who have no such interest. The Party apparatus, the military and the security police are but the most powerful agencies who may broadly be placed in that category. What might change the attitude of the Party leadership and even of the military (who, ultimately, could not flourish in a declining economy) would be a continuation of economic setbacks on a scale which meant (in the words of Seweryn Bialer) that a policy of 'muddling through' became synonymous with a 'muddling down'.[54]

The issue of equality, in both its legal and social aspects, has been raised by two contributors to this volume. John Hazard has predicted that Soviet citizens will achieve a greater equality before the law in the course of the decade and sees the legal profession as being prepared increasingly to combat bureaucratic arbitrariness on the part of state officials, even if they have to tread much more carefully when dealing with Party officials. Alastair McAuley, in contrast, predicts no dramatic move towards greater social equality in the Soviet Union in the period until 1990 'in the absence of civil unrest'. Those in the Soviet Union who would like to see more attention paid not only to legal norms but to the law of supply and demand are not usually, in an economic sense, egalitarians. It can be argued, however, that a Hungarian-style economic reform where goods are available at something approximating a market price in the shops and, at the same time, the problem of poverty is faced more squarely than in the USSR and social services directed at those most in need, is at least as consistent with the promotion of a greater socio-economic equality as the Soviet system of veiled inequalities in the distribution of foodstuffs, consumer goods and services. The extent, it may be added, to which more fortunately-placed Soviet citizens now place orders for their weekly shopping at their workplace – and the higher the office they occupy, the better the selection available – could in time become a significant source of social tension, even if it lacks the immediate impact of a sharp price rise in the shops.

Two persistent, and interconnected, problems on the Soviet political agenda – and ones likely to remain there not just for the rest of the decade – are the demographic question and the nationalities issue. Increasingly serious attention has been paid, as Ann Helgeson has documented in Chapter 5, to the elaboration of a demographic policy, but Helgeson sees little sign of the policies adopted thus far being successful in producing population growth where it is economically most needed or, alternatively, of change in economic policy which adapts to the growth prospects and distribution of the population. The Party leadership, anxious to attract workers from labour-surplus areas to Siberia and for them to remain there, is aware that higher wages alone are not the answer[55] and Soviet scholars are being urged to adopt an interdisciplinary approach to the study of demographic problems.[56]

In his broad survey of trends and problems within the Party, John Miller, in Chapter 1, pinpoints the related ethnic question as the one which is turning out to be the most intractable problem for the 'Party managers'. The Party response to ethnic pressures has, he observes, varied remarkably from one republic to another[57] and in some cases a declining proportion of Russians in the republican Party (as in Georgia, Azerbaydzhan, Kazakhstan and Uzbekistan) may well be linked with a greater assertiveness on the part of the titular nationality within those republics and the decline in the strength and standing there of Russians. One reaction of the Party leadership to this, as Miller's analysis of the composition of the new Central Committee brings out, would appear to be a somewhat defensive but also deliberate bolstering of the centre against the periphery. Not only did the representation of the Central Committee of the CPSU apparatus show a significant increase from 6.3 to 9.4 per cent of the elected Central Committee membership, but the overall expansion of that membership produced a significant reduction in regional representation as part of an attempt, Miller suggests, 'to curb the influence at the centre of regional lobbies'.

Finally, and perhaps the most important of all the problems facing the present leadership and their successors, is the entire area of foreign and defence policy surveyed by David Holloway in Chapter 2. The enormous concern felt by the Soviet leadership in the face of events in Poland in 1980–81 was reflected in Brezhnev's report to the Party Congress which spoke of the 'pillars of the socialist state in Poland' being 'in jeopardy'.[58] While the imposition of martial law in December 1981 was a vast improvement, in Soviet eyes, on what had gone before, it scarcely contributed to the long-term betterment of Polish-Soviet relations, and while Eastern Europe, especially in the (very different) shapes of Hungary and the GDR, sometimes provides inspiration for Soviet policy-makers, it creates at least as many headaches (including a major crisis approximately once a decade) and has become a net economic liability at a time when the Soviet Union cannot afford to be indulgent in the dispensation of largesse. Other aspects of Soviet foreign relations give no less cause for concern. As Holloway observes: 'Soviet policy in the decade of detente has drawn the Soviet Union's adversaries closer together; and this must be considered a major failure of policy'. The fact that the USA, China and Japan have established much better relations with each other than any one of them has with the Soviet Union is, indeed, a failure on a sufficient scale to force some hard thinking on foreign policy, and no doubt some new initiatives, when the leadership succession takes place. It is doubtful whether the present top leadership, having failed to do so thus far, could establish relations of trust with the United States or China, but a younger successor to Brezhnev will start off with some advantages and it would be surprising if a serious effort to improve relations with both the United States and China were not to be undertaken. The change in Chinese domestic policy since the death of Mao has removed at least one of the impediments to improved Sino-Soviet relations and progress in that direction (though falling far short of a relationship of complete trust and co-operation) must indeed be counted a realistic possibility when the battle-scarred, elderly leadership on both sides passes on. Foreign policy is almost certainly an area in which contention and pressures to move in not wholly compatible directions will become a significant feature of the early post-Brezhnev period.

One of the reasons why leadership change leads to policy innovation is that particular leaders acquire a vested interest in the correctness of a line they have long taken and in persistence with a policy they have long supported. This applies also to officials below Secretary of the Central Committee or ministerial rank who do, nevertheless, make significant inputs to the policy process in particular areas. The head of the China desk in the Ministry of Foreign Affairs, M. S. Kapitsa, may serve as a case in point. Kapitsa (who has published numerous articles and books on China) has taken an anti-Chinese line for so long that it is very difficult to imagine him playing a constructive role in the improvement of Sino-Soviet relations. Indeed, inasmuch as such improved relations might well lead to his replacement by an official without a long record of excoriating the Chinese, he may be seen to have no particular interest in good Sino-Soviet relations.

Leadership succession and policy innovation go together in the Soviet Union for a number of reasons which have been discussed earlier in this chapter. The fact that changes in the top leadership – especially in the General Secretaryship but also in the Chairmanship of the Council of Ministers – facilitate change further down the hierarchy is also conducive to policy shifts. Yet nothing is more important than the extent to which great policy-making power is concentrated in the hands of the top Party leadership itself. No General Secretary in the 1980s is likely to be as unconstrained in his use of personal power as was Stalin for the last twenty years of his life. Because of the fact that he 'inherits' a number of senior colleagues whom he cannot instantly replace, he may even start off in a weaker position, so far as individual political power is concerned, than the American or French President. But he is the *de facto* 'chief executive' within a collective executive organ which has a power not only to take policy initiatives but also to implement policy changes without facing a critical legislature, a potentially hostile press and the other impediments familiar to his western counterparts. When that factor is taken in conjunction with the political longevity of Soviet General Secretaries and the super-power status of the USSR, it is fair to conclude that nowhere is there likely to be a more important political succession in the 1980s than the choice of successor to Leonid Brezhnev.

NOTES

1. For two thoughtful and significant books which discuss these matters within a broad context (and on the basis of extensive research on the career patterns of Soviet officials), see Seweryn Bialer, *Stalin's Successors: Leadership, stability, and change in the Soviet Union* (Cambridge and New York, 1980); and Jerry F. Hough, *Soviet Leadership in Transition*, Brookings Institution (Washington, DC, 1980).
2. For fuller discussion of the Brezhnev leadership up until the middle or late 1970s, see Archie Brown in Brown and Kaser (eds), *The Soviet Union since the Fall of Khrushchev* (2nd edn., London, 1978), pp. 234–49, 305–13; Grey Hodnett, 'The Pattern of Leadership Politics' in Seweryn Bialer (ed.), *The Domestic Context of Soviet Foreign Policy* (Boulder, Colorado, 1981), pp. 87–118; Jerry F. Hough, 'The Brezhnev Era: The Man and the System', *Problems of Communism*, xxv, No. 2 (March–April 1976), 1–17; Archie Brown, 'The Power of the General Secretary of the CPSU' in T. H. Rigby, Archie Brown and Peter Reddaway (eds), *Authority, Power and Policy in the USSR* (London and New York, 1980), pp. 135–57; and Richard M. Mills, 'The Soviet Leadership Problem', *World Politics*, 33, No. 4 (July 1981), 590–613.
3. For comparison of Brezhnev in this respect with Stalin and Khrushchev, see Brown, 'The Power of the General Secretary of the CPSU', op. cit.
4. Podgorny, according to well-informed sources, accused Brezhnev of seeking personal aggrandisement and the abandonment of the principle of collective leadership.
5. For Soviet biographies of Tikhonov, see, for example, *Pravda*, 24 October 1980, p. 1; and (for somewhat fuller details *Deputaty Verkhovnogo Soveta: Desyatyy sozyv* (Moscow, 1979), p. 436; and *Ezhegodnik bol'shoy sovetskoy entsiklopedii 1981* (Moscow, 1981), p. 604.
6. Mazurov was born in 1914 and Tikhonov in 1905. Katushev was born in 1927 and Rusakov in 1909.
7. *Pravda*, 24 October 1980, p. 1.

8. See *Pravda*, 27 April 1976, p. 1; *Pravda*, 28 April 1976, p. 2; *Pravda*, 29 April 1976, pp. 1–2; and *Pravda*, 30 April 1976, pp. 1–2.

9. See *Pravda*, 18 July 1978, p. 1; *Pravda*, 19 July 1978, p. 1; and *Pravda*, 20 July 1978, pp. 1–2.

10. See *Pravda*, 27 January 1982, p. 1; *Pravda*, 29 January 1982, p. 1; and *Pravda*, 30 January 1982, pp. 1–2.

11. See *Pravda*, 21 December 1980, pp. 1–2; and *Pravda*, 23 December 1980, p. 1.

12. See *Pravda*, 24 December 1980, pp. 1–2.

13. L. I. Brezhnev, *Otchet Tsentral'nogo Komiteta KPSS i ocherednye zadachi partii v oblasti vnutrenney i vneshney politiki: doklad XXV s'ezdu KPSS 24 fevralya 1976 goda* (Moscow, 1976), pp. 79–80.

14. L. I. Brezhnev, *Otchetnyy doklad Tsentral'nogo Komiteta KPSS XXVI s'ezdu Kommunisticheskoy partii Sovetskogo Soyuza i ocherednye zadachi partii v oblasti vnutrenney i vneshney politiki, 23 fevralya 1981 goda* (Moscow, 1981), p. 94.

15. See Brown, 'The Power of the General Secretary of the CPSU', op. cit., pp. 140–1, 155.

16. Brezhnev, *Otchetny doklad Tsentral'nogo Komiteta KPSS XXVI s'ezdu*, op. cit., p. 94.

17. On the theme of 'tranquillity', see Brown, 'The Power of the General Secretary of the CPSU', op. cit., pp. 146–7.

18. Valerie Bunce, *Do New Leaders Make a Difference? Executive Succession and Public Policy under Capitalism and Socialism* (Princeton, NJ, 1981), p. 255.

19. After studying the pattern of budgetary allocations in a number of Communist states, Bunce notes (p. 148) that changes in priorities 'occur early on in the administration and tend to endure'. That, however, leaves open the question whether the removal of the previous, well-entrenched and powerful leader was essentially a facilitating condition for such changes which may then be the result of a variety of pressures from different sources or whether the changes reflect the personal priorities of the new leader.

20. Most unambiguously 'Brezhnev men' among those who joined the Politburo between 1971 and 1980 were D. A. Kunaev and V. V. Shcherbitsky (full members from 1971), K. U. Chernenko (full member from 1978) and N. A. Tikhonov (full member from 1979). Those whose relations with Brezhnev most evidently ranged from relatively cool to critical and who departed from the Politburo during the same period were P. E. Shelest and G. I. Voronov (removed 1973), A. N. Shelepin (removed 1975), D. S. Polyansky (dropped at regular five-yearly election, 1976), N. V. Podgorny (removed 1977), K. T. Mazarov (removed 1978) and A. N. Kosygin (resigned due to ill-health, 1980).

21. As David Holloway has noted in Chapter 2 of this volume, p. 35.

22. See Holloway, pp. 49–50 and Brown, pp. 223–224, in Brown and Kaser (eds.), *The Soviet Union since the Fall of Khrushchev*, op. cit.

23. As Valerie Bunce interprets it in *Do New Leaders Make a Difference?* op. cit., pp. 172–3.

24. Exceptionally, it can pave the way to systemic change. Thus, the

replacement of Antonín Novotný by Alexander Dubček as First Secretary of the Communist Party of Czechoslovakia in January 1968 was a necessary, though not sufficient, condition for the promotion of the fundamental changes in the Czechoslovak political system which were rapidly to get under way and which took a massive military intervention to arrest.

25. It is the main thesis of Bunce's *Do New Leaders Make a Difference?* op. cit.
26. Ibid., p. 171.
27. A single exception which might be proposed would be that of Shelepin and the abolition of the Committee of Party-State Control. As chairman of that body, Shelepin was presumably less than enthusiastic when Brezhnev announced its demise in December 1965, though Brezhnev himself had every reason to play a particularly active part in securing that result.
28. I have in mind the two major works on the Soviet leadership in this period: Carl A. Linden, *Khrushchev and the Soviet Leadership 1957–1964* (Baltimore, 1966); and Michel Tatu, *Power in the Kremlin: From Khrushchev's Decline to Collective Leadership* (London, 1969).
29. Bunce, op. cit., p. 173.
30. In calculating the average age of the Politburo at the time of previous successions, I have counted only full, not candidate, members of the Politburo.
31. Bunce, op cit., especially pp. 218–21, 239–42.
32. For one of the best accounts of relevant characteristics of contenders for the post of General Secretary (even though many of the names of the personalities involved have changed in the meantime), see Grey Hodnett, 'Succession Contingencies in the Soviet Union', *Problems of Communism*, XXIV, No. 2 (March–April 1975), 1–21.
33. Even by Hodnett in his otherwise thorough analysis (see note 32, above) of the ' "probabilistic" rather than "causal" ' chains of interaction relevant to the succession process.
34. By this I mean the *de facto* party leadership. Stalin is exceptional in that he became a Secretary of the Central Committee and General Secretary simultaneously, but it was not until after Lenin's death that he emerged as top leader.
35. A qualification must again be made in the case of Stalin. Between Stalin's accession to the General Secretaryship and Lenin's death, Lenin chaired the Politburo when he was fit enough to attend. In his absence it was chaired by Kamenev who continued to take the chair in 1924. It was Stalin who first made the General Secretaryship the top job, but he did not achieve this overnight (Cf. T. H. Rigby, *Lenin's Government: Sovnarkom 1917–22* (Cambridge, 1979, esp. p. 139).
36. Brezhnev, *Otchet Tsentral'nogo Komiteta KPSS* . . ., op. cit., p. 80.
37. Among full members of the Politburo (as of early 1982 and after Suslov's death) there are nine Russians and four non-Russians, the latter comprising two Ukrainians (N. A. Tikhonov and V. V. Shcherbitsky), one Kazakh (D. A. Kunaev) and one Latvian (A. Ya. Pel'she). In the nine-man Secretariat of the Central Committee there is only one non-Russian, the Belorussian M. V. Zimyanin. Non-Russians have even representation with Russians only among candidate members of the Politburo. In the

entire top leadership – full and candidate members of the Politburo and Secretariat of the Central Committee – there are sixteen Russians and nine non-Russians.

38. Khrushchev was both First Secretary of the Moscow regional party organisation and a Secretary of the Central Committee at the time of Stalin's death.

39. It should be added that in spite of the highly negative portrayal of Stalin by Khrushchev and the downplaying to this day of Stalin's immense role in Soviet history in accounts of the Stalin era published in the USSR, an official anathema was not pronounced, even by Khrushchev, on his entire General Secretaryship. Criticism of Stalin in Khrushchev's speech to the XX Party Congress focused especially on the post-XVII Congress (1934) period. (See N. S. Khrushchev, *The 'Secret' Speech*, with an introduction by Zhores and Roy Medvedev, Nottingham 1976, especially p. 32.) It was only in retirement that Khrushchev went so far as to criticise Stalin's forcible collectivisation of agriculture as an 'utter perversion' of Lenin's principles and the work of 'a barbarian'. (See *Khrushchev Remembers: The Last Testament*, edited and translated by Strobe Talbott, London, 1974, pp. 107–9).

40. The various editions of *Deputaty Verkhovnogo Soveta SSSR*, which include biographies of Party leaders (in their capacity as deputies of the Supreme Soviet), give the individual's nationality, unlike the biographical notes of Soviet politicians contained in the yearbooks of the *Bol'shaya sovetskaya entsiklopediya*.

41. The Politburo was officially known at that time as the Presidium of the Central Committee.

42. Brezhnev had earlier brief experience as a Secretary of the Central Committee during the last year of Stalin's life (1952–53).

43. Brezhnev's official title was initially that of First Secretary of the Central Committee, the style employed between 1953–1966, when there was a reversion to the earlier title of General Secretary.

44. Some Soviet intellectuals take the view that he 'would last no longer than Malenkov' or 'would last only fifteen minutes'.

45. The major Soviet reference books imply that Gorbachev left school at 15 since they state that 'from 1946–50 he was an assistant to a combine operator on a Machine-Tractor Station in the Stavropol' region'. (See *Ezhegodnik bol'shoy sovetskoy entsiklopedii 1981* (Moscow, 1981), p. 573; also *Deputaty Verkovnogo Soveta SSSR: Desyatyy sozyv* (Moscow, 1979), p. 119.) Jerry Hough has, however, cast doubt on the view that Gorbachev was ever a full-time worker by citing a local (Stavropol') newspaper biography which suggests that his agricultural work was done in the summers while he was still a school pupil. See Hough, *Soviet Leadership in Transition*, op. cit., p. 58.

46. This may, indeed, lend support to the local biography of Gorbachev cited by Hough (see note 45 above). Yet the weight of evidence still suggests that Gorbachev was something more than merely a school-holiday agricultural worker. Apart from the Order of the Red Banner which he had already acquired before entering Moscow University as a student, there is the evidence of Brezhnev himself to be considered. Presenting

Gorbachev with the Order of Lenin a few days after the latter's fiftieth birthday, Brezhnev remarked: 'Thirty-five years ago he began his working life as an assistant to a combine operator' (*Pravda*, 6 March 1981, p. 2).

47. Gorbachev's funeral tribute to Kulakov is published in *Pravda*, 20 July 1978, p. 2.

48. Biographical information on Gorbachev comes mainly from *Deputaty Verkhovnogo Soveta SSSR: Desyatyy sozyv* (Moscow, 1979), p. 119; *Pravda*, 22 October 1980, p. 1; and *Ezhegodnik bol'shoy sovetskoy entsiklopedii 1981* (Moscow, 1981), p. 573. A few additional points relating to his student days at Moscow University are based on the recollections of several of his contemporaries.

49. *Pravda*, 21 January 1982, p. 2.

50. For these arguments, see L. I. Brezhnev, *Voprosy razvitiya politicheskoy sistemy sovetskogo obshchestva* (Moscow, 1977), pp. 434–5; and *Pravda*, 19 June 1977, p. 1; and for discussion of them, see Brown, 'The Power of the General Secretary of the CPSU', op. cit., pp. 141–3.

51. A number of scholars in recent years have emphasised the extent to which the Soviet system, and Communist systems generally, may (to borrow the words of Stephen White) be more dependent than 'liberal democracies, buttressed by the "come rain or come shine" legitimacy which their political institutions confer upon them' on economic growth and rising living standards. Ralf Dahrendorf (cited by Seweryn Bialer) notes the closer link in Communist than western states between 'economic growth and political organization'; and it would be understandable if Soviet citizens, accustomed to their political leaders taking a large share of the credit for economic successes, were to draw the conclusion that the leaders must bear responsibility also for economic failures. To a considerable extent, western leaders, too, get blamed by citizens for economic failure, but there are easy mechanisms – most notably, competitive elections – whereby the entire top leadership team can be changed and somewhat different policies pursued without threat to the political system itself. See Ralf Dahrendorf in Michel J. Crozier, Samuel P. Huntington and Joji Watunaki, *The Crisis of Democracy* (New York 1975), p. 189; Stephen White, *Political Culture and Soviet Politics* (London, 1979), pp. 189–90; and Bialer, *Stalin's Successors*, op. cit., especially Chapter 15, 'The Politics of Stringency', pp. 283–305.

52. L. I. Brezhnev, *Otchetnyy doklad Tsentral'nogo komiteta KPSS XXVI s'ezdu*, op. cit., p. 9.

53. Ibid.

54. Bialer, *Stalin's Successors*, op. cit., p. 305.

55. See the interesting recent book by G. I. Litvinova, *Pravo i demografi-cheskie protsessy v SSSR* (Moscow, 1981), especially pp. 151–3, 188.

56. Ibid.

57. On this point, see also Mary McAuley, 'Party Recruitment and the Nationalities in the USSR: A Study in Centre-Republican Relationships' in *British Journal of Political Science*, 10, Part 4 (October 1980), pp. 461–87.

58. Brezhnev, *Otchetnyy doklad Tsentral'nogo komiteta KPSS XXVI s'ezdu*, op. cit., p. 12.

Calendar of Political Events: 1971–July 1982

1971

5, 14 and 19 March   Series of measures announced by the Council of Ministers, the Central Committee of the Party, and the Presidium of the Supreme Soviet on the strengthening of the powers of the soviets and the codification of their existing rights.

22 March   Plenary session of the Central Committee approved the draft Central Committee report prepared for the XXIV Party Congress and the draft Five-year Plan, 1971–5.

30 March–9 April   XXIV Party Congress held in Moscow. Emphasis on foreign policy goal of seeking a new European security settlement based on the territorial division reached at the end of the Second World War. It was agreed that Party Congresses should in future be held once in five years (previously – in principle – they had met every four years). Party rules changed to strengthen the supervisory role of primary Party organisations.

9 April   Announcement of composition of leading Party organs following the first meeting of the Central Committee newly elected by the Congress. *Politburo*: L. I. Brezhnev, G. I. Voronov, V. V. Grishin, A. P. Kirilenko, A. N. Kosygin, F. D. Kulakov, D. A. Kunaev, K. T. Mazurov, A. Ya. Pel'she, N. V. Podgorny, D. S. Polyansky, M. A. Suslov, A. N. Shelepin, P. E. Shelest and V. V. Shcherbitsky. *Candidate members*: Yu. V. Andropov, P. N. Demichev, P. M. Masherov, V. P. Mzhavanadze, Sh. R. Rashidov and D. F. Ustinov. *Secretariat*: L. I. Brezhnev (General Secretary), P. N. Demichev, I. V. Kapitonov, K. F. Katushev, A. P. Kirilenko, F. D. Kulakov, B. N. Ponomarev, M. S. Solomentsev, M. A. Suslov and D. F. Ustinov.

27–29 July   Adoption by annual Session of Comecon of 'Comprehensive Programme' for further socialist economic integration.

11 September   Death of N. S. Khrushchev (aged 77).

22–23 November   Plenary session of the Central Committee discussed foreign policy and international activity since the XXIV Congress. M. S. Solomentsev elected to candidate membership of the Politburo, relinquishing his position in the Secretariat.

1972

11–15 January   Widespread arrests and flat-searches in the Ukraine and Moscow designed to suppress the *samizdat* journals, the *Ukrainian Herald* and the *Chronicle of Current Events.*

6 March   Publication in *Pravda* of severe censure of the Party organisation of the Georgian capital of Tbilisi.

18–19 May   Riots in Kaunas following the self-immolation of Romas Kalanta in support of greater political and religious freedom in Lithuania.

19 May   Plenary session of the Central Committee approved a report by L. I. Brezhnev on the international situation. I. V. Kapitonov reported on the forthcoming exchange of Party cards. B. N. Ponomarev became a candidate member of the Politburo.

May   P. E. Shelest replaced as First Secretary of the Ukrainian Party Central Commitee by V. V. Shcherbitsky.

22–30 May   Visit of United States President Nixon to the Soviet Union. Signing of Anti-Ballistic Missile Treaty, the Interim Agreement on Offensive Missiles, and the Agreement on the Establishment of the Joint US-USSR Commerical Commission.

29 September   V. P. Mzhavanadze replaced by E. A. Shevardnadze as First Secretary of the Georgian Party Central Committee.

18 October   Signing of Soviet-United States Trade Agreement in Washington.

18 December   Plenary session of the Central Committee approved the state economic plan and state budget for 1973. V. I. Dolgikh elected a secretary of the Central Committee, and V. P. Mzhavanadze removed from candidate membership of the Politburo following his forced retirement from the First Secretaryship of the Georgian Party.

1973

2 February　D. S. Polyansky appointed Minister of Agriculture (in succession to V. V. Matskevich) while retaining his seat on the Politburo.

26–27 April　Plenary session of the Central Committee devoted to foreign affairs. P. E. Shelest and G. I. Voronov removed from the Politburo and Yu. V. Andropov, A. A. Gromyko and A. A. Grechko appointed; G. V. Romanov elected to candidate membership of the Politburo.

18–22 May　Visit by Brezhnev to the Federal Republic of Germany for talks with Chancellor Brandt. Relations between the USSR and the FRG reached a 'new, normal for peacetime' level; economic and cultural agreements signed.

18–25 June　Visit by Brezhnev to United States for talks with President Nixon. Signed Agreement on the Prevention of Nuclear War and agreements to promote trade between the USSR and the United States.

11 July　Presentation in Moscow of International Lenin Peace Prize to Brezhnev.

10–11 December　Plenary session of the Central Committee approved Brezhnev's report on the activities of the Politburo in domestic and foreign policy and approved the state economic plan and state budget for 1974.

1974

11 and 17 February　Demonstrations in Moscow and Tallin by Germans demanding to emigrate to West Germany.

12–13 February　Arrest and deportation from the USSR of Solzhenitsyn.

18–21 June　Twenty-fifth anniversary Session of Comecon, 'for the first time . . . working out an agreed plan for multilateral measures of integration', and co-ordinating 1976–80 plans as part of a fifteen-year programme.

3 July Brezhnev and Nixon signed agreements on nuclear arms control at end of Nixon's visit to the Soviet Union.

24 July Plenary session of the Central Committee addressed by Brezhnev.

18 October Letters between Senator Jackson and Henry Kissinger claim agreement on the part of the Soviet leaders to ease emigration restrictions.

23–24 November Talks between Brezhnev and President Ford at Vladivostok.

16 December Plenary session of the Central Committee approved the state economic plan and state budget for 1975. P. N. Demichev removed from the Secretariat of the Central Committee following his appointment as Minister of Culture on 14 November in succession to Ekaterina Furtseva, who died on 25 October.

24 December New regulation on internal passports under which such passports to be extended to all Soviet citizens, that is, including the peasantry.

1975

14 January Soviet decision not to ratify the USSR-USA Trade Agreement of 1972.

21–23 January Executive Committee of Comecon abrogates system of quinquennially-fixed prices for inter-member trade and introduces a moving average of world prices.

4–7 February First meeting (in Moscow) of secretariats of Comecon and EEC.

11 February Ratification by Presidium of the Supreme Soviet of the agreement to renounce bacteriological and toxic weapons.

16 April Plenary session of the Central Committee. Report by A. A. Gromyko 'On the international situation and the foreign policy of the Soviet Union'. Date of the start of the XXV Party Congress fixed for 24 February 1976. A. N. Shelepin removed from membership 'at his own request' (removed from Chairmanship of Central Council of Trade Unions on 22 May).

8 May   Completion of first section of the Baikal-Amur Magistral (BAM), the second railway to link Siberia with the Pacific Ocean.

25 June   Government and Party decision to codify economic legislation.

1 August   Signing in Helsinki (by Brezhnev for the USSR) of the Final Act of the Conference on Security and Co-operation in Europe.

28 August–5 September   Visit to Vietnam by Soviet Party and Government delegation led by M. S. Solomentsev, candidate member of the Politburo (following unconditional surrender of South Vietnam on 30 April).

9 October   Nobel Peace Prize awarded to Dr A. D. Sakharov (announced on 13 November that he would not be given exit visa to attend ceremony in Oslo).

17 October   Nobel Prize in Economics awarded to L. V. Kantorovich (jointly with an American, T. Koopmans).

1 December   Plenary session of the Central Committee approved draft of the Five-year plan, 1976–80.

1976

20 February   Plenary session of the Central Committee approved texts of the Report of the Committee to the XXV Congress to be delivered by Brezhnev and of the Report on the Five-year Plan to be delivered by Kosygin.

25 February–5 March   XXV Party Congress held in Moscow. Report of Central Committee to the Congress noted that in foreign policy 'the achievements of the past five years are of truly everlasting significance' and that the improvements in relations with the United States had decisively reduced the danger of world war.

5 March   Announcement of composition of leading Party organs following the first meeting of the Central Committee newly elected by the Congress. *Politburo*: L. I. Brezhnev, Yu. V. Andropov, A. A. Grechko, V. V. Grishin, A. A. Gromyko, A. P. Kirilenko, A. N.

Kosygin, F. D. Kulakov, D. A. Kunaev, K. T. Mazurov, A. Ya. Pel'she, N. V. Podgorny, G. V. Romanov, M. A. Suslov, D. F. Ustinov and V. V. Shcherbitsky; *Candidate members*: G. A. Aliev, P. N. Demichev, P. M. Masherov, B. N. Ponomarev, Sh. R. Rashidov and M. S. Solomentsev. *Secretariat*: L. I. Brezhnev (General Secretary), A. P. Kirilenko, F. D. Kulakov, M. A. Suslov, D. F. Ustinov, B. N. Ponomarev, I. V. Kapitonov, V. I. Dolgikh, K. F. Katushev, M. V. Zimyanin and K. U. Chernenko.

16 March   D. S. Polyansky (dropped from Politburo at the first meeting of the XXV Congress Central Committee) removed from office of Minister of Agriculture and replaced by V. K. Mesyats.

26 April   Death of Marshal A. A. Grechko, member of Politburo and Minister of Defence, aged 72. (D. F. Ustinov named new Minister of Defence, 30 April; Ustinov relinquished his position in the Secretariat but kept his place in the Politburo.)

10 May   L. I. Brezhnev created a Marshal of the Soviet Union.

28 May   Signature by Brezhnev in Moscow and President Ford in Washington of bilateral Treaty on Underground Nuclear Explosions for Peaceful Purposes.

29–30 June   Conference of European Communist Parties held in Berlin.

15 July   Departure of Andrey Amalrik from the Soviet Union.

30 July   D. F. Ustinov created a Marshal of the Soviet Union.

25–26 October   Plenary session of Central Committee heard reports on the State Budget and economic plan for 1977 and on the Five-year Plan, 1976–80. Brezhnev, in a wide-ranging speech, stressed need to raise farm efficiency as unprecedented investments were being made in agriculture. The plenum also considered Party organisational questions and elected Ya. P. Ryabov to the Secretariat of the Central Committee.

17 November   EEC proposals on draft agreement and exchange of information put to Comecon.

30 November   Death of Marshal I. I. Yakubovsky, Commander-in-Chief of Warsaw Pact Armed Forces, aged 64.

19 December   Celebration of Brezhnev's seventieth birthday.

19 December   Departure of Vladimir Bukovsky from Soviet Union in exchange for Luis Corvalan, General Secretary of the Chilean Communist Party (Bukovsky was released from Vladimir prison and Corvalan from detention in Chile).

1977

5 January   First significant retail price increases (partly offset by decreases) since 1962 (increases also took place in subsequent years).

9 January   Announcement that Army General V. G. Kulikov had succeeded Yakubovsky as Commander-in-Chief of Warsaw Pact Armed Forces.

9 February   Diplomatic relations between the Soviet Union and Spain resumed after a break of thirty-eight years.

28–30 March   Proposals by United States Secretary of State, Cyrus Vance, at bilateral talks in Moscow on SALT II rejected by Soviet side.

18 April   Counter proposals made by Comecon to EEC on trade concessions.

24 May   Plenary session of the Central Committee approved the basic draft of the Constitutional Commission for a new Soviet Constitution and recommended the Presidium of the Supreme Soviet to publish the draft for an 'all-people's discussion'. The Central Commitee also approved the text and music of a revised National Anthem. N. V. Podgorny removed from membership of the Politburo and K. F. Katushev replaced as a Secretary of the Central Committee by K. V. Rusakov.

27 May   E. M. Tyazhel'nikov relieved of post of First Secretary of the Komsomol (to become head of the Propaganda department of the Central Committee of the CPSU) and replaced by B. N. Pastukhov.

4 June   Publication in *Pravda* of the text of the draft of the new Constitution.

12 June   Publication in *Pravda* of the text and music of the new National Anthem.

16 June   Supreme Soviet of the USSR relieved N. V. Podgorny of

Chairmanship of the Presidium of the Supreme Soviet and unanimously elected L. I. Brezhnev to that office.

21 September   Meeting (in Brussels) at ministerial level between EEC and Comecon.

3 October   Plenary session of the Central Committee approved report by Brezhnev on the new Constitution following the 'all-people's discussion' of the draft. K. U. Chernenko, while remaining a Secretary of the Central Committee, and V. V. Kuznetsov elected to candidate membership of the Politburo.

7 October   Supreme Soviet adopted the new Constitution of the USSR.

7 November   Sixtieth anniversary of the Bolshevik Revolution.

13 December   Plenary session of the Central Committee heard reports on the economic plan and state budget for 1978 and considered progress over the first two years of the Five-year Plan.

1978

20 February   By decree of the Presidium of the Supreme Soviet, Brezhnev awarded the Soviet Union's highest military honour, the Order of Victory.

3–4 July   Plenary session of the Central Committee devoted mainly to agricultural problems.

17 July   Death of Politburo member and Secretary of the Central Committee (responsible for agriculture), F. D. Kulakov (aged 60).

27 November   Plenary session of the Central Committee heard reports on the economic plan and state budget for 1979; organisational questions also discussed. K. U. Chernenko promoted from candidate to full membership of the Politburo, while retaining his Secretaryship of the Central Committee. N. A. Tikhonov and E. A. Shevarnadze elected candidate members of the Politburo, and M. S. Gorbachev elected as a Secretary of the Central Committee; K. T. Mazurov removed from Politburo membership 'on account of his health and at his own request'.

1979

17 April Plenary session of the Central Committee considered matters coming up at the Supreme Soviet the following day and approved Politburo proposals for the organisation of the Supreme Soviet session. Ya. P. Ryabov relieved of his Secretaryship of the Central Committee on his transfer to the post of First Deputy Chairman of Gosplan (the State Planning Committee).

22 April Brezhnev awarded the Lenin Prize for Literature for his three volumes of memoirs.

16–18 June Talks between Soviet delegation led by President Brezhnev and United States delegation led by President Carter at Vienna.

19 June Publication of agreement between the Soviet Union and the United States on strategic arms limitation, signed the previous day in Vienna by Brezhnev and Carter (SALT II).

28 June A. N. Kosygin, leading the Soviet delegation to the Annual Session of Comecon, promised other member-states an increase in USSR energy supplies during 1981–5.

29 July Publication of a decree 'On the Improvement of Planning and the Strengthening of the Influence of the Economic Mechanism over Raising the Efficiency of Production and the Quality of Work.'

28 August Death of Soviet writer, Konstantin Simonov (aged 63).

27 November Plenary session of the Central Committe heard reports on the economic plan and state budget for 1980 and considered organisational questions. N. A. Tikhonov transferred from candidate to full membership of the Politburo; M. S. Gorbachev elected a candidate member of the Politburo while remaining a Secretary of the Central Committee.

27 December Soviet military intervention in Afghanistan.

1980

3 January President Carter requested United States Senate to delay consideration of SALT II and (4 January) restricted sales of grain and 'high technology' to the USSR.

22 January   Academician A. D. Sakharov removed from Moscow and exiled to city of Gork'y.

23 June   Plenary session of the Central Committee determined date of opening of next Party Congress (23 February 1981). Reports delivered by Brezhnev on domestic and international problems and by the Minister of Foreign Affairs, A. A. Gromyko, on 'The international situation and the foreign policy of the Soviet Union'. The plenum 'fully approved the measures of help rendered to Afghanistan'.

19 July–3 August   Olympic Games held in Moscow.

4 October   P. M. Masherov, candidate member of the Politburo and First Secretary of the Central Committee of the Belorussian Communist Party, killed (aged 62) in a car accident.

21 October   Plenary session of the Central Committee heard reports on the economic plan and state budget for 1981 and a speech from Brezhnev on the socio-economic development of the country which paid special attention to agricultural administration. M. S. Gorbachev, while remaining a Secretary of the Central Committee, promoted from candidate to full membership of the Politburo. T, Ya. Kiselev (First Secretary of the Central Committee of the Belorussian Party in succession to P. M. Masherov) elected a candidate member of the Politburo.

23 October   A. N. Kosygin replaced as Chairman of the Council of Ministers by N. A. Tikhonov.

12 November   Death of Andrey Amalrik (aged 42) in car accident in Spain.

12 November   Departure from the Soviet Union of human rights campaigner and literary scholar, Lev Kopelev.

14 November   L. F. Il'ichev, Deputy Foreign Minister, reaffirms 'profound devotion to all the principles and provisions of the Final Act' at the opening session of the Helsinki review conference in Madrid.

18 December   Death of A. N. Kosygin (aged 76).

29 December   Death of Nadezhda Mandel'shtam (aged 81), author of *Hope Against Hope* and *Hope Abandoned* and widow of Osip Mandel'shtam.

29 December   Work begins on the 600 km railway from Surgut to Urengoy to open up the large natural-gas fields on the Arctic littoral and in the Yamal' peninsula.

1981

20 February   Plenary session of the Central Committee approved the text of the Report of the Central Committee to the XXVI Party Congress to be delivered by Brezhnev and of the Report on the Five-year Plan for 1981–5 to be delivered by N. A. Tikhonov.

23 February–3 March   XXVI Party Congress held in Moscow. Report of the Central Committee to the Congress noted that the period since the previous Party Congress had 'not been a simple one' and that there had been 'no few difficulties in the country's economic development and in international affairs'. Strong concern expressed over developments in Poland in 1980–1 where 'the pillars of the socialist state' were in jeopardy. Preparations announced for a new Party Programme to take account of the extensive experience 'of socialist and communist construction in the USSR' which had accrued since the current programme was drawn up in 1961.

3 March   Announcement of composition of leading Party organs following the first meeting of the Central Committee newly elected by the Congress. *Politburo*: L. I. Brezhnev, Yu. V. Andropov, M. S. Gorbachev, V. V. Grishin, A. A. Gromyko, A. P. Kirilenko, D. A. Kunaev, A. Ya. Pel'she, G. V. Romanov, M. A. Suslov, N. A. Tikhonov, D. F. Ustinov, K. U. Chernenko and V. V. Shcherbitsky; *Candidate members*: G. A. Aliev, P. N. Demichev, T. Ya. Kiselev, V. V. Kuznetsov, B. N. Ponomarev, Sh. R. Rashidov, M. S. Solomentsev and E. A. Shevardnadze. *Secretariat*: L. I. Brezhnev (General Secretary), M. S. Gorbachev, A. P. Kirilenko, M. A. Suslov, K. U. Chernenko, B. N. Ponomarev, N. V. Kapitonov, V. I. Dolgikh, M. V. Zimyanin and K. V. Rusakov.

28 March   Death of Soviet writer, Yuriy Trifonov (aged 55).

30 March   Promulgation of decree 'On Measures to Strengthen Government Help to Families with Children'.

24 April   President Reagan lifts the United States restrictions on grain exports to the USSR.

5 June   Letter from the Central Committee of the CPSU to the Central Committee of the Polish United Workers' Party expressing concern at the course of events in Poland.

29 September   Contracts signed in Düsseldorf by Mashinoimport with firms from the FRG, France, Italy and the UK to provide equipment for a 5000 km gas pipeline from the Urengoy fields to Western Europe.

16 November Plenary session of the Central Committee heard reports on the economic plan and state budget for 1982 and a speech from Brezhnev placing emphasis on 'the food problem', urging economic reform and calling for improved efficiency in the economy.

22–25 November Brezhnev, visiting Bonn, urges 'mutually-beneficial cooperation' between the USSR and the FRG. Parallel meetings between I. V. Arkhipov, First Deputy Chairman of the USSR Council of Ministers, and O. Lambsdorff, FRG Minister of Economics.

12 December Martial law imposed in Poland. Reported in the Soviet Union as a response to attempts by 'counter-revolutionary forces' to overthrow the Polish Party and government and to seize power.

19 December Reception in Kremlin in honour of Brezhnev's seventy-fifth birthday attended by East European Party leaders and other members of the Soviet leadership and addressed by M. A. Suslov. Brezhnev granted the award of Hero of the Soviet Union for the fourth time and his seventh Order of Lenin.

30 December President Reagan places restrictions on United States sales of technology to the USSR as response to alleged Soviet involvement in the imposition of martial law in Poland.

1982

1 January General revision of wholesale prices (which had been operative since 1 July 1967); energy prices increased by only some 50 per cent.

17 January Death of the writer and long-term prisoner in Soviet labour camps, Varlam Shalamov (aged 74).

20 January Death of the First Deputy Chairman of the KGB, S. K. Tsvigun (aged 64).

26 January Death of long-standing Politburo member and Secretary of the Central Committee, M. A. Suslov (aged 79).

29 January Suslov buried in Kremlin wall following funeral oration by Brezhnev.

5 March   A. I. Shibaev replaced as chairman of the Soviet trade union organisation by S. A. Shalaev.

24 May   Plenary session of the Central Committee devoted to the agriculture and food situation. Heard report from Brezhnev 'On the Food Programme of the USSR for the period up to 1990 and the measures for its realisation'. Approved this comprehensive programme with its emphasis on the agro-industrial complex, on increased investment in agricultural infrastructure and increase in procurement (but not retail) prices of basic foodstuffs. Politburo member Yu. V. Andropov elected a Secretary of the Central Committee. Secretary of the Central Committee V. A. Dolgikh elected a candidate member of the Politburo.

26 May   Announcement of Yu. V. Andropov's replacement as chairman of the KGB by the head of the Ukrainian KGB, V. V. Fedorchuk.

15 June   In a speech to the United Nations General Assembly, the Soviet Foreign Minister, A. A. Gromyko, declared that the Soviet Union would not be the first to use nuclear weapons.

16 July   Strong attack on the foreign policy of the Reagan Administration published in *Pravda* by G. A. Arbatov, Director of the Institute of US and Canadian Studies in Moscow.

Note: All known meetings of the Central Committee of the CPSU and all movements into and out of the Politburo and Secretariat of the Central Committee within the 1971–July 1982 period are recorded in the above Calendar. Any remarks within quotations are either from the annual Yearbook of the Great Soviet Encyclopedia (*Ezhegodnik bol'shoy sovetskoy entsiklopedii*) or from *Pravda*. In the book to which the present volume is, *inter alia*, a sequel, *The Soviet Union since the Fall of Khrushchev*, the Calendar extends back to the beginning of the Brezhnev era in October 1964.

Postscript: July 1982

Archie Brown

Since this book went to press, several political and economic developments have occurred which are worthy of note and which have a direct bearing on some of the issues raised in previous chapters (especially 7 and 9). So far as the leadership succession is concerned, there have been signs of contenders pressing their claims and two significant promotions were announced at the May 1982 plenary session of the Central Committee of the CPSU. A comprehensive 'Food Programme' was adopted by the same plenary session, though one which may not be commensurate with the scale of Soviet agricultural problems as the country apparently heads for its fourth bad harvest in a row.[1]

The main development of potential relevance to the coming change in the top leadership was the promotion of Yuriy Andropov to a Secretaryship of the Central Committee (while retaining his full Politburo membership) and the promotion of Vladimir Dolgikh to candidate membership of the Politburo (while he retained his Secretaryship of the Central Committee). These elections at the May plenum restore the size of the Secretariat to ten (cf. page 227) and, in terms of my argument on the importance of an incoming General Secretary already combining full Politburo membership with a Secretaryship of the Central Committee (see page 233), strengthen Andropov's chances of succeeding Brezhnev.

It means, among other things, that there is now a second person with a foothold in each of these vital institutions who is under the age of seventy, though Andropov (who celebrated his sixty-eighth birthday less than a month after his latest promotion) is seventeen years older than Gorbachev. The corollary of that, however, is that he is vastly more experienced than Gorbachev and, indeed, if one chooses to put equal weight upon familiarity with foreign and domestic policy, his qualifications are more impressive than those of either Kirilenko or Chernenko (not to mention Grishin). Though his fifteen-year occupancy of the chairmanship of the KGB will scarcely count in Andropov's favour with foreign statesmen, there is no longer the potential embarrassment of moving him straight from being security chief to General Secretary (and so *de facto* diplomat-in-chief).

If, as of mid-1982, Andropov has clearly become a leading contender for the succession, the issue of who will be next General Secretary remains a very open one. Much depends upon how much longer Brezhnev's considerable powers of survival will, in fact, sustain him as well as upon the health of his leading colleagues.[2] It seems likely that Brezhnev's own preferred successor is still his closest colleague, Chernenko, and the latter has shown every sign of wishing to win friends and influence people.

Chernenko published a broad-ranging article in the journal *Kommunist* in April 1982[3] which may be seen as part of an attempt to broaden his appeal and to demonstrate, perhaps, that he can match the range of Andropov (who achieved greater prominence in the same month as the principal speaker at the Kremlin Palace of Congresses on the 112th anniversary of Lenin's birth, thus receiving the customary extensive coverage accorded to this annual celebration by *Pravda*[4] for his review of the domestic, international and ideological scene). If Chernenko's *Kommunist* article is viewed as a surrogate election manifesto, it is noteworthy that he takes pains to present himself as a not entirely uncritical supporter of the status quo, that he explicitly disagrees with those who see the answer to the Soviet Union's problems in 'more discipline' and 'less democracy',[5] and that he stresses (conscious of his handicap of having spent more time in ideological and narrowly secretarial work than in running parts of the country or sectors of the economy) the unity and indissolubility of ideological and organisational work.[6]

The relevance of such publications to the leadership succession is that even if a short-list of one is eventually drawn up by the inner party leadership, that selection is not made in a vacuum. It is reasonable to assume that when Brezhnev finally goes, a majority within the selectorate – as in 1964 – will be secured for one member of the Politburo who will then be presented to the Central Committee as the single candidate in the formal election to the General Secretaryship. It is, however, more than probable that opinion outside the ranks of the Politburo and Secretariat (most notably, within the Central Committee apparatus, the military, the KGB and, not least, among elected members of the Central Committee) will have been informally communicated to, and taken into consideration by, the Politburo and thus have some bearing on the nomination of General Secretary which they place before a plenary session of the Central Committee.

The May plenum of the Central Committee which brought Andropov into a very strong position to contend for the leadership (or to play a Suslovian role of king-maker) saw the promotion also of Vladimir Dolgikh who, though not yet a full member of the Politburo, could in due course become a serious candidate for either the General Secretaryship or the Chairmanship of the Council of Ministers. Dolgikh, a Secretary of the Central Committee since 1972 (and head of the department of the Central Committee responsible for heavy industry since 1976) was accorded candidate membership of the Politburo while retaining his Secretaryship. His background, prior to entering full-time party work, is that of a qualified engineer and factory manager, and he is one of the abler Soviet leaders as well as being one of the few people in the entire top leadership team under the age of sixty. (He was born in 1924.)

Recent events do not, however, alter my view (expressed in Chapter 9) that the qualifications of the youngest Politburo member, Mikhail Gorbachev, for the General Secretaryship should be taken very seriously indeed. Much may depend upon the outcome of the struggle which is bound to accompany the attempt to implement the May 1982 'Food Programme' (summarised by Alec Nove on page 185). As Secretary of the Central Committee responsible for agriculture and for the agro-industrial complexes (the importance of the development of which was stressed in the materials presented to the May plenum of the Central Committee[7] and by Gorbachev himself at a conference of republican and regional party secretaries and representatives of relevant ministries and industrial enterprises in July 1982[8]), he is in day-to-day charge of the domestic policy area to which the party leadership is currently according the highest priority. That does not, of course, mean that Gorbachev has a completely free hand. If I was correct in suggesting in Chapter 9 that Gorbachev wishes to see a more radical agricultural reform than has been attempted in the Soviet Union thus far, that he is sympathetic both to Hungarian innovation in this regard and to the *beznaryadnoe zveno* (see pages 241 and 244), then it must be said that he failed to get authoritative support for reform along such bold lines incorporated in the programme presented to the May plenum. The rather surprising fact that Gorbachev was not one of the twenty-two speakers who addressed that plenary session on 'his' subject may, indeed, lend support to the view that the programme fell short of his assessment of what was required. Furthermore, in an article in July 1982 on 'The Food Programme and the Tasks of its Implementation',[10] Gorbachev explicitly accords to Brezhnev the 'leading role' in initiating and formulating this programme,[11] thus further freeing himself of full responsibility for its limitations as distinct from the task of its implementation.[12]

Two appointments in the most recent period, in addition to the changes at Politburo and Secretariat level, deserve mention. In returning to the Secretariat (which he left in 1967 to become Chairman of the KGB), Andropov naturally had to vacate the headship of the KGB. His place was taken not by one of the deputy chairmen of that organisation in Moscow but by the head of the Ukrainian KGB, V. V. Fedorchuk. The appointment departs from recent practice in two ways. First, Fedorchuk is a career officer in the security forces, having joined the NKVD in 1939. Second, he is not even a candidate member of the Central Committee, whereas Andropov for his last nine years as KGB chairman was a full member of the Politburo. If the fact that the new chairman is a KGB insider (taken in conjunction with what is known of his role in the Ukraine) has led commentators to suggest that 'the KGB will in future be rougher, tougher and more ruthless in its crack-down on dissidents and nationalists',[13] less attention has been paid to Fedorchuk's subordinate political status as compared with Andropov, whose new duties as a Secretary of the Central Committee are, moreover, likely to include oversight of the security organs. There is thus little reason to believe that the KGB will cease to be the instrument of the top party leadership and subject to political controls imposed by them.

The other appointment alluded to above is that of S. A. Shalaev as chairman of the Soviet trade union organisation in succession to A. I. Shibaev, a change which took place on 5 March 1982. This is also a departure from recent practice in that the outgoing trade union head, like Shelepin and Grishin before him, came to the top union post as an outsider,[14] whereas his successor, Shalaev, has spent much of his career in trade union work.[15] Though the change could be explained in terms of the age difference between the two men (Shibaev was born in 1915 and Shalaev in 1929), it is almost certainly also related to the party leadership's concern with the Polish example and their realisation that excessive official trade union moribundity has its dangers for the system, even if the kind of trade union activity on behalf of workers which they seek represents a differentiation of functions rather than a division of powers.[16]

Finally, mention should be made of two decisions by the Reagan adminstration in the United States in July 1982 which illustrate the interconnection of politics and economics and of foreign trade and international political relations. On the one hand, the US extended its ban on the sale of equipment for use in construction of the Soviet gas pipeline to Western Europe and forbade West European subsidiaries of American companies to step into the breach. On the other hand, President Reagan sought an extension for another year of the US grain agreement with the Soviet Union in the hope of encouraging the USSR to import more American wheat. By slowing down the construction of the gas pipeline and by offering a one-year, rather than long-term, grain agreement, the US contributed to the Soviet Union's economic difficulties and added more substantially to the deterioration of Soviet–US political relationships. Soviet leaders could, however, draw consolation from the growing gap between American and West European perceptions of East–West relations in general and of the benefits to be derived from the gas pipeline in particular.[17] Thus, having formed a negative view of the possibilities of doing business with the United States under Reagan, Soviet policy-makers and propagandists are focusing increasing attention on Western Europe.

NOTES

1. The *East European Markets: Financial Times* fortnightly business review forecast (Vol. 2, No. 15, 26 July 1982, p. 2) a Soviet grain harvest for 1982 of around 185 million tonnes as against a target of 238 million tonnes.
2. On 30 June 1982, Dmitriy Ustinov, noting Brezhnev's 'constant attention to military construction, to the development and perfecting of the armed forces, and to the training of military cadres' wished him 'good health and *many years* [my italics, A.B.] of fruitful work for the good of the people' (*Pravda*, 1 July, p. 2).
3. K. Chernenko, 'Avangardnaya rol' partii kommunistov. Vazhnoe uslovie ee vozrastaniya', *Kommunist*, No. 6, April 1982, 25–43.
4. *Pravda*, 23 April 1982, pp. 1–2.
5. Chernenko, op. cit., p. 41.
6. Chernenko continues, at the time of writing, to be accorded great prominence by the Soviet mass media. *Pravda* (22 July 1982, p. 2) gave extensive, and highly positive, coverage to a book published under his name which was but a second, revised edition of a previously published work.
7. 'Prodovol'stevennaya programma SSSR na period do 1990 goda i mery po ee realizatsii: Materialy mayskogo Plenuma TsK KPSS 1982 goda', *Partiynaya zhizn'*, No. 12, June 1982.
8. See *Pravda*, 17 July 1982, p. 2.
9. See *Pravda*, 25 May 1982, p. 1.
10. M. Gorbachev, 'Prodovol'stvennaya programma i zadachi ee realizatsii', *Kommunist*, No. 10, July 1982, 6–21.

11. Ibid., p. 6.
12. In the same article Gorbachev devotes much attention to the real problems of life in the countryside which hamper Soviet agriculture (including some of those discussed by Alec Nove in Chapter 7) and refers to 'links' (or 'teams'), albeit not 'autonomous teams', as well as 'brigades' (ibid., p. 16). Cf. Nove, Chapter 7, p. 185.
13. Michael Binyon, 'Tough Ukraine boss means rougher KGB', *The Times*, 28 June 1982.
14. He spent most of his career in party secretarial work, but part of it (1947–55) as a factory manager. See *Ezhegodnik bol'shoy sovetskoy entsiklopedii 1981* (Moscow, 1981), p. 610.
15. Ibid., pp. 609–10.
16. Cf. Brezhnev's report to the XXVI Party Congress: *Otchetnyy doklad Tsentral'nogo Komiteta KPSS XXVI s'ezdu* (Moscow, 1981), pp. 89–90.
17. Part of the rationale for a policy of economic sanctions by the United States was a study of the dependence of the Soviet economy on foreign trade cited by the director of the US Census Bureau, Bruce Chapman. The suggestion that Soviet imports accounted for as much as 15 per cent of Soviet GNP and 20 per cent of national income was greeted with widespread scepticism in Western Europe. See, for example, the leaders in *The Times*, 21 July 1982, and *East European Markets: Financial Times*, Vol. 2, No. 15, 26 July 1982.

Index

273